Alex Brummer has, since 1989  and Economics pages, where he previously the paper's foreign e Washington correspondent. He politics from Southampton U Bradford University Manageme

Roger Cowe, who works for the .............. pages, is a prize-winning journalist and former deputy editor at *Accountancy Age*, and was editor of *The Guardian Guide to the UK's Top Companies*. He has an MBA from Manchester Business School.

Together Alex Brummer and Roger Cowe wrote *Hanson: A Biography* (1994), which was one of the most successful business biographies of recent years.

## Further praise for *Weinstock*:

'A remarkable life-story.'    ANTHONY HOWARD, *Sunday Times*

'A fascinating account of the rise of a Polish-Jewish orphan who took command of an ailing GEC in 1963, steered it through financial turbulence in the 1960s, perfected the art of the hostile takeover, and built Britain's premier industrial powerhouse. His contribution to UK industry has been huge and this is a worthy chronicle of his achievements.'    *Business Age*

'Fascinating insights into Weinstock's character.'
LESLIE HANNAH, *Times Literary Supplement*

'An engaging read.'    JOHN BIFFEN, *Independent on Sunday*

'A perceptive and fascinating book which goes far beyond the normal narrow scale of business biography.'
ROBERT BRUCE, *Accountancy*

'An excellent biography of a remarkable man. It paints an absorbing picture of the whole man, strengths and weaknesses, successes and failures, fads and foibles, family background and influences . . . a well researched, well written, thoughtful and balanced record of a distinguished man who was a pioneer in many ways.'    BASIL W. DENNING, *Strategy*

'Very readable and englightening.'
KENNETH HARRIS, *The Herald* (Glasgow)

'A fascinating book about a very complex character.'
JOHN GARRETT, *Tribune*

# WEINSTOCK

*The Life and Times of*
*Britain's Premier Industrialist*

**Alex Brummer**
and
**Roger Cowe**

*To Robert*
*with warmest*
*regards*
*Alex*

HarperCollinsBusiness
*An imprint of HarperCollinsPublishers*

HarperCollinsBusiness
An Imprint of HarperCollins*Publishers*
77–85 Fulham Palace Road,
Hammersmith, London W6 8JB

This paperback edition 1999
1 3 5 7 9 8 6 4 2

First published in Great Britain by
HarperCollins*Publishers* 1998

ISBN 0 00 638745 4

Set in PostScript Linotype Meridien by
Rowland Phototypesetting Ltd, Bury St Edmunds, Suffolk

Printed and bound in Great Britain by
Caledonian International Book Manufacturing Ltd, Glasgow

# CONTENTS

# ILLUSTRATIONS

Arnold Weinstock at the Stoke Newington Central School before being evacuated from Warwickshire. (*Gordon Hill*)

Freddie Fogg, the schoolmaster who guided Weinstock to matriculation and the LSE, and who inspired his lifelong love of music. (*Gordon Hill*)

Weinstock's father-in-law Sir Michael Sobell, founder of Radio & Allied Industries.

Weinstock after GEC's takeover of AEI, 1967. (*Copyright Hulton Getty*)

Workers protest against the closure of AEI's Woolwich plant. (*Peter Johns/Guardian*)

Kenneth Bond, Weinstock and Lord Aldington during the battle for English Electric, July 1968. (*Guardian*)

Lord Nelson and Weinstock announcing the GEC–English Electric merger, 13 September 1968. (*Press Association*)

Weinstock and Nelson at the first annual general meeting of GEC–AEI, September 1969. (*Guardian*)

Weinstock in 1973, characteristically conducting business over the telephone.

Baron Weinstock of Bowden at his introduction to the House of Lords, 15 October 1980. (*Universal Pictorial Press*)

Weinstock with his right-hand man, Sir Kenneth Bond, 1985.

Riccardo Muti, Weinstock's musical hero and devoted friend. (*Lelli & Masotti/Teatro alla Scala, Milan*)

Peter Reynolds, manager of the Ballymacoll Stud in County Meath. (*Alex Brummer*)

Troy, the pride of the Sobell–Weinstock racing partnership, winning the 1979 Derby with Willie Carson. (*E.G. Byrne/Guardian*)

Weinstock at the races in 1985. (*Bespix*)

Henry Kissinger, briefly a GEC adviser, with Weinstock and Lord Rothschild. (*Sidney Harris*)

Two future GEC chairmen, Lords Carrington and Prior, leaving 10 Downing Street after a Cabinet meeting. (*Leith Butler*)

Chairman Lord Prior celebrates GEC's centenary, April 1986.

Simon Weinstock in 1993, three years before his untimely death at the age of forty-four. (*Colin Beere/Financial Times*)

Weinstock at his country mansion at Bowden, Wiltshire, 1987. (*S. Smith/Guardian*)

In the study at Bowden. (*S. Smith/Guardian*)

The Hon. Sara Morrison, Weinstock's confidante and GEC director. (*Universal Pictorial Press*)

Weinstock and Lady Netta. (*Mark Beddall/Camera Press*)

Weinstock in his office at Stanhope Gate, surrounded by pictures of racehorses. (*Sue Adler/Observer*)

Weinstock in 1995.

# FOREWORD

The genesis of this book lies in our 1994 biography of Lord Hanson. Having finished that book, we looked for another figure who had made a dramatic impact on the post-war British industrial landscape. We did not have to look far, for there is no one comparable to Arnold Weinstock. His longevity alone – thirty-three years at the head of the General Electric Company – qualifies him as one of the outstanding industrialists of the modern era. His unconventional background, fascinating personality, idiosyncratic style and uncompromising beliefs made him an irresistible subject. He has attracted controversy throughout his career: fiercely criticised by those who regard him as having wasted a golden opportunity to keep Britain in the lead in the advanced electronics and new communications technologies of the late twentieth century, he has been praised by others for having saved what he could from the minefield laid for manufacturers by the inept policies of successive British governments – as chronicled in his private memoranda, to which we gained exclusive access. It seemed to us at the time we began researching this book, in the autumn of 1994, that he was a business leader whose influence on a generation of industrialists was unmatched, and whose attitudes, formed in the white heat of an earlier Labour revolution, were especially relevant to the New Labour era which was approaching.

But Weinstock is a very private figure, and little light has ever been shed on how he reached the top of British industry, why he remained there, and what motivated him. Our first step was to approach him to seek his cooperation, although there was never any intention that this should be an 'authorised' biography. His response was polite but firm: he would do nothing to stand in our way, but while he remained managing director of GEC, that was his priority. He was not prepared to spend company time talking to us, even though he was keen to give a wider airing to his views on industrial policy and the mess which governments had made of it.

This relatively benign position was enough to set us on our way. Our researcher, Debbie Gordon, began trawling through records of births, marriages and deaths to establish Weinstock's family background and relationships. She followed his early life as a wartime evacuee, and discovered invaluable contacts in Warwickshire, where the unpromising boy from Stoke Newington in north-east London was transformed into university material. Her work was crucial to our understanding of the Weinstock family, and was the foundation for the first chapter. Her brother Daniel Gordon contributed equally valuable work in Poland, where he uncovered the background of the Weinstock family in the provincial manufacturing town of Lodz.

Otherwise our researches have been largely focused on the people who have worked with, or in rivalry to, Lord Weinstock in industry and in government during his three decades at the top. They include an impressive array of business and political figures, who have been involved in policy-making at company and government level for many years, as well as less eminent, but no less helpful, people who have known and worked with him, including schoolfriends from Stoke Newington. Few of those we approached, including leading politicians of the era, were unwilling to talk about this man, who has provoked such strong feelings – both positive and negative – in those who have come across him. We are grateful for their time and assistance. Many of them, however, as is particularly the case in the world of business, preferred to remain anonymous. We have respected their wish for confidentiality; other conversations are fully referenced.

The biography of an industrial figure such as Lord Weinstock must be as much about his company as about his personality. A substantial section of the book, therefore, is concerned with the history of GEC during his tenure. We have relied to some extent on GEC's annual reports for those years, and are grateful to the company, and in particular to company secretary Norman Porter, for supplying us with copies of the relevant documents. We have also made use of the extensive reporting of the company's financial results and other press coverage, which provides a thorough and continuous commentary on companies of GEC's size. Our understanding of the background to the electrical industry, and especially of the crucial takeovers of the 1960s, was helped by a previous book by two journalists: *Anatomy of a Merger*, by Robert Jones and Oliver Marriott. We have leant on their work especially for Chapter Four. The account of the Weinstock racing and bloodstock interests was largely made possible as a result of the hospitality of Peter Reynolds, manager of the Weinstock-owned Ballymacoll stud in Ireland. Weinstock's love of music was illuminated with the help of the musical director of La Scala, Milan, Riccardo Muti.

The progress of our research was sadly impeded by the fatal illness of Lord Weinstock's son Simon, which took his life in May 1996. This tragedy became a key element in our story, but also delayed the point at which we could talk to Lord Weinstock himself: it was not a time when we could impose on him for interviews. True to his word, however, he agreed to answer our questions in the autumn of 1996, once he had stepped down from the position he had occupied for so long. We are immensely grateful to him for sparing us time and for being prepared to answer our questions at what must have been among the most difficult times of his life. We must pay special tribute to GEC director Sara Morrison for her patient handling of our approaches and of her managing director. Equally importantly, it was through her that we were eventually to obtain entrée to the Weinstock memoranda, a unique collection of Arnold Weinstock's confidential missives to his senior executives covering thirty years of GEC history, from 1963 to 1993. This was the essential Weinstock management guide, leavened with wry humour and bracing political views.

Thanks are also due to many others. Generally to all our colleagues on the *Guardian*, who have had to put up with our distraction while we worked on this project, and who have been a constant source of support and advice. More specifically to librarian Maryvonne Grellier, City Office librarian Nick Pandya, picture researcher Nick Richmond and City Office administrator Primrose Williamson. The biggest burden of a book researched and written around a busy working life on a daily newspaper has inevitably fallen on our families, who have had to put up with substantial loss of quality time. So our deepest gratitude is due to our spouses, Tricia Brummer and Christine Asbury, and to our children, Jessica,

Justin and Gabriel Brummer and Timothy, Robbie and Gabriel Cowbury. Our thanks to them for their forbearance, and to everybody else who has made this book possible: in the first instance our agent, Mike Shaw of Curtis Brown, who encouraged us to pursue the project; in the most literal sense to Richard Johnson and Robert Lacey at HarperCollins, who have inspired us, prodded us, honed our words and kept us on the right track. The ultimate responsibility, including any errors, remains with us.

*Alex Brummer and Roger Cowe*
*London, November 1997*

# PRELUDE: FINAL DAYS

## 4 October 1996

THE DOORS OF the Royal Opera House were still closed as the guests, dressed darkly and elegantly, formed a sombre throng in the bright autumnal sun. Some greeted each other with smiles and kisses; others chatted in low tones or sheltered in the large doorways from the gusty wind. It was a mainly metropolitan crowd, with pinstriped businessmen accompanied by sleekly attired women with well-groomed hair and plummy accents. But scattered among them were others up from the country, the racing fraternity in trilby hats and tweeds, and a few more ruddy-faced and less well turned-out figures up from rural Wiltshire, or from the Ballymacoll stud across the Irish Sea.

Shortly before 3 p.m. the doors swung open and the waiting crowd moved forward in an orderly way, clutching small cream-coloured seating cards in their hands as they were ushered towards the orchestra stalls to the sound of Bach's *Fantasia in G* from the organ. The occasional familiar face crossed the field of vision as people took their seats. The magnificent sweep of Raine Spencer's hair was unmistakable; the chiselled face of jockey Lester Piggott, sitting in the side stalls; the tall, slightly dishevelled figure of Lord Rees-Mogg; in the centre stalls a dozen or so rows from the front was Sara Morrison, a director of the General Electric Company and long-time confidante of Lord Arnold Weinstock; standing at the front of the House, conducting a proprietorial check on the seating arrangements and looking like the *maître d'* in a grand restaurant, was Sir Jeremy Isaacs, the pink-faced general director of the Royal Opera House.

In the front row, slightly hidden from view, sat the main celebrants – members of the Weinstock family, there to honour the memory of Simon Weinstock, the lost scion, whose life and career

13

had been cut short at the age of forty-four after a losing fight with cancer. The death of any offspring is a searing experience, leaving a permanent scar on those left behind, but the passing of Simon on 18 May 1996 was far more than just the loss of a son for Arnold Weinstock. Simon was his son, friend, trusted business colleague and potential successor as managing director of GEC. The two men had had an exceptionally close relationship and understanding of each other. Even as Simon's health was ebbing away Lord Weinstock was having to struggle with the momentous choice of an outside successor for the global company he had effectively created himself; he had been cruelly denied the opportunity of considering his son's place in the new hierarchy, the possibility that even if Simon did not succeed him directly he might eventually take charge of the business built on his wisdom and skills and those of his father-in-law, Sir Michael Sobell. Simon's departure was to destroy Weinstock's dreams and confidence. As he wrote in a scrawled, handwritten letter from his holiday retreat at Cap d'Antibes in August 1966: 'It is not possible for me to accept that the world continues to exist without Simon.'[1]

As the final notes of Bach's *Adagio and Fugue* died away in the expanse of the Opera House there was a momentary silence before a tall, serene, fair woman dressed in a black suit strode purposefully to the microphone at the front of the stage. In the days following Simon Weinstock's death, as the tributes poured in and the obituaries appeared, his wife Laura had been referred to simply as the daughter of Sir Francis Legh, equerry to the Queen Mother and Private Secretary to Princess Margaret, with an unspoken hint that she was something unusual, in terms of background, in a family dynasty with Polish-Jewish origins. Now it was Laura's moment. Her voice was steady and cool, her tribute to her late husband wry and affectionate. She told, through a series of amusing anecdotes, how the couple had first met at a dinner party at which he never spoke a word to her until ordering her into his Aston Martin for a ride to a hunt ball; of Simon's disregard for social etiquette; of his perfectionism and his obsession with the finest foods – rejecting, on one occasion, the entire menu at Harry's Bar in Paris in a seductive Italian accent. 'He was always right,' Laura observed ruefully; 'maddeningly so.' He was a man who 'never wasted a moment of his life'.

Laura explained that the fact that Pergolesi's *Stabat Mater*, which was played at the memorial concert, was part of the Catholic liturgy was of no religious significance; it was simply a piece of music loved by her late husband. To underline the point, and to make a generous nod towards her father-in-law and the intense religious tradition which is so much part of Arnold Weinstock's makeup, she added: 'Simon was born a Jew, and we buried him as a Jew.' While alive Simon had made few concessions to the traditions of his ancestors, but he had been laid to rest in Willesden Jewish Cemetery with simplicity, among his own people – in much the same way as generations of Weinstocks had been buried in the family seat of Lodz in Poland. This meant that Laura would never be able to lie by his side. As Simon lived his life in his father's footsteps, so he had been laid to rest in a bare pine coffin to the sound of the *Kaddish* – the prayer of sanctification and consolation – in the way of his forefathers.

The conductor for Simon's memorial concert was Riccardo Muti, who had flown in specially from La Scala in Milan. Muti and Weinstock are extremely close, brought together by their love of classical music. When Weinstock appeared on the BBC's *Desert Island Discs* in 1993 he chose eight pieces conducted by Muti. 'I have a special relationship with Muti; we have been friends for very many years,' he told Sue Lawley.[2] The affection is mutual, Muti regarding Weinstock not simply as a patron or admirer but as 'a brother'.[3] Weinstock, who in business has a reputation for toughness and instilling fear in those who work under him, acknowledges that music is so fundamental to his character that it often reduces him to tears.

As Muti appeared on the podium, tall, dressed starkly in a high-buttoned, black double-breasted suit, Laura Weinstock let it be known that he, the members of the Philharmonia Orchestra who accompanied him and the soprano soloists Barbara Frittoli and Anna Caterina Antonacci had requested that there be no applause. The unbroken hour of music which followed, beginning with a sequence from Pergolesi's *Stabat Mater*, was a rare interval of peace and beauty, far from the bustle of London outside the doors.

The final act of the afternoon was a brief tribute from Lord Prior, a large, florid-faced figure who escaped from the Northern Ireland

Office and the government of Margaret Thatcher in September 1984 to become GEC chairman. In his first years at GEC Prior had found it difficult to become close to Arnold Weinstock and the small coterie of directors who formed the 'inner cabinet' at GEC. But with the passage of time he warmed to his dominant managing director, enjoying his Jewish humour and sharing in his enthusiasms, including music. Prior needed all his political and social skills to steer GEC through the succession crisis which dominated Weinstock's final years as the head of GEC. It was he who had to persuade Weinstock that the City of London would not stand for Simon, whatever his experience and abilities, moving into his father's seat. Now Prior told the audience inside the opera house that Simon had not wanted to leave the investment bankers S.G. Warburg, where he had been working, to join GEC, but had moved to the company 'because his father had wanted it'. Simon, he said, had brought 'honour and intellectual argument' to the GEC headquarters at Stanhope Gate in Mayfair, and he would always be remembered for his loyalty and affectionate nature.

In the foyer the slim, slightly stooped figure of Lord Weinstock stood, looking vulnerable and grief-stricken as the guests gently and diffidently shook his hand, exchanging the fewest of words. The final, formal goodbye to Simon, in the company of so many associates from the diverse worlds of business, bloodstock racing and music, brought down the curtain on a period of turbulence and change in GEC and in Arnold Weinstock's personal life which might have destroyed a man of lesser strength.

After his son's death Weinstock had instinctively retreated to the place where he felt most comfortable and secure: his office. It was only after his final annual general meeting as managing director of GEC on 6 September 1996 at the London Hilton in Park Lane, and the memorial concert later that month, that the extent of the void in a life filled with ambitions for GEC and for his son was to become apparent.

The air of crisis which hung over the question of Weinstock's successor at GEC coincided with the death of his son. Almost from the time Simon had joined GEC from the merchant bank S.G. Warburg in 1983 there was an expectation at Stanhope Gate and in the City that his father was grooming him for the GEC succession, in much the same way as he had already taken over Weinstock's stud and horse-racing interests. The speculation intensified after 1987, when Simon was made commercial director of GEC. His experience in corporate finance at Warburgs had acquainted him with the art of mergers and acquisitions, and in the period that he was part of his father's inner cabinet a series of important deals was struck which fundamentally changed the shape of the General Electric Company. Simon was also involved in piecing together a number of strategic alliances which were intended to bolster GEC's defences against takeover while taking advantage of the increasing globalisation of the industrial world, giving him the blooding he needed in the sphere of global power, defence and technology industries. Moreover, his work after 1992 when he took over supervision of GEC-Marconi, the high-technology company at the core of Britain's defence industry, appeared, in his father's eyes, to have bolted onto his academic credentials the practical experience required to take on the running of a multi-billion pound enterprise.

The speculation as to who would succeed Weinstock as managing director at GEC intensified after he turned seventy on 29 July 1994. Under pressure from the City, he had let it be known that he would relinquish his position within two years, thereby imposing a deadline on himself and the selection committee – on which he would be the dominant figure. He had always seen Simon, then forty-two years old, as his natural successor. 'Of course I would like it, but only on the condition that it fulfilled his life and not that he did something to please me,' he declared in a 1992 interview.[4] Moreover, inside GEC, where Weinstock was such a dominant presence, there were few who would publicly disagree with him.

But the early 1990s were a very different time from 1961, when Arnold Weinstock and his father-in-law Michael Sobell had merged their family business Radio & Allied into GEC, and from the 1980s, when Simon had seamlessly been brought into Stanhope Gate and rapidly made a main board director. It was an age of stronger corporate governance in the City, with the institutional shareholders, the large insurance companies and pension funds demanding a greater say over management. At British Aerospace, a rival of GEC in the defence sector and one of the largest customers for the advanced avionics manufactured by GEC-Marconi, the senior management was twice turfed out by the institutions because it had failed to perform satisfactorily. There was no such problem at GEC. In the deep and long recession of 1990–91, when profits fell across British industry, GEC remained as steady as a rock, its profits close to £1 billion and its assets among the healthiest of Britain's top companies. But good corporate governance also meant smooth transition, so that the interests of shareholders – the owners of the business – and other stakeholders were not disturbed. In this new world the ability to manage assets was seen as the key to industrial succession, not bloodlines, and the possibility that Simon Weinstock might succeed his father at the head of Britain's flagship manufacturer and exporter was not viewed with unalloyed joy.

Even inside GEC there were deep-seated uncertainties. 'He should never have been on the board, let alone a candidate for the succession,' argued Richard Reynolds, the chairman of GPT, GEC's 60 per cent-owned telecoms offshoot. Reynolds was forced off the GEC board in November 1996 after privately briefing the *Sunday Telegraph* about his reservations before Simon's death.[5] Weinstock had established Reynolds' responsibility for the leaks by inspecting the phone records at Stanhope Gate.

Some among Weinstock's inner circle felt that his ambition for his son to succeed him was foolish. 'He [Simon] is away with the fairies,' one observed, expressing frustration that Lord Weinstock, as wise as he is, could never come to terms with the perceived shortcomings of his son. The chairman, Lord Prior, left little doubt that he regarded Weinstock as the problem: 'It's been a difficult area, because Arnold has been so dominant in the company for so long and, frankly, has not really wanted to let go of the reins. But I think there is a sort of inevitability about age, like everything else, that you can't get over. This was very much found out because he was hoping that Simon was going to take over from him. And although I think Simon might have grown into the job in years to come ... I think it was a bit cruel to Simon. And it took quite a long while to convince father that son was not the right person.'[6]

Despite his ambitions for his son, Weinstock was too astute a businessman to have discounted other possibilities. There was a flurry of excitement when in 1994 he added two younger executives to GEC's board: Peter Gershon, managing director of GEC-Marconi, and Jim Cronin, managing director of GEC–Alsthom, who is widely credited with having stitched together what is arguably GEC's only genuinely world-class business, in power engineering and locomotive systems.

But Weinstock never really believed that either Gershon or Cronin, or the young finance director David Newlands, had the breadth of vision GEC required. Instead, he explored the possibility of making an outside acquisition which would bring its management – and perhaps his own successor – with it. Among the companies considered were Carlton Communications, whose chairman was Michael Green, and Amstrad, run by Alan Sugar. Faced with increasing pressure to make a decision, and with Simon's illness, which shattered his hopes for a third generation at the pinnacle of the British electrical engineering industry, he opted for an experienced industrialist, British Aerospace's deputy chief executive George Simpson, as his successor.

Lord Weinstock's handling of the succession was not his finest hour. It left a stain on his final days as managing director of GEC, and a lingering anger which surfaced at his last annual general meeting, at the London Hilton on 6 September 1996. There he took the opportunity to lecture the shareholders who had demanded a modernisation of GEC's management structures and on the shortcomings of the corporate governance system which had demanded his retirement. His brutalist view was that shareholders who did not trust their directors should sell their shares.

Even Weinstock's closest admirers regard the handover of power as having been calamitous. 'It was a mess,' one of his closest associates observed: 'Arnold had to take the blame because he had been warned three years earlier that he needed to take steps on the succession, but had just ploughed on.'[7] By October 1995, when director Richard Reynolds had surreptitiously spoken to the press, the game was up, although Reynolds' main target had not been Weinstock but Prior, whom he hoped to follow as chairman. At that point even Weinstock began to recognise that an internal appointment, including a succession structure involving Simon, was no longer possible: the moment had passed.

Neither Weinstock nor Prior was particularly well suited for the search process. Prior had never fulfilled the traditional chairman's role of cultivating the City and investors, but had been used more as a super-ambassador for GEC in the Far East and as a link to Whitehall, which was responsible for so much of the group's domestic business. In the event it was Weinstock who took the initiative. When the succession issue was finally resolved, an enormous burden was lifted from his shoulders, only to be replaced by another – his son's health. With Simon's death, a huge vacuum opened in Arnold Weinstock's life which could only be filled by work. The office is still the place he is most likely to be found, or with Simon's children – his eldest granddaughter, thirteen-year-old Pamela, was at his side at his last annual meeting as managing director.

# CHAPTER ONE

# *New Beginnings*

ARNOLD WEINSTOCK'S PARENTS migrated to London from the prosperous Polish city of Lodz in the early years of the twentieth century. A relatively modern city, which grew rapidly in the nineteenth century, Lodz is located a hundred miles south-west of the capital Warsaw, and three hundred miles east of Berlin. It has strong industrial and manufacturing traditions. The Russians, who controlled the region in the early nineteenth century, declared it an industrial zone, attracting German manufacturers to the area who harnessed the latest technology to develop a thriving textile industry. By the 1840s Lodz had become a commercial centre and Poland's second city. Large numbers of Polish peasants were drawn there in search of work, swelling the population to three hundred thousand by the end of the century. Among the incomers were many members of the surrounding rural Jewish populations, who started to settle in the city in the 1820s, arriving in huge numbers in the 1830s. A second wave of Jewish immigration to Lodz was sparked later in the century as Russian Jews fled from an outbreak of pogroms and persecution.

From 1825 to 1860 the Jewish population of Lodz was confined to a tiny area in the older part of the city, where restrictive laws confined their activities to the traditional areas of shopkeeping, tanning and tailoring. These laws were lifted in the 1860s, opening new residential and commercial opportunities for the community. Soon they were starting small industries and moving into banking and trading, and newly-arrived Russian and Lithuanian Jews saw an opportunity to develop Lodz as a trading centre with the east.

But although the Jews of Lodz had begun to move up the economic ladder, only a few made the top rung, which was largely occupied by the German entrepreneurs who first developed the city. The most celebrated Jewish industrialist was the textile magnate Izrael Pozanski, whose factory employed thousands of Poles and Jews and became the suppliers of clothing to much of Eastern Europe. The Pozanski family built itself three magnificent palaces, one of which now serves as Lodz's municipal offices, and Izrael Pozanski's exploits reached almost mythical proportions among the city's 250,000-strong Jewish community. Some forty thousand of Lodz's poor working-class Jews were crowded into the Baluty area north of the city, which during the Second World War would become the notorious Lodz Ghetto.

Lodz's Jewish community was economically better off than those in Warsaw and Krakow, and enjoyed far more tolerance than in other Polish cities. They may not have been fully integrated, but many were successful enough to break down barriers and form businesses. The elegant main thoroughfare, Piotrkowska, renowned as the longest shopping street in Europe, provided testimony to the commercial achievement of the Jews of Lodz. A road of well-built, ornate stone buildings, the businesses on one side of Piotrkowska were dominated by Jewish-owned banks, stores and merchants, while on the other side were those owned and controlled by German and Polish entrepreneurs. Piotrkowska has claimed a place in the *Guinness Book of Records* as the site of the most lengthy tug-of-wars in history in 1938, shortly before the German army arrived in Lodz. Located at Piotrkowska 60 at the turn of the century was a paper merchant and stationers which bore the legend 'Weinstok', one of several enterprises bearing the family name at the time. Another was the Kommissionerzy, a second-hand store in an affluent neighbourhood, and in the same period a Boruch Weinstok operated an ironmonger's/iron merchant's store close to the centre of the city.

The commercial success and social acceptance of the Jews of Lodz contrasted with the conditions in nearby towns and villages, where poverty and outbreaks of anti-Semitism drove many Jews to the cities or abroad. Even after the First World War, when Lodz moved from Russian to Polish control, it remained a magnet for Jewish refugees, constantly on the move in Europe between the world wars. Among those who arrived in the city in large numbers were traditional Jews from Russia, some of whom bore the Weinstock name, which had formerly been comparatively rare in Poland.

The main traces of the Weinstock family in Lodz prior to the First World War are to be found in the vast, overgrown Jewish cemetery to the north-east of the city, one of the most beautiful and best preserved in Eastern Europe, covering more than a square mile and containing an astonishing 180,000 graves. The rows of elaborately carved granite memorial stones are dominated by the gold-domed tomb of the Pozanski family. Among those buried in the cemetery is one Sucher Weinstock, who died in January 1925, aged fifty-three. His grave is decorated with a carving of a goblet being filled with wine. This could indicate a connection with the wine trade, or it could be no more than an illustration of the family name. Nearby is the grave of Sucher's wife Mundla, who died a year earlier than her husband, on 24 December 1924, aged fifty-four. Both graves are unkempt and overgrown, suggesting that any relatives who might have cared for them moved away many decades ago.

Among the most famous Jewish sons of Lodz is an Aleksander Weinstock, whose paintings – signed 'Weinsztok' – decorate the walls of the modern Jewish Community Centre. Aleksander Weinstock was a self-taught artist who painted advertising posters on the streets of Lodz in the inter-war period. During the war he escaped to Russia, returning to Lodz after the liberation. His prints and paintings were exhibited at the Union of Lodz Artists in 1955, 1956 and 1960–61. He has since emigrated to Victoria, Australia, where he is still painting.

On the surface, the decision by Arnold Weinstock's father Simon to uproot his wife Golda (Gertie) Schag and their three young sons in 1904 is somewhat puzzling. But despite the comparatively good conditions enjoyed by the Jews of Lodz, Simon and Golda were acutely aware that the whole history of the Jewish communities of Russia and Poland was littered with pogroms and outbreaks of persecution. Their decision to emigrate from Poland was prescient. In the late 1930s, by which time Simon Weinstock's sons had settled into successful careers in London, many of Lodz's wealthier Jews were fleeing for safer pastures in Western Europe and the United States.

Left behind were two hundred thousand Jews, who in 1941 were herded into a small section of the city which became infamous as the Lodz ghetto. Tens of thousands of those trapped inside the ghetto's walls were shipped off to unknown destinations – the death camps. Yet despite the grief, exhaustion, starvation and fear in the ghetto, the civilised culture of 'family, art, education, sex, religion and hope' lived on.[1] By the time of the German defeat, just thirty-eight thousand of Lodz's pre-war Jewish population of a quarter of a million survived, including four bearing the name of Weinstock. The city, stifled by the domination of the Soviet Union, ceased to be the thriving commercial centre of the late nineteenth and early twentieth century. It rapidly became apparent that the surviving remnant of Lodz's Jewry was no longer welcome, and following anti-Semitic outbursts in 1948, 1956 and 1968, the Jewish community dwindled to nothing.

Arnold Weinstock was born on 29 July 1924 in Stoke Newington, in the London Borough of Hackney. It was a remarkable birth for its time because of the age of his parents: his father was fifty, and his mother forty-six. The oldest of the new baby's five brothers, Samuel, was twenty-four, and the closest to him in age, Henry, was fifteen. Arnold was the third of the Weinstock clan to have been born a British citizen, following Harry, born in 1906, and Henry, born in 1909. The family home at 50 Belgrade Road, Stoke Newington, was a modest two-storey Victorian terraced house, one of forty-eight built by the developer Thomas Pryor. In the late-nineteenth century Stoke Newington was largely inhabited by professional people working in the City of London, and was regarded as a cut above the nearby working-class neighbourhoods of Islington and the East End, where poor Jewish immigrants, mainly from Russia, lived in squalid conditions in hazardous tenement buildings. It had a sizeable German community, and Belgrade Road was originally called Wiesbaden Road, but the name was changed during the First World War.

In the early years of the twentieth century, after Arnold Weinstock's parents settled there, the traditional agrarian-based industries of Stoke Newington, nurseries and cow-keeping, had given way to small-scale manufacture, including pram- and bicycle-

24

making, sometimes in sweatshop conditions, and outworking was common. By 1914 larger factories began to appear, including the 'Hygienic Steam Laundry', wallpaper factories and a piano-maker. The Alexandra Theatre – which played host to Lily Langtry and other artists – was a popular venue, and there were several cinemas. None of these, however, could challenge the popularity of Hackney Downs as a favourite courting location for young people freed from the drudgery of appalling workshop conditions.[2]

More than fifty years later the residents of Belgrade Road are more West Indian than Jewish. The street is still respectable. Many of the houses surrounding Arnold Weinstock's birthplace have been gentrified, and just a few houses down from the Weinstock home – currently derelict – behind a wrought-iron fence is a small, peaceful garden belonging to the nearby Princess May Road School, where the young Arnold received his first education.

At the time of Arnold's birth his father Simon, a master cutter, was working for Hitchcock & Willis, a specialist firm making 'Ladies' Coats and Mantles' in the area to the north of Oxford Street in London's West End, which was and remains the centre of the women's tailoring business. It was Simon's job to draw the patterns and cut the cloth. This is a skilled trade, as the ability to cut accurately and avoid wastage of expensive materials can make a real difference to the profits of the business: Simon's son Arnold would bring similar abilities to the electrical trade later in his life. Among Arnold's earliest memories is being taken by his father to his workplace and being fussed over by his co-workers.

Simon Weinstock was not the only immigrant to gravitate towards the clothing trade. As in Lodz, where textile manufacture had been the dominant business, tailoring and the rag trade were the most likely occupations for the immigrant Jewish population of North and East London. In the East End of the 1920s, Jewish textile workers were beginning to organise, forming trade unions and negotiating hours and conditions of work and a minimum wage of £3 per week.

Through his work Simon Weinstock improved his family's fortunes, allowing them to live a reasonably comfortable life. His work in the West End also gave him and his sons an insight into where best to attempt to make the transition to Britain's moneyed classes.

By the mid-1920s Arnold's elder brothers were beginning to make their way in the world. The second eldest son, Michael, had struck out on his own as a hairdresser in the Old Kent Road. On 27 January 1924 he married Annie Gelblatt, a West End dressmaker, at the Wellington Road Synagogue in Stoke Newington. The third of the brothers, Jack (Jakob), also a hairdresser, was married in the same synagogue to Fanny Bond, the daughter of a draper, in 1928. Jack was later to open his own hairdressing salon on Well Street, in the West End garment district, where he attracted a 'swish' range of clients who would be vital to Arnold's progress after the Second World War. Marriage is among the most sacred institution of Judaism, and for Simon and Golda the weddings of two of their sons, in the country they had adopted as their own, were particularly symbolic, and events of great pride and rejoicing.

Just a month before Arnold's fifth birthday, and less than a year after Jack's wedding, tragedy struck the family when Simon died of heart failure on 28 June 1929, after contracting acute pneumonia. Although he was only a small boy, Arnold felt the loss deeply. His father, a tall, dignified figure, had instilled in his children the value of having a trade and a love of their Jewish roots. Among Arnold's enduring memories of his father was the ritual of dressing up in dark coat, trousers and hat on the Jewish Sabbath, with his gold fob watch and chain nestled in his waistcoat, and setting out for the *shul* (synagogue) at Wellington Road.

The loss of her husband placed enormous pressure on Golda, who was now left with the full responsibility of looking after her eldest son, Samuel, who had been born with a handicap (later to be diagnosed as motor neurone disease). But, in the tradition of Jewish mothers, she was a strong, dominant woman who as 'the boss' of the household was able to cope with most of life's vicissitudes.[3]

Shortly after his father's death, Arnold began his schooling at the Princess May Road School, just a block south of the family home. The school is an impressive three-storey Victorian structure built of yellow and red brick, capped by a vast, airy loft, a small white tower and a lightning rod decorated with a small globe. It faces Stoke Newington Road, the main street, and is built around a large quadrangular play area. As was the custom with schools of the day there was one entrance for boys and another for girls and infants.

The years at the Princess May school were not happy ones for Arnold. He began his education there under the shadow of his father's death, but when he was nine years old he was to suffer an even greater tragedy. His mother had contracted breast cancer, and Arnold, confused and told very little about what was happening, was sent away from Belgrade Road, in the company of one his brother's wives, to Walton-on-the-Naze, a small Essex seaside resort. By the time he returned to London his mother, who had held the family together after his father's death, had lost her struggle with her illness, dying at the age of fifty-six on 12 May 1934. Arnold, the late child of his parents' marriage, was now an orphan.

In the wider world, the British economy was lumbering under the burden of three million unemployed, Sir Oswald Mosley had opened his campaign of hatred against the Jews, and in Germany Adolf Hitler had ruthlessly crushed all political opposition to become sole master of the country. All of these would play a part in shaping the course of Arnold Weinstock's life.

With no parents to care for him, the responsibility for bringing up Arnold now shifted to his older brothers. He does not recollect this experience with any great enthusiasm: 'One of my brothers took me in for a bit, until the war,' he has noted flatly.[4] The brother who opened his doors was the twenty-eight-year-old Harry, a master hairdresser who four years earlier had married Annie Waltzer, a fur machinist. Arnold moved into their house at 91 Carysfort Road, a few streets to the west of Belgrade Road, on the edge of Clissold Park. By 1936 he was living at Petherton Road, a little to the south-west, on the borders of Highbury, with various Waltzer in-laws.

It was in the Highbury years that Arnold's great love of music was born. His inspiration was Cantor Koussevitzky at the nearby Poet's Road Synagogue, one of three brothers, all of whom were musically accomplished and had outstanding voices. Arnold, who had an alto voice, joined the Synagogue choir, and would perch with the other choir members high above the ark containing the scrolls of the law, mesmerised by the beauty of the liturgy and

Cantor Koussevitsky's tenor voice: it was from this choral ground-
ing that his love of opera would develop. Apart from music, though,
his interest in Jewish culture was not always strong: 'There used
to be a rabbi who came to teach me Hebrew, but I used to stand
at the top of the road with my bicycle and when I saw him coming
I used to ride in the opposite direction,' he remembered many years
later.[5]

The period of rootlessness and wandering which followed the
death of his mother would profoundly affect Arnold's character. It
developed in him a deep need for his own home, or territory, of
which he was master and where his control was absolute. It was
this need, rather than a ruthless desire to make money, which was
to shape his subsequent business career.

In September 1935, at the age of eleven, Arnold moved on to
the Stoke Newington Central School. Central schools, while they
did not share the prestige of the grammar schools, were considered
far more challenging than the normal run of secondary schools,
which provided a rudimentary education until the then school leaving age of fourteen. Entry to a central school required a strong
recommendation from the headmaster of the junior school, and
interviews were held with candidates drawn from the local area.
Gaining a place at the central school must have been an early
confidence-booster for the young Arnold, given his difficult personal circumstances.

The Stoke Newington Central School (SNCS) placed an emphasis
on practical commercial training, but its curriculum was broad
enough to encourage in Arnold, and in many of those who were
at school with him, an interest in music. The school also had a
strong sports tradition, notably in cricket, football and athletics,
although there is no indication that the young Arnold, who was
pitifully thin, showed much interest. Indeed, his physique was a
subject of some amusement for his classmates. 'He was so skinny
that we would play the xylophone on his ribs,' Gordon Hill, a school
friend picked out by the school magazine as a 'budding football
champion', who would later work for GEC, recalls.[6]

There was a great deal of pride in what SNCS stood for. Writing
in the school magazine at the end of Arnold's first year, the headmaster, Captain W.H.L. Jones, reported that the school had 'con-

tinued to progress', with the average roll at 395 pupils, boys and girls, and attendance 93 per cent. He noted that 'all pupils who complete the school course are quickly placed in employment, and the numerous letters received from Old Scholars giving accounts of happy progress are a source of great pleasure.' His goal, he declared, was that a larger number of pupils would enter for the Royal Society of Arts and London Chamber of Commerce examinations.[7] The high quality of the school's teaching and the success of its students made it something of a showcase for the London County Council. During Arnold's first year, visitors from all over the world came to visit the school, including delegations from France, Czechoslovakia, Australia, Sweden, Norway and the USA. There was also a visit from Poland, the land of his late parents.

The pupils of Class 1X, including Arnold, settled in well according to one pupil who wrote in the school magazine: 'Soon after our arrival the Headmaster paid our class a compliment by saying how quickly we all had our uniform, and our hymn books; we are proud of this, and also our classroom, which we think is the cheeriest in the School.' Arnold's own recollections are not so rose-tinted. He remembers taking a beating for failing to complete his homework, an indication that he had not yet discovered the value of learning, although he was later to be regarded by his fellow pupils as something of a swot.

More to his taste was SNCS's focus on the world of commerce, finance and expenditure. This partly reflected the interests of Captain Jones, an honours graduate in economics. All the children were required to learn shorthand and typing. French was also compulsory, which would prove useful for Weinstock later in life, when his favourite vacation spot would be Cap d'Antibes and when he would forge a series of commercial alliances with French industrial groups. But perhaps most important of all to the young Weinstock was the study of double-entry bookkeeping, by no means a standard part of the school curriculum. As he was to record several decades later: 'It [SNCS] was a secondary school and it was supposed to teach commercial things. It did actually teach me bookkeeping. Simple double-entry bookkeeping. That stood me in good stead, better than accounting really! That was a very valuable thing to have learned at an early age!'[8]

29

In his later life as a captain of industry, Arnold Weinstock would keep track of what was happening in GEC's dozens of constituent companies by means of a series of accounting and financial ratios. Accurate cost-accounting was at the core of the discipline he would bring to the British electrical and defence contracting industries. His admiration for the power of accounting had been nurtured at the Stoke Newington Central School.

There were also lessons on how the SNCS graduate entering the workforce should deal with the practical side of life, as a fellow student recalls: 'One of the things we learnt was about finance and when you leave school and go to work, how you should work out your expenditure. They told us that 25 per cent of your money should go on housing, 25 per cent on food, and so much on clothes, and so much on savings.'[9] Captain Jones was also very keen to have as many pupils as possible sign up for the School Savings Society and learn the value of thrift – another lesson which Weinstock, who always liked to operate his businesses with a cash cushion, never forgot.

Culturally, there was much to commend SNCS to the young Weinstock. At least 25 per cent of the school's intake was Jewish, many of the children travelling from nearby Stamford Hill, where they lived in flats run by the Guinness Trust and the London County Council. Although Stamford Hill and Stoke Newington were both considered Jewish areas in the 1930s, the highly orthodox sects which have now colonised this part of North London did not arrive until after the liberation of the concentration camps. Nevertheless, there was a strong Jewish atmosphere in the neighbourhood, with a good scattering of kosher butchers and bakers, as well as the vibrant synagogue on Poet's Road where the young Arnold Weinstock sang in the choir. SNCS was generally free of anti-Semitism, despite the bitterness in the nearby East End, where in 1936–37 Sir Oswald Mosley's British Union of Fascists was fomenting trouble by marching through Jewish neighbourhoods, boycotting and defacing Jewish-owned businesses.[10] In these potentially disturbing times the science teacher D.R. Newton, who was Jewish, provided some reassurance to the Jewish students at SNCS. But the actions of Mosley and his black-shirted thugs were to have a strong influence on the teenage Weinstock's developing political outlook:

'Before the war, in 1939, when I was fourteen or fifteen years old, the two people I most admired were Churchill and Stalin' because of their willingness to stand up to the Fascists.[11]

SNCS's greatest cultural inspiration was its music teacher, Frederick (Freddie) Fogg. He had the rare gift of being able to instil a love of music in the children, to the point that they would happily give up their lunch hour to practise. An article in the school magazine captures Freddie Fogg's pulling power. The writer describes going in search of strange wails reverberating through the school during the lunch break:

> Surely what I hear is a wail of agony from some poor tortured native, or a starving family? Can there possibly be such atrocities in the happy, peace loving Borough of Stoke Newington? . . . or even worse, has one child killed another in amiable play, or has someone speared a friend with a window pole, gouged their eyes with a lino-cutting tool, or playfully caught someone's head in a guillotine? Dreadful pictures flit across my mind as I rush downstairs. There, under the stimulating tuition of a smiling, rotund mentor, some two dozen youths and maidens of Stoke Newington are eagerly and happily practising their scales . . . the wails and shrieks which had so terrified me are but the scratchings of a group of violin enthusiasts, and the usually harassed faces of three masters who are participating become almost seraphic with delight . . . even so are discovered the Kreislers, Milsteins and Menuhins of the rising generation.[12]

Many of the students were captivated by Freddie Fogg's teaching, both in music and his other subject of mathematics, and by the vitality he would invest in school productions of Gilbert and Sullivan, in which he would take the comic lead. In *The Yeomen of the Guard*, produced shortly before Christmas 1938, Fogg played the role of Jack Point, the strolling jester. Among the chorus, dressed up in red Beefeater costume, was Arnold Weinstock, now fourteen years old. Pursuing his interest in light opera, he had also taken to visiting Sadler's Wells and viewing from the gallery. Freddie Fogg's production of *The Yeomen of the Guard* was a sell-out, and he was to become an inspiration for the teenage Weinstock, a sort of surrogate

31

father. He was an accomplished enough teacher to combine his job at SNCS with part-time teaching at the North London Polytechnic, and he instilled a lifelong love of music in many of his pupils, including Gordon Hill.

*The Yeomen of the Guard* would be the last Gilbert and Sullivan light opera to be heard at the Stoke Newington Central School for several years. The hopes of 'peace in our time' which Neville Chamberlain brought back from his ill-starred meeting with Adolf Hitler in Munich on 30 September 1938 proved short-lived, and by the spring of 1939 the positions of the British and French governments had hardened against any potential Nazi incursion into Poland. Plans drawn up by the London County Council to evacuate priority groups to the countryside were revived. In conjunction with the Ministry of Health and the Board of Education, the LCC decided that preference for evacuation should be given to schoolchildren, young children with their mothers or guardians, and pregnant women. By August 1939, shortly before war was declared, some 70 per cent of London's schoolchildren, including Arnold Weinstock and the other pupils of SNCS, had been registered for evacuation. The Germans invaded Poland, the land of Weinstock's parents, on 1 September, and the British declaration of war followed within forty-eight hours.

The plans for moving six hundred thousand schoolchildren to the countryside were triggered, and the children of SNCS assembled for a train journey to an unknown destination. Each child had a small case containing their personal effects, and they were issued with a lapel badge with their name and a cardboard box containing a gas mask. For the fifteen-year-old Arnold Weinstock, evacuation meant leaving the central school, the Poet's Road Synagogue and Sadler's Wells, his brothers and extended family and the urban environment for the countryside, about which he knew little. It was a wrenching experience for a child who had already suffered the trauma of being orphaned.

There were rumours among some of the parents that the children were to be taken to Northampton, but instead the locomotive steamed into Rugby station, in Warwickshire. The party of children and teachers was directed a few hundred yards north of the station

32

to the town's cattle market, where the families who had agreed to take evacuees had assembled. If they had been expecting neatly dressed little children in pretty frocks and smart uniforms, they were quickly disabused. As a chill wind whistled across the large, flat expanse of the cattle market they were greeted by the sight of a knot of awkward teenagers, most of whom had never left their native North London before. Arnold, tall and skinny with a mop of dark hair, cut a particularly unprepossessing figure. No one could have guessed that this youth would one day be the largest employer in the Rugby area. Within a short walking distance of the cattle market stood the British Thomson-Houston engineering plant, now part of GEC–Alsthom, the world-beating Anglo–French power-turbine group.

The situation at the cattle market was an uncomfortable one. There was no pre-assignment of children to families, but instead a crude selection, a little like that in a school playground before a pick-up football match. The smaller children were selected first, then the girls, and finally the gangling teenage boys. The sense of rejection for those picked towards the end of this process, especially if life had already delivered them hard knocks, as in Arnold's case, must have been severe.

Arnold was eventually chosen by Harry and Florence Smith, who lived in a two-storey end-of-terrace council house just outside the picturesque village of Churchover. The house was slightly isolated from the village, with its smartly restored brick-built houses, cottages and stables, and neatly mowed village green. It stood on the road to Coton, an elegant stone-built manor house built by Mrs Astor. At the time of Arnold's stay Coton was occupied by the formidable figure of Mrs Arthur James, the godmother of the present Queen Mother, who was reputed to have been a mistress of Edward VII and who took a strong interest in the well-being of the evacuees. Harry Smith was employed at Thomson-Houston, while Flo worked part-time at Coton. They had a young son, Roger.

The assembly point for the evacuees and the families with whom they were staying was the village hall at Harborough Magna, three miles or so as the crow flies from the Smiths' house. It was in this plain wooden structure that the children were formally registered by the local education authorities before beginning their new lives.

They were broken up into groups of about twenty and distributed among the village schools throughout the area, although Harborough Magna would serve as the effective centre. The SNCS headmaster's wife Mrs Jones would teach typing classes at the rectory at Harborough Magna; Captain Jones would be in charge of English teaching throughout the school in exile; and Freddie Fogg, based in Monks Kirby (five miles north of Harborough Magna), would teach algebra, geometry and maths as well as music.

The arrival of the SNCS students was as disconcerting to the residents of rural Warwickshire as it was to the children themselves. Many of the local families had never travelled to London, and they certainly had no knowledge or understanding of the Jewish children among the refugees. One of the foster mothers recalls that when the headmistress of the village school came to ask if she would take some of the evacuees, 'she had to inform us that they were Jewish boys. We found them quite likeable, but they took a lot of keeping when they were ten years old until they were sixteen years old. The ones I had were Jewish boys, and I said it did not worry me, because none of us asked to be born, do we? We received ten shillings per boy per week.'[13]

The village schools, in which children of all ages would learn together, were very different from SNCS, with its emphasis on commercial examinations, matriculation and preparing its pupils for careers in the City of London. In the early days, the head teacher of the small, single-storey red-brick Harborough Magna school, Mary Bounds, clearly found the new arrangements a little trying. By November 1939 enough resources had been marshalled to resume full-day schooling, but Mrs Bounds was plainly not a happy woman. On 6 November she wrote in her diary: 'All the time we have done half-day school, no complaints have been made, about the way Stoke Newington people have finished their work, but yesterday, when I only had one and a quarter hours to look after eleven dinners, children and myself, I had so much tidying to do that I had no lunch at all. When I left a polite note for Mr Hope [Norman Hope, the SNCS deputy head], he rudely said to me to write through the correspondent. He is in no position to give me orders so I am ignoring him.'[14]

Dissatisfied with the direction in which things were going, Mrs Bounds set a new series of requirements for the Stoke Newington teachers. She asked that blackboards be cleaned and dusters shaken; that the SNCS teachers get their own duster; that dirty water be emptied and buckets put away; and that school be dismissed at the proper time, and without gossiping. She added: 'I have taken three children on my register. But I will not have other children crouching over the fire in my room, where my children and I eat, as they eat out of papers, strew their crumbs, and no hot drink is provided for them.' But the musical talents of the SNCS pupils, as drilled by Freddie Fogg, made even the acerbic Mrs Bounds more receptive to the visitors. On 22 December, just before the first Christmas of the war, she wrote: 'This week the evacuees entertained us at the hall on Wednesday with the concert which they will be giving their billet mothers.' The evacuees broadened their sporting horizons during their exile. SNCS was a soccer school, but the boys had to adjust to rugby union for games with Rugby school, as well as an annual cricket match arranged by 'one of the rich farmer's sons'.[15]

Although the Smiths' house on the outskirts of Churchover was one of a terrace, its setting in the lush Warwickshire countryside was a world away from the choked streets of Stoke Newington and Highbury. Arnold's daily three-mile walk to Harborough Magna took him along attractive country lanes and across a stream whose waters sometimes submerged the narrow footbridge.

After less than a year with the Smiths, Arnold was told he was moving. This time he found himself billeted in a remote farmhouse, set in 120 acres of land, near the tiny hamlet of Withybrook. It was a primitive place, with almost no plumbing. There were, however, advantages. He was now assigned to the school at Monks Kirby, and so fell within the sphere of influence of Freddie Fogg. Moreover, the wife of his new host, Percy Dawkins, was a schoolteacher, and she helped to enthuse the young Weinstock in his learning. 'They [the Dawkinses] were very good to me,' he remembers. He also encountered a totally different musical experience from the Poet's Road Synagogue – singing in a Church of England choir at Monks Kirby, encouraged by Fogg: 'I used to walk four miles a day to school, and there I was taught by a master who in London had taught us mathematics and music. He was a lay preacher, and he helped me enormously and made me take an interest in work which no one had been able to do before. I took four months, I remember, learning the whole of *Macbeth* walking backwards and forwards to school. I never had a look at the thing in class at all.'[16] Now firmly under the wing of Freddie Fogg, the young Arnold began to make astonishing progress in his school work. 'He revived my interest in learning,' he recalls, which had been at a low ebb 'for five or six years'.

Along with some of his classmates from SNCS, Weinstock sat his Matriculation in the parish hall at Harborough Magna midway through 1941. He was confident enough to sit six subjects, and gained a distinction in mathematics, putting him in a strong position to become the first member of his family ever to gain a place at university. Supported by good references from Captain Jones and from Fogg, who had guided him through his Matriculation, he applied to the London School of Economics to read for a B.Sc. (Economics) degree in statistics. On the basis of his Matriculation results and shining recommendations, he was accepted without interview.

Weinstock's stay in rural Warwickshire left little lasting impression on the villagers of Churchover, Monks Kirby and Harborough Magna. He was not one of the youths who is remembered for dancing with the local girls and learning to drink beer at the Golden Lion in Harborough Magna. Nevertheless, as he progressed through industry, memories of his stay in rural Warwickshire were stirred, and he never lost touch with Flo and Harry Smith or with the Dawkins family. His generosity allowed the Smiths to take family holidays, and when Harry had a bad accident at Thomson-Houston Arnold anxiously enquired about his well-being. Each Christmas Florence would receive flowers from GEC headquarters at Stanhope Gate.

When the villagers of Churchover wanted to commemorate Queen Elizabeth II's Silver Jubilee in 1977, it was to Arnold Weinstock that they turned for help. A member of the parish council, Hazel Bell, contacted him, and the result was a circular lattice metal seat, constructed at an AEI plant nearby, which now surrounds the magnificent old oak on Churchover village green. A small steel plaque reads: 'This seat commemorates the Jubilee of Queen Elizabeth II. It was provided by funds raised from the Parish and with the assistance of GEC Machines Ltd whose first-year apprentices manufactured it.' There is no reference to Weinstock's Warwickshire interlude, or to the contribution it made to his education and eventual achievements.

Weinstock has never publicly paid a sentimental return visit to Warwickshire. In October 1991 he sent his apologies when many of the surviving evacuees gathered for a reunion at the old wooden village hall at Harborough Magna on the fiftieth anniversary of their journey from London. In his capacity as GEC's managing director he did visit the Willans Works in Rugby, now a maker of turbines for GEC–Alsthom, in 1979. Gordon Hill, who was works manager at Willans, told a sceptical local director Sir Robert Davidson that he wished to meet Arnie Weinstock, as they had been at school together. The managing director duly arrived, accompanied by fellow director Sara Morrison, whose dog proceeded to pee on the bowling green. The reunion between the two Stoke Newington evacuees, the one who had stayed in Warwickshire and the other who had made a remarkable journey to the heights of industry, was brusque. Arnold's first words to his old classmate were: 'You used to bully me,' to which Gordon Hill replied, 'Not in a million years.'[17] When Hill retired from Willans in 1989 he received a personal fax from Stanhope Gate: 'I have heard from Bob Davidson that you are hanging up your boots today. This is to send you my very best wishes for a long and happy retirement doing what you like.'[18]

At the outbreak of war the Ministry of Works had laid claim to the central London home of the London School of Economics, Britain's leading temple of learning for students of the social sciences. Appropriately, the LSE buildings were to be the base of the Ministry of Economic Warfare, headed by Hugh Dalton, who had trained at the LSE and who went on to be the Labour Party's first post-war Chancellor of the Exchequer. The School found shelter in Cambridge, at the Master's Lodge opposite the main gate at Peterhouse, which was called New Court at the time but was subsequently renamed The Hostel.

At first it was thought that the LSE's exile in Cambridge would be a temporary affair, but soon it became apparent that the School would be part of Cambridge for some time, and it remained there for six years in all. At the time of its removal to Cambridge the LSE, founded in 1895 by the Fabian socialists Sidney and Beatrice Webb, enjoyed a high reputation. Under the direction of William Beveridge, the architect of the modern Welfare State, it had been transformed from a 'flimsy semi-academic institution geared to part-time teaching and learning and certain special courses into a modern research university with a strong undergraduate component'.[19]

Between 1919 and 1937, Beveridge attracted some of the most notable teachers and scholars of the era to the LSE. Among the glittering names who would move to Cambridge under Beveridge's successor Alexander Carr-Saunders were Friedrich von Hayek, who in the 1980s would become the high priest of Thatcherism; R.H. Tawney, the influential socialist economic historian; Nicholas Kaldor, who was to become economic adviser to the Wilson governments of the 1960s; the brilliant anthropologist Bernard Malinowski; Harold Laski, the much-admired socialist political scientist and philosopher; and Lionel Robbins, who directed the economic section of Churchill's war cabinet and went on to write the 1963 Robbins Committee report on higher education. Beveridge had also attracted to the School many of the most accomplished young academics from Continental Europe, some of them seeking safe haven before the Nazi onslaught. Their presence, and the generally socialist leanings of the academic faculty, bestowed upon the LSE a glamour which made it a magnet for students like Arnold Weinstock growing up in the late 1930s: the brightest of their generation.

By the time Arnold, then aged seventeen, arrived at Cambridge in the autumn of 1941, the integration of the LSE with its wartime host was well under way. The choice of Cambridge for the LSE's sojourn had appeared somewhat odd. Many of the School's most famous names, including Robbins, Laski and Tawney, had Oxford degrees. Moreover, the LSE had partly been established as a counterweight to the prevailing classical orthodoxy of Alfred Marshall and Cambridge. Oxford, a more worldly place, was in many ways more like the LSE, whereas the emphasis at Cambridge was more bound up with mathematics and the work of the scientific community. Nevertheless, the LSE and its faculty were welcomed: the Director Alexander Carr-Saunders and one of his senior colleagues, L.G. Robinson, who lectured in international history, were given high-table privileges at Peterhouse, which were later extended to other members of the faculty. Students were found private lodgings in the town. Grove Lodge, a large house with a garden, became the LSE's lending library and the centre of student life for the university-in-exile.

The task for the shrunken faculty at Cambridge was a difficult one: the ethos and exclusivity of the School had to be preserved at a moment when there was a great deal of integration of lectures and teaching because of low staff numbers as a result of the war. The student body also changed. The evening and part-time students disappeared, and the post-graduate contingent, very strong in the 1930s, shrank to a fifth of its pre-war size. The results were a largely undergraduate LSE and an increasing number of women students as young men were called up by the armed forces. By the time Arnold Weinstock received his degree in 1944 the majority of the intake was women, a great turnaround.

Intellectually, being at the LSE in Cambridge during the war was an exciting experience. There was a great deal of crossover between faculties. Many Cambridge undergraduates were enticed by the high-octane lectures of Harold Laski, while the LSE students had the opportunity to attend lectures by John Maynard Keynes, whose economics would become the guiding light for post-Second World War governments everywhere. 'Keynes' lectures in economics were so popular [with LSE students] that they had to be restricted to senior undergraduates to give Cambridge students a chance,' a wartime Cambridge student remembered.[20]

The presence of the LSE faculty and students also put a strain on Cambridge's accommodation. Many lecturers and teachers took flats in the city, although it was always said that R.H. Tawney, who came up from London to deliver his lectures, only required a cupboard to sleep in. The students were scattered all over Cambridge. Some managed to find shelter with friends and relatives, while others were in university lodgings, where 'the landladies never ceased to compare the LSE students unfavourably with "my young gentlemen"' – the Cambridge undergraduates.[21]

Arnold Weinstock was among those in lodgings. He supported himself financially with a combination of a London County Council grant of around £70 per year, special LSE funds made available to less-well-off undergraduates evacuated to Cambridge worth up to £26 per term – regarded as quite generous – and some top-up help from his elder brothers. An LSE friend remembers calling on Weinstock in his rooms with another acquaintance from London's East End: 'Arnold was sitting in his armchair in his rooms listening to classical music, of which he was very fond. He must have had good hearing, because the music was not playing very loudly, and his own voice was rather muted: he never shouted or raised his voice.'[22] Weinstock's developing passion for music is a recurring theme of the Cambridge period. Many years later he recalled: 'Most of the institutions in Cambridge are in Trumpington Street and beyond it. Trumpington Street is very, very wide, and if you were on one side of the road there was no way in the blackout of knowing who was on the other side of the road. So the little clique with whom I hobnobbed, mainly a table-tennis-playing clique, used to whistle the theme from the last movement, the choral movement, of Beethoven's 9th Symphony as we were walking along. By that means we could recognise each other, and this was a rather useful way of making contact.'[23]

Few of Weinstock's fellow students found it easy to break through the shell which he built around himself while at university. He was regarded as a self-possessed and self-contained person who went his own way, and avoided socialising. His childhood experiences of losing his parents young, never having a real place he could call home and winning his way to university through sheer hard work, meant that he was more able than most students to run his own life. Stanley Bloom, a friend from the LSE days, saw him as a loner with whom it was difficult to become close. Efforts by the strong Jewish contingent at Cambridge to entice Weinstock into the Jewish Society failed; he told his would-be recruiters that he was not a society man – a characteristic he would later display in his industrial life when he scorned the Confederation of British Industry. Even though Cambridge offered many distractions, particularly for someone as fond of classical music as Weinstock, he played a less than enthusiastic part in university life, and as a result he may have missed out on many valuable experiences. The political scientist Norman MacKenzie wrote that the LSE at Cambridge was like a 'liner at the start of a long voyage ... uprooted and crowded together we found it easy to make friends.' It was also a 'market place for ideas'.[24]

The atmosphere among the LSE's students and staff crackled with politics and sex. The left's original extreme antagonism to the war turned to strong support after the Germans abrogated the Molotov–Ribbentrop Pact and turned their guns on the Soviet Union. Weinstock, however, missed out on much of this. When he did visit Grove Lodge, the focus of LSE activity, he spent most of his time in a side room playing table tennis, rather than discussing politics. And as for the sex, he regretfully acknowledges that he didn't see any of it. Instead, he chose to immerse himself in the intricacies of statistics. 'He was an avid student, determined to do well. We all expected him to get a first-class degree,' Stanley Bloom remembered.[25]

Although statistics was at the core of his degree course, Weinstock was also obliged to take a broader range of papers across the social science area. His economics lecturer was Friedrich von Hayek, later to become famous as the author of *The Road to Serfdom*, but at the time more concerned with making connections between monetary policy and fluctuations in the trade cycle. Despite the grandeur of his ideas, he did not impress the undergraduate Weinstock, who remembered him as 'the most boring teacher'. Nor, after a time, was he greatly thrilled by Harold Laski, despite the queues of Cambridge students for his lectures. 'I used to listen to him, until I realised he was a fraud,' says Weinstock. As economic history was not one of his main subjects, Weinstock missed out on the great and eccentric R.H. Tawney. If there was a significant intellectual influence on Weinstock at the LSE, it was the Reader in Statistics E.C. Rhodes, a very strong mathematician. Rhodes caused a flourish of excitement when he proposed that when it returned to London after the war the LSE should relocate itself in a semi-rural setting like Hampstead or Malden (where its sports ground was), and rename itself 'Webb College', after its founders. The idea found little support among Rhodes's colleagues. Weinstock also drew inspiration from the teaching of George Schwartz, who was Lecturer in Commerce.[26]

The student body of which Weinstock was part at the LSE in Cambridge was an eclectic mixture. There were Jewish acquaintances, like Stanley Bloom, with not dissimilar backgrounds to his own. There were a large number of women, who might not have been there but for the war, and foreign nationals in flight from Hitler, including a substantial number of Poles. There were also some students who had not met the exacting standards of the armed services. Among this group was Peter Richards, who went on to become Professor of Government at Southampton University, where in 1963 he wrote *Patronage in British Government*, the classic work on the subject. And there was a group of high fliers who after the war would go on to make their mark in academe and public life. These included (Sir) Klaus Moser, the statistician, educationalist and academic who formed a firm intellectual bond – based on music and mathematics – and a friendship with the slightly younger Weinstock which was to remain intact over five decades. Moser, who was a year ahead of Weinstock, was awarded a first-class B.Sc. Economics degree in 1943, as was Harold Laski's protégé Norman MacKenzie. Weinstock was less impressed with MacKenzie, who years later went on to gain a politics chair at Sussex University. MacKenzie, an activist in the Socialist Society, made repeated efforts to involve Weinstock, who stoutly refused to become involved: 'All he wanted to do was interfere in people's lives. It was very offputting.'[27]

Other luminaries of Weinstock's time at the LSE included Oliver (Lord) McGregor, who graduated with a first in 1944, and went on to head a department at the University of London before collecting a string of quangos, including the Press Complaints Commission; (Sir) Kenneth Berrill, who was to head the Cabinet Office think tank from 1974 to 80; and the industrialist (Sir) Gordon Brunton.

Despite the high expectations of his fellow students, and an abundance of hard work, Weinstock was to be awarded only a lower second – a clear disappointment in view of the intelligence he was later to demonstrate in the real world of business. But given the unhappiness and unevenness of his pre-university education, his degree was still a remarkable achievement which presaged well for the future.

The journey which brought Arnold Weinstock's parents from

Lodz, and ended with him receiving a degree from the London School of Economics, was hazardous and rough. Along the way he had to live through the devastating experiences of being orphaned before reaching the age of ten, having to move out of his childhood home and effectively camp out with relatives before being shipped off, like baggage, to an alien environment in rural Warwickshire. His early years left Arnold Weinstock with deep scars. Instead of a childhood filled with happy memories of family outings, his parents' love and the joyous discovery of his Jewish roots, he experienced only loss. There were no parents to provide him with the normal moral compass, to guide him through the physical and mental turmoil of adolescence; his was 'an orphanic existence'.[28] By the time he was being shuffled around Warwickshire during the war, Weinstock could endure almost anything. He had developed an inner strength built on the need to survive the constant changes in the people and environment around him. Although there were friends and mentors along the way, he could not rely upon them, and had to learn to fend for himself.

It was in Warwickshire, under the guidance of a gifted teacher, that Arnold Weinstock began deploying the strengths he had developed to combat the bad times. He became determined to lift himself above the ethos of simply learning a trade, which had taken his older brothers into hairdressing and cabinet-making. He wanted something more, and when the opportunity came along, in the shape of possible entry to the LSE, he seized it, achieving his goal with seeming ease after a very unpromising beginning. The young Weinstock had also picked up some other traits, including a love of music and a gambler's instinct. But above all, his early life experiences had inculcated him with a determination to succeed.

# CHAPTER TWO

## *Man of Property*

TWO DAYS AFTER Arnold Weinstock graduated from the LSE in June 1944 he received his call-up papers. His degree in statistics made him more valuable at home than at the front, and he was told to report to the Production and Priority Branch of the Admiralty, at Bath, where he would work on procurement. This was to be a formative experience for the man who fifty years later would be master of Britain's entire naval warship production and facilities, through his control of shipyards at Barrow in Furness and Yarrow.

Although at Cambridge Weinstock had acquired a technical competence in statistics, and had moved some social distance from his Stoke Newington background, at the age of twenty he remained fairly unsophisticated. Unlike many of the officers serving at the Admiralty, his education, largely acquired while evacuated in Warwickshire, was extremely patchy. He lacked the finish of his contemporaries in Bath, who had had the benefit of stable family backgrounds and public-school educations. In many ways the Admiralty was to serve as a finishing school for Weinstock, educating him about life in ways not possible in the Warwickshire countryside, and which he had failed to avail himself of in wartime Cambridge.

The young Weinstock had a useful knack of attaching himself to older, wiser people who would help to guide him through life. In much the same way as he had attracted the attention of Freddie Fogg in rural exile, who smoothed his path to the LSE, at the Admiralty Weinstock came under the influence of the charismatic figure of James Mackay. The Scottish major was a striking figure, who at six foot four towered above the spindly Weinstock. He was also intellectually accomplished, having been an academic before

44

the war. Mackay's knowledge of the classics greatly impressed the young Weinstock, who determined to make the most of the opportunity to fill the gaps in his own education. It was the task of Mackay and his young assistant to compile war production reports for the Board of the Admiralty, which would then be passed to the Cabinet Production Committee. 'He gave me enormously responsible jobs,' recalls Weinstock, who in effect was writing Cabinet papers while still in his early twenties.

Among the tasks Weinstock was assigned was to write draft minutes, work out production budgets and edit two Admiralty bulletins. It quickly became apparent to him that while he knew how to analyse the raw statistical material provided by ordnance and production units, he was ignorant of basic report-writing skills. Mackay took him in hand, going through his reports word by word, correcting his grammar and language, reorganising the material in a logical way and instructing him on how to frame an easy-to-follow summary and conclusions which would command action and respect. The precision drafting skills he learned at the Admiralty would remain with Weinstock all his life. In later years he would delight in sending back reports to senior colleagues with corrections scribbled in the margins. The experience also taught him the high quality of documentation necessary for companies seeking to procure government contracts.

Weinstock thoroughly enjoyed his years in Bath, but he realised that working in the Admiralty was not going to provide him with the material and financial independence for which he yearned after his nomadic childhood: 'I was always a bit extravagant, and I loved the Admiralty. I spent three years in the Admiralty working very hard, but I really could not stay because I needed more money than that. I like to spend money, I like to buy nice things and I like to eat well.'[1]

To augment his income, Weinstock took up lecturing on economics and statistics to the local Workers' Education Association, which was good for his confidence as well as his pocket. This earned him £100 per year, in addition to his Admiralty stipend of £250. Even so, he ran through his cash quickly, spending his monthly income in five or six days of good living before being forced by economic circumstances to return to the staff canteen. And although in his early years in Bath he was happy enough living in lodgings on Lawson Road, by the time he left the city he had moved to the more agreeable – and considerably more expensive – Carfax Hotel. The conflict between personal extravagance and professional caution, even meanness, was to be evident throughout Weinstock's career.

Weinstock returned to London in 1947. It was to the third of his elder brothers, Jack, who had contributed to his education while at the LSE, that he again turned for help. With his busy hairdressing salon on Wells Street in the West End, a favourite gathering spot for young Jewish businessmen making their way in post-war London, Jack had an excellent range of commercial contacts. He arranged for his brilliant younger brother, with his LSE degree and administrative experience at the Admiralty, to meet Louis Scott, one of a group of entrepreneurial property developers who were to recognise that despite the destruction of the war, which had led to a collapse in London's property values, reconstruction and the housing needs of returning soldiers offered enormous opportunities. Louis Scott was a small man with a swarthy complexion and an engaging personality. His base was a small suite of offices in Berkeley Street, opposite the Mayfair Hotel. He did not confine his business activity to property development, but had a wide range of interests, including finance. Having met the young Weinstock, he agreed to take him on as his assistant.

Among Scott's business associates was the Russian-born Joe Littman, who during the war years was one of the few investors brave enough to commit himself to the property market, buying several shops on Oxford Street. Littman was essentially an investor rather than a developer, but he was one of the early exponents of the sale and leaseback, one of the prime tools in the developer's armoury. The freehold of an occupied commercial property would be sold by the occupant to a third party, usually a property investment company like Littman's or a big insurance group, who leased it back to the original owner. This would allow the occupant – whether it be ICI or a small corner shop – to release a substantial cash sum for other purposes. The technique was so closely associated with Littman – who began his career selling hats and furs on Kilburn High Road – that it became known for a time as a 'Littman cocktail'.[2] Arnold Weinstock was introduced to the tough and street-smart Littman by Louis Scott, and came to regard him as one of the towering figures in the property world of the 1940s and 1950s. Scott and Littman jointly owned the fashionable Empress restaurant, also on Berkeley Street, which was a second home to many of the property fraternity. Saul L. Magrill, then a partner in the West End commercial property agents Dudley Samuel & Harrison, recalls the intense but friendly rivalry of the period, and a brief encounter with Weinstock:

> The Empress was a popular lunchtime venue for the Mayfair property people, agents, their clients and general hangers-on. It was a hotbed of intrigue and gossip and when we lunched there with colleagues, we spoke in whispers surrounded by competitors. Close by, the Grill Room in the old Berkeley Hotel was also favoured but less dangerous. When I had an appointment with Louis Scott I walked the few yards from my office round to his to be greeted by a very laid-back young man with his legs up on the desk who said 'Whaddya want?' I mentioned my appointment and he added, 'Louis Scott is out,' in a rather arrogant manner, although he looked rather bored.[3]

In fact the young Weinstock was using his time at Louis Scott's side wisely. He was still a shy and reserved young man, his apparent arrogance a cover for a lack of confidence in the new world of business. His shyness led him to prefer to deal with people over the telephone rather than face to face, a tendency which remained with him throughout his career. But Scott quickly came to recognise his great talent, particularly for absorbing information, and his capacity for hard work. As always, Weinstock was absolutely determined to be on top of his new brief, and he soon became an expert in two areas of great importance to Louis Scott's business: planning law and taxation. Every transaction which crossed his desk would be subjected to vigorous scrutiny: 'He was cautious and thorough: he would examine every deal most closely, questioning, teasing out the meaning of words in contracts. No matter how good it looked he would go into it from every angle. Already he was developing a reputation for being invariably right.'[4]

Knowledge of planning laws was essential in the post-Second World War environment in which Weinstock began his commercial career. Wartime Britain had become a command economy, in which much commercial London property had been commandeered by the government. Property was subject to a baffling array of controls, rules and regulations. There were distinctions between different types of building work: essential and non-essential, dangerous and safe war-damaged structures, even between turfing a lawn and building a summerhouse. No building work costing more than £50 (later increased to £100) was allowed without a licence. The rules were strictly enforced – the Ministry of Works reported in 1947 that there had been 454 successful prosecutions for breaches, resulting in fines of £152,466, an enormous sum at the time.

Theoretically at least, it was almost impossible for even the most enterprising property developer to prosper. Licences and controls covered almost every situation, although the more skilled operators could circumvent some of the rules, for instance by certifying a bombed building as dangerous, which would allow it to be refurbished. There were, however, no restrictions on the buying and selling of buildings, and pre-war property tycoons were able to make huge profits from the rise in prices partly brought about by the new restrictive regime.

The first breakthrough for the new breed of property tycoons, including Louis Scott, came in 1954 when the Churchill government, having fulfilled its 1951 election pledge to build three hundred thousand houses a year, lifted the regulations which had suppressed development and construction under Attlee's Labour administration. Speaking in the Commons on 2 November 1954, the Minister of Works Nigel Birch told cheering Tory backbenchers that the system of building licences had become obsolete: 'Licences are now issued freely in nearly all areas, and neither the cost nor the inconvenience caused to architects and contractors can any longer be justified.'[5] A shoal of developers, many of them trained in the offices of commercial estate agents, moved rapidly to take advantage of the new situation, and the property boom was under way. Among the most successful was Charles Clore, who went on to build Sears Holdings, one of the most enduring retail empires of the post-war period. Others whose fortunes were made in these years included Harry Hyams, best known as the developer of the landmark Centre Point building; Walter Flack, whose Murrayfield company was involved in innovative shopping-centre development from Huddersfield to Preston; Jack Cotton, whose City Centre Properties was eventually to merge with Charles Clore's businesses; and Gabriel Harrison, who founded Amalgamated Investments and Property, one of the victims of the 1973–75 property crash.

Through his position as Louis Scott's assistant Arnold Weinstock was both a participant in and an observer of this heady period, in which some of Britain's greatest property fortunes were founded. His mentor Louis Scott exercised his skills in buying and merging businesses, often with a strong property content. He would cut surplus costs, rebuild the businesses and then sell them off once they were profitable. In effect he was a company doctor. While property was the main focus of his activities, Weinstock also obtained his first experience of industry in the shape of a ballpoint pen manufacturer, which Scott allowed him to take in hand. He would also gain insight into the catering business through Scott's two restaurants, which included the Persian Room, part of the Empress.

Scott had bought the Empress because of its promising location close to Piccadilly. He decided to divide it into two businesses: the first a sort of residential hotel, the second a fashionable restaurant. Under Scott's direction the Persian Room became a popular venue, largely because of its pianist, brought over from Switzerland. The pianist claimed to have composed the 'Harry Lime Theme', made famous by Carol Reed's 1949 film *The Third Man*, but Weinstock regarded him as little more than a peasant, as he had difficulty coping with any other tune. Despite its popularity, the finances of the Empress were a mess, and Scott was unable to sell it off because of government restrictions on property investment. He asked his young partner to sort matters out, and make him happy again. Weinstock thus came to be in charge of the Empress for a couple of months.

His main task was to sort out the finances. This was largely done by splitting the Empress into two, a common practice in the property market at the time, which allowed the investor two mortgages or secured bank loans. Weinstock approached the nearby Williams Deacon Bank in Piccadilly, which came up with two separate loans of £50,000 each, which secured Scott's ownership of the Empress until such time as he could sell it on. The connection with the Manchester-based bank proved a useful one for Weinstock, and it would eventually assist him and his father-in-law-to-be Michael Sobell in the expansion of their television manufacturer Radio & Allied.

More than anything else, Weinstock came to admire Scott's skills as a valuer of property and businesses. He had an instinct for making quick valuations which rarely let him down, whereas it would take Weinstock, equipped with all the tools of the trade, including valuation tables and plans, far longer. Observing Scott's business techniques, like the other skills Weinstock had picked up from mentors at school and in the Admiralty, was an essential part of the learning process for a business career which would soon advance rapidly. Within a decade Louis Scott would be assigned by his former assistant, now managing director of one of Britain's biggest manufacturers, to handle the General Electric Company's property needs.

Weinstock's work for Scott was not entirely satisfying for an ambitious young man with a lively mind, but after the frugality of his Admiralty pay he very much enjoyed the good salary he was now receiving, and he now had the opportunity to indulge his taste for the finer things in life. He was living in rooms in Mayfair, and liked nothing better than to spend the weekend in Paris, returning with the finest silk ties and other stylish and expensive accoutrements.

After his exiles in Warwickshire, Cambridge and Bath, where he was largely separated from the scenes of his Jewish childhood, the return to London brought the young Weinstock back in touch with the community from which he came. His sense of Jewish identity was tenuous, despite the love of cantorial music he developed as a choirboy at the Poet's Road Synagogue; he has described the traditional Jewish world as 'not my style'.[6] Nevertheless, the clients of his brothers' hairdressing shop on Wells Street, in the centre of the drapery/clothing district, were largely Jewish business people who had made the transition from East End tailoring shops to the more upmarket world of central London. The larger Jewish population was beginning to make the transition from inner-city terraced houses to more spacious homes in the leafy suburbs of North London and well-proportioned apartments in the West End, and from the trades into commerce, big business and the professions. The property world which Weinstock joined in 1947 was dominated by Jewish entrepreneurs, and it was to this group that he looked for his personal and social advancement.

Weinstock's sense of identity with Judaism was, however, strong enough for him to pay his first visit to Israel in 1949, only a year after the creation of the Jewish state, when it was still a place for pioneers, barely independent and struggling against the odds for economic and political survival. (On a stopover in Cyprus he was amused to spot a plane on the runway bearing the insignia 'Sobel-air', and speculated that his future father-in-law was following him.) Though he was only twenty-five at the time, this visit to Israel suggests Weinstock's growing confidence. During the course of it he met two of the great heroes of Zionism: Teddy Kollek, later to become the long-standing Mayor of Jerusalem and an early advocate of peace with the Palestinians; and Isaac Persky, father of the future Prime Minister Shimon Peres. With remarkable self-assurance, Weinstock told the Zionist leaders that if their government was to gain economic credibility it ought to fund itself through the issue of bonds; better that than become a nation of *schnorrers* (beggars), he said. His advice was largely ignored, and in its early years Israel was highly dependent on contributions from the Jewish communities of the diaspora. Although in later years as a defence contractor Weinstock could not be regarded as an overt friend of Israel, privately his commitment to and support of the Jewish state was unwavering.

It was through Louis Scott, with the encouragement of the hotelier Maxwell Joseph, that Weinstock made the most important connection of his life. He was invited to drinks at Joseph's apartment at Carlton House in St James's before going on to a charity dinner at the Dorchester Hotel on Park Lane. Weinstock was given no warning by Joseph, but the seating plan for the dinner had been carefully arranged. Sitting next to him was one of London's most eligible young women, the vivacious Netta Sobell, who at twenty-nine was four years older than Weinstock, and at an age when her parents might have expected her to have been married off long before. The slightly diffident young man and the daughter of the entrepreneur who had built one of the most successful consumer electric businesses in Britain spent the evening engrossed in each other's company. The relationship blossomed, and dates followed at a number of fashionable restaurants and night-spots.

Despite the great distance in wealth between the orphaned Weinstock and his future bride, their family backgrounds were not that different. Michael Sobel (the second 'l' would be added later) had been born of Polish-Jewish stock at Boryslav, in Galicia, then part of the Austro-Hungarian empire. The Sobel family had been wealthy, owning oil wells and factories, but anti-Semitism and persecution were ever-present threats, and in 1903 – a year before Arnold Weinstock's father made the journey from Lodz to London – Lewis Sobel, his wife Esther and their children Lora and Michael travelled from Galicia to London. They settled in Dalston, then a respectable, middle-class London suburb and the neighbouring area to Weinstock's Stoke Newington.

Lewis Sobel set up in business as a confectioner. At the age of eleven his son Michael was sent to the Central London Foundation School on Cowper Street, *alma mater* to many bright Jewish children of the era. At sixteen, with some capital provided by his father, Michael went into business importing fancy leather accessories and electrical goods from abroad. It was a fortunate piece of timing: by the early 1920s radio was becoming a popular form of entertainment, and the enterprising Michael was well placed to take advantage of this. Soon he found he could not keep up with the public demand for radios through imports alone, so he established manufacturing facilities at Stonebridge Park in North-West London, at Hirwaun, near Aberdare in the Rhondda Valley, and at Amersham in Buckinghamshire, where he continued to make wireless sets throughout the war. It was during this period that Michael, now an extremely wealthy entrepreneur, added the second 'l' to his name, so as to turn the title of his firm to Sobell Industries. He believed that the suffix 'bell' would more easily be identified by the public with the electrical industries which he was pioneering.[7]

At the end of the First World War Michael Sobel had married

Anne Rakusen, a member of a prominent Leeds family best known in the Jewish community for its domination of the trade in *matzos*, the unleavened bread traditionally eaten at Passover. There were two daughters from the marriage: Hilda, who was to marry Stanley Rubin, and Netta, who would do much better by marrying a future peer of the realm. Netta Sobel was born on 8 September 1920 at 2 Fairholt Road, a wide, tree-lined road in Stoke Newington, just a mile or so north of where her future husband would be born four years later. By the time Arnold and Netta were married in 1949, both would have journeyed economically and socially a long way from the London Borough of Hackney. Weinstock described himself on the marriage certificate as a company director living at 18 Berkeley Street in Mayfair, which was actually his place of work. He was in fact living in nearby rooms at 7 Deanery Street. Netta was living at the family mansion in Buckinghamshire.

The wedding took place on 23 October 1949 at the St John's Wood Synagogue, a bastion of the more prosperous elements of Anglo-Jewry. Arnold's brother Jack stood in for his late parents under the canopy, acting as the surrogate father as he had on many previous occasions, having helped his younger brother financially through university and enabled him to climb the first rung of business by recommending him to Louis Scott.

The marriage was an important alliance. Traditionally Jewish fathers with no sons to carry on their family business would look to their daughters' husbands to provide the necessary continuity. Michael Sobell's elder daughter Hilda's husband Stanley Rubin was already involved in Sobell Industries, but was not regarded as having any great aptitude for business. He was a fine fellow to book the family vacations in France, but would rather be breezing around town in his Bentley than calculating the cost of valves at the Sobell plants. Michael Sobell saw straight away that in his second son-in-law he had potentially acquired a more valuable asset for Sobell Industries.

Although Weinstock would continue to work for Louis Scott for five years after his marriage to Netta, Sobell recognised that his superior analytical and administrative intellect could help him transform his radio and embryonic television manufacturing business into a serious global competitor. In later years Netta would laugh off the question of whether Arnold's career was assisted by marrying the boss's daughter: 'He's a brilliant man, he was bound to make progress.'[8] In fact she was determined that her talented husband would eventually work at her father's side.

The Britain in which the Weinstocks began their married life was just beginning to emerge from the siege atmosphere of the Second World War and the frenzy of nationalisation and change, including the creation of the Welfare State, inaugurated by Clement Attlee's Labour government. The strains in the nation's economic and industrial policy, with which Weinstock would struggle for much of his career, were beginning to show. On 18 September 1949 the pound was devalued by 30 per cent, from \$4.03 to \$2.80, in a move designed to reduce Britain's huge war debt to America, halt the build-up of the trade deficit and encourage exporters. The first signs that Britain was on the verge of a new television age, which would have an even greater impact on the populace than the radio age on which the Sobell family fortunes had been based, also became clear. The BBC, preparing for the new era, bought the Rank film studios at Shepherd's Bush and Lime Grove to begin making television programmes. Although Laurence Olivier's *Hamlet* had just won five Oscars, concern for the future of film in Britain was growing. The BBC's investment in a network of television transmitters which could reach some 75 per cent of the population was the signal for electrical manufacturers like Sobell Industries to turn their attention to the coming technology.

Arnold Weinstock immersed himself in the family life that he had always yearned for, and which had been among the factors that had led him to an early marriage. In 1950 he and Netta set up house in a restored sixteenth-century farm building, the Old Barn, which had been moved brick by brick from Sussex to Denham in rural Buckinghamshire. Denham had been made famous by the film producer Sir Alexander Korda, who was in many respects the nearest Britain had to its own Hollywood-style mogul. In 1936 he had set up his studios at Denham, and their output included such classics as *Things to Come*, *Anna Karenina* and Laurence Olivier's *Richard III*.

Denham was as different a place as could be imagined from the Stoke Newington of Arnold and Netta's childhoods and the Mayfair of their recent past. Netta was determined that her children would be reared in the country, away from the distractions, smog and noise of London. As Weinstock remembers nostalgically, in those days the main arteries into London were not yet clogged with traffic, and it took him only twenty-five minutes in his bull-nosed Ford and later in a Vauxhall to commute from Denham to his offices on Berkeley Street.[9]

Arnold and Netta's first child, a son, was born at Devonshire Place in London on 24 February 1952. The boy was to be called Simon Andrew, taking his first name from a revered dead relative, in this case his paternal grandfather, as is the custom in Judaism. This was both a recognition of the life of Weinstock's father and of his own deep-seated attachment to the customs of Jewish life. In April 1955 the couple had their second child, a daughter, Susan Gina, whose second name was an Anglicised echo of Weinstock's mother Golda (Gertie). At the age of thirty-one, Weinstock gave the appearance of having achieved almost everything he wanted from life. He had a happy, supportive marriage, a spacious home in the country, two young children and a comfortable income.

Labour held on to power in the 1950 general election, but with a greatly reduced overall majority of just five seats. British troops were again involved in a war, this time in Korea, even though the country could ill afford the cost. Chancellor of the Exchequer Hugh Gaitskell's budget in April 1951 was an austere affair, increasing taxation so as to shift resources from consumption, which was beginning to surge, to defence. The incentives for a new generation of would-be capitalists like Arnold Weinstock must have looked limited as the top rate of tax climbed to 97.5 per cent. When Gaitskell proposed to introduce charges for spectacles and false teeth provided by the new National Health Service, the government began to disintegrate. The Minister of Labour Aneurin Bevan resigned in protest, followed by the President of the Board of Trade, the young firebrand Harold Wilson. With Prime Minister Clement Attlee in hospital, Bevan and Gaitskell fought a public battle for the soul of the party. The resulting chaos contributed to the Conservatives' return to power in October 1951.

Weinstock, who was now director of property investments in the Louis Scott group of companies, was faced with a clear choice. He could either be part of the coming commercial property boom, or he could leave the limiting world of property, in which the skills needed were entrepreneurial rather than managerial, and move across to his father-in-law's sphere of manufacturing for the new consumer economy. The takeover, administrative and pruning skills he had developed under Louis Scott's guidance could be used to great advantage in industry.

In addition, Weinstock was becoming restless working for Scott. Although he had enormous respect for him, and had learned a great deal, he felt he was marking time – 'tinkering', as he would call it – rather than making a direct contribution to Britain's post-war prosperity. He needed a bigger canvas on which to work.

The golden age of radio had been the 1940s, when programmes like *ITMA* and *Family Favourites* attracted enormous audiences. But it was already becoming apparent that television was the medium of the future. In 1946 there were only fifteen thousand television licence-holders in Britain, most of them in London. A decade later there were five million, and 98 per cent of the population was in reach of a television signal.[10] The BBC's huge investment in television was reinforced by its coverage of major events, notably Queen Elizabeth II's Coronation in June 1953. In much the same way as Rupert Murdoch would use sport to attract viewers to his Sky satellite channels forty years later, the BBC was using the big events of the 1950s to cultivate public interest in television. It succeeded to such an extent that demand for television receivers far exceeded supply.

Netta Weinstock felt it was time for her husband to move on in his career. Stanley Rubin, the husband of her sister Hilda, had been working alongside her father in Sobell Industries, which was now one of Britain's biggest makers of television receivers, and she desired a similar career path for Weinstock. 'My wife nagged at me to talk to my father-in-law about joining him,' he says.[11]

Weinstock, however, remained reluctant. He was well aware of the potential pitfalls and tensions of giving up an independent life to work in what was, in effect, a family business. But he was also aware that the demand for television receivers was taking off, and saw the electrical business as one where he could exercise his talents for cost-cutting and reorganisation, gained under Louis Scott.

Much of Arnold Weinstock's life to this point had served to equip him for the challenges which were to come. His personal history provided him with the technical skills he needed to be an efficient manager and the drive he needed to make a success of his life. His modest education at the Stoke Newington Central School gave him an understanding of double-entry bookkeeping, an essential pre-requisite when it came to turning businesses around and putting sound cost controls in place. At the LSE he gained theoretical know-ledge of how an economy works, and also developed a healthy sense of scepticism about the swagger of politics, which would prove extremely useful later on, when a great deal of his business would be with the public sector. But most significantly, his mastery of mathematics and statistics, the major elements of his degree, would allow him to develop a statistical framework for analysing businesses, and a sound basis on which to conduct discussions with the technologists and engineers who would be vital associates in the electrical industries. At the Admiralty Weinstock had been put through a kind of finishing school by James Mackay, one of the most influential figures in his life, who taught him the value of writing clear, understandable and forceful reports – a requirement which Weinstock would impose on staff and colleagues, including, on occasions, those who did not even work for him.

Experience of the realities of business life came with the seven years at the right hand of Louis Scott. In these years Weinstock also developed from a shy, callow graduate to a more worldly family man – although he never entirely lost his youthful diffidence. He learned to respect instinct and judgement in business, and to appreciate the techniques of the company doctor and the role of law and taxation in shaping business decisions. But above all his seven years as a man of property had equipped him with an enor-mous and enduring range of business contacts, so he would not be dependent on the circle into which he had married.

If there was a weakness in the Weinstock armoury it was that he never had the opportunity to master the art of marketing, a lack which would become apparent in later years when it came to converting the advanced technologies he controlled into consumer products.

In addition to the practical skills he had acquired, the insecurity and loss of Weinstock's childhood years had inculcated other qualities which would make him a driven and focused businessman. At work he would always be a loner, with a strong determination to plot his own destiny, with the help of a few close associates, rather than relying on others. He was guided by a strong sense of moral obligation, and a conviction that the workers in his businesses, including the managers, were as important as the shareholders, with whom he would show limited patience in later years. Weinstock was also a natural leader, who could inspire loyalty and respect from his staff. His unhappy childhood and youth had inspired in him a self-motivation and a belief in the art of the possible which he would bring to bear on the family television business, before embarking on a far grander adventure.

# CHAPTER THREE

## *Into the Hot Seat*

ARNOLD WEINSTOCK shot to the top of British industry because his family business was taken over by one of Britain's biggest companies, General Electric. But there was very nearly no family business for the young Weinstock to move into. Without a fortuitous chain of events and his father-in-law's canny negotiating skills, Britain's top post-war industrialist might have been destined for a lifetime in property. Weinstock habitually complains that had he stayed in property he would have become 'very, very rich' rather than merely very rich as the boss of, and a major shareholder in, GEC. But GEC would undoubtedly have been the worse without him, as would much of the rest of the British electrical industry. Such eminence must have seemed a long way away in the mid-1950s, when Weinstock finally bowed to his wife's repeated pressure to join her father in business, seizing an opportunity which presented itself thanks to a curious episode involving the music and electronics group EMI.

Michael Sobell's attempts to capitalise on the post-war demand for electrical goods had met with limited success. He registered his company, Sobell Industries, on 16 January 1946. But it traded only fitfully at first, as lack of money in consumers' pockets was matched by difficulties in obtaining parts and materials. Britain was still a long way from the affluent society it had begun to aspire to be. Industry was only slowly picking up the pieces of peacetime manufacturing, attempting to re-establish supply lines and customer contacts which had been broken by war, and in many cases physically converting factories back from military production.

Clement Attlee's post-war Labour government had attempted to balance socialist intervention with the dismantling of wartime controls. But its wider industrial and economic aims were hampered by the financial legacy of war – huge government debts and urgent requirements for investment in housing and infrastructure. As a result, taxes remained high and consumer demand subdued. Nevertheless, there was clearly huge potential in the electronics industry. The demand for television was stoked by the visions of affluence from America, the first hints of which had come with the GIs during the war, followed by tantalising glimpses of what might be as Britain struggled through post-war austerity.

Michael Sobell's big break came in March 1951, when he signed a deal with the music and electronics group EMI to assemble radios and televisions. Under the contract Sobell would assemble between fifty and 150,000 televisions and radios a year, over the next five and a half years.[1] This would allow him to fill the factory he had rented in South Wales, as regional development criteria meant it would be allocated a guaranteed number of electronic valves by the government.

It looked like a highly profitable deal, but it proved disappointing. Despite the boom following the Conservative election victory in October 1951, EMI's orders were much lower than anticipated. In July 1952 volumes for the coming year were cut to just twenty-five thousand units. Sobell required loans from EMI in the form of advance payments in both July and September. By the end of the year, the contract had collapsed.

At the same time, Sobell was facing a patent infringement action, because he had been making television sets without a licence. That might have been the end of Sobell Industries – and of Arnold Weinstock's industrial career, even before it had begun. But EMI's lack of attention to detail came to the rescue, creating not only the opportunity for Weinstock to get out of property, but also the beginnings of a partnership with Kenneth Bond which was to last until the end of the 1980s. It also showed him the value of aggression in business dealings.

EMI's contract with Sobell had been intended to fulfil a deal with the retailer Great Universal Stores (GUS). GUS was one of the most notable post-war retail success stories, built up by Isaac Wolfson to become a conglomerate embracing such High Street names as Times Furnishing and Burberry, as well as the country's leading mail-order operation. Wolfson was perspicacious, and he had included a clause in GUS's contract with EMI allowing cancellation if the government tightened hire-purchase regulations. Almost inevitably, given that it was a key weapon in controlling consumer spending, this happened in 1953. Unfortunately for EMI, it had omitted to include a similar clause in its agreement with Sobell. EMI was therefore faced with a substantial damages claim when it cancelled its order from Sobell. As a solution, Sobell proposed in spring 1953 that he should sell his business to EMI. The deal took a long time to go through, much to Sobell's annoyance. On 29 August 1953 he wrote angrily to EMI director E.J. Emery:

> I was amazed to find on my return from holiday that the Heads of Agreement are still unsigned . . . I am sure you will agree that I have been very patient throughout these negotiations, but I cannot in fairness to my company and myself allow this uncertain state of affairs to continue what would appear to be interminably . . . I am reluctantly compelled to confirm to withdraw the offer for the sale of the shares in my company and to discontinue further negotiations.

The tactic worked. Heads of agreement were signed on 15 September, providing for a purchase price of £250,000. Sobell would retain the leases on the Hirwaun factory in South Wales and the offices on the Langley Park industrial estate in Slough.[2] He and his son-in-law Stanley Rubin guaranteed that profits for the year would be at least £50,000, and agreed to continue running the business until the end of March 1954.

But having acquired the business, which continued making the Sobell trademark radios and televisions, its new owner did not know what to do with it. EMI was more interested in music and high-technology electronics than in the mass manufacturing of consumer goods.[3] And it was faced with the imminent departure of Michael Sobell and Stanley Rubin, which would leave it to run the operation. Once again Sobell came up with a solution. In December 1953, just three months after they had bought his company, the EMI board agreed to let Sobell effectively take it back, paying EMI a royalty of 4 per cent. Sobell was back in business without ever having left it. All that remained was to buy back the rights to the Sobell trademark, which he was to do in May 1955 for £78,750. He was back where he had started before the EMI contract, and £150,000 better off.

Although Sobell was now approaching his mid-sixties, like many such businessmen, the concept of retirement was alien to him. But he did want to build up capital for his old age, and he didn't want to do it all himself. The answer was to swap one son-in-law, Stanley Rubin, who had been happy to cash in his 10 per cent interest in Sobell's business on the first sale to EMI, for the other, Arnold Weinstock, and to look for a flotation on the stock market to realise his capital.

Weinstock joined the newly-independent company, Radio & Allied Industries, in 1954, and soon took charge of the business, although he was not formally a director. Sobell had promised directorships to many of his former staff when the business was being resurrected, but Weinstock objected to so many non-family faces on the board. 'All right,' said his father-in-law, 'but in that case you can't be a director either.'[4] As a result Weinstock always described himself as 'the manager'.

Weinstock's first task was to help extricate Sobell from the clutches of EMI. On the EMI side in the negotiations over the sale of the Sobell trademark to Radio & Allied was an accountant called Kenneth Bond, who had been taken into partnership at the small firm of Cooper & Cooper during 1954. The firm (which had no connection with the better-known Cooper Bros, now Coopers & Lybrand) mainly served clients in the London produce market with the normal run of accounting and audit work, but it also had connections with EMI, and Bond was called in occasionally to help on various financial transactions. Weinstock was impressed by Bond's financial acumen, and invited him to join the new company. But Bond was not yet ready to leave the accounting profession for industry, and resisted Weinstock's offer for several years. He still remembers the date he finally joined: 1 April 1957. By then Weinstock was firmly in the driving seat, and was set on expanding the business quickly in the classic British fashion, by making takeovers. But his introduction into his father-in-law's business had not been without difficulty.

At thirty, Weinstock was still a young man, but while he had run several businesses for Louis Scott, he had no experience of manufacturing or of selling consumer products. To take care of production matters, Sobell brought in an engineer, John Banner, whose own company, Banner Radio & Television, was subsumed into Radio & Allied. And John James, a friendly radio and TV dealer introduced Sobell to a brilliant salesman, Leslie Bentley-Jones, who had been with EMI and Thorn and who was well known and respected by the retailers. James was to be even more important subsequently, when he introduced Sobell and Weinstock to the merchant banker who would lead them to GEC.

Leslie Bentley-Jones was nominally joint managing director with Weinstock, but there was little doubt who was in charge. Weinstock was still very shy, despite his years in the fashionable world of Mayfair property men. That shyness had become brusqueness, and an apparent lack of interest in other people and their opinions. This, combined with a self-confidence based on a powerful mind and a difficult childhood which had required him to be independent from an early age, was often seen as aggression and rudeness. Yet Weinstock also had a finely developed sense of humour and a deep concern for any troubles which might befall his staff, especially illnesses (perhaps this appealed to his own strong streak of hypochondria). This combination of characteristics stayed with him throughout his career, leaving many who came into contact with him either puzzled, hurt or charmed by his mixture of humour, humanity and hardness.

Despite his youth, his comparative lack of experience and his debt to Michael Sobell for bringing him into the company, Weinstock showed little deference to anybody, even his father-in-law. At first Sobell continued to come into the office every day, and was closely involved in the business. But then he became quite ill after a prostate operation, and spent some months recuperating. Weinstock became used to operating without him during his long absence, and when Sobell returned, everything was different. Like his son-in-law forty years later, however, he did not find it easy to let go, and continued to inspect the purchase invoices, and generally to try to ensure that Weinstock and his team had everything under control.

Weinstock remembers that on one occasion his father-in-law strayed into what Weinstock regarded as interference, suggesting that the company introduce an export model television. Weinstock, sitting nonchalantly with his feet on a desk, rejected the idea dismissively, as he felt it would over-complicate the operations of the small factory.

Sobell was not impressed. 'Remember your place,' he snapped at his son-in-law.

Weinstock promptly stormed out, saying: 'If you want to run the business, you run it.'

Sobell rang Netta that night to ask where Weinstock was, and she told him he was never coming back. But Sobell soon persuaded him to return, and Weinstock now accepts he was wrong to show disrespect to his father-in-law, who owned most of the business and who was entitled to his views. Nevertheless, the incident marked the end of Sobell's direct involvement in the company, although he never completely let go. Well into his nineties he remained notionally chairman of Radio & Allied, or GEC (Radio and Television), as it had become. In the 1980s the chief executive of the division, Jeff Sansom, used to travel to Sobell's home in Englefield Green, Surrey, for tea on the last Friday of every month. Even after all those years the old man would ask: 'Is Arnold doing all right?'

Arnold had been widely acknowledged to be doing fine more or less from the moment he took over in 1955. His lack of experience of the industry, combined with an eye for detail and a self-assurance which has often been misinterpreted as arrogance, made him an exciting, if sometimes irritating, boss. Kenneth Bond remembered: 'He would question people, go on and on and on. You would get the impression he didn't like what they were doing, but it wasn't that. He was trying to find out what the position was, what was the truth, and satisfy himself that they were right. It's that ability to investigate in depth which has been one of his great attributes.'[5]

One convention he challenged was the launch of new models of televisions in the autumn of each year. It was a practice followed by every other company in the industry, but Weinstock argued that a spring launch would offset the pre-Christmas selling peak and even out sales over the year. It made him highly unpopular with his competitors, but Weinstock has never been interested in popularity, except with his customers, and they were delighted to have something new in the shops in the slack summer months.

Weinstock's early management experience set the style which he was to employ throughout his career, and the nature of the business he had moved into also affected the way he was to run GEC for more than thirty years. His understanding of and approach to manufacturing was heavily influenced by the nature of Radio & Allied's business as an assembler of consumer equipment. The key to success in such a business is controlling costs. Of course it was essential to achieve sales, and to do that, the products had to be right. Other companies in the industry, usually dominated by engineers, spent a fortune developing over-specified products. Weinstock was no engineer, which helped him to concentrate on producing a basic product that worked, and which could be sold cheaply but at an adequate profit. The banker who subsequently brokered R&A's marriage to GEC said: 'He was among the first to see that all television sets were alike and that they were fashion articles, not engineering problems.'[6]

The early days also illustrated Weinstock's aversion to overwork, which continued throughout his career. He had become interested in horse-racing through his father-in-law Michael Sobell, and despite his alertness to any suggestion of slacking by the company's staff, he and Kenneth Bond would spend occasional afternoons at the races when everything was running smoothly and one of his horses was running at Windsor or Kempton Park.

Nevertheless, Weinstock made a success of Radio & Allied using the small businessman's classic approach of attention to detail and a tight grip on the purse-strings. It was the approach which he adhered to throughout his career, and which made him one of the most unusual managing directors of a large company in the 1980s and 1990s, leaving him open to the criticism that he had no vision. Yet while on the one hand he was intensely interested in detail, he was also aware of and thoughtful about issues at the highest level. At the same time as spending much of his energy ensuring that the Hirwaun plant churned out televisions, radios and radiograms as efficiently as possible, he also worked to expand the business.

His first move was the acquisition of McMichael Radio in 1956. Like Radio & Allied, McMichael was based in Slough, and Weinstock recalls that he used to pass it once a fortnight when he took the train from his home in Gerrards Cross to South Wales. He also knew a couple of the directors, from whom he gathered how vulnerable this public company was. The owner seldom went near the place. His son was the export director, although, as Weinstock observed: 'He was paid more than the exports.'

Weinstock's first thought was to agree to Radio & Allied being acquired by McMichael, which would have achieved a flotation on the stock exchange. This, though, would not have released any cash, which Michael Sobell wanted, rather than having it all tied up in the business. So R&A simply bought it, with a £270,000 loan from Williams Deacon, whom Weinstock knew from his days with Louis Scott.

Raising the money for such a deal was not easy for a small company with a limited record, especially at a time when bank lending was very tightly controlled by the Bank of England. R&A had some trade bills (effectively IOUs) as a result of a rash deal by Sobell to win an order by granting two years' credit to an important customer. Weinstock hoped to use the bills to raise cash, but S.G. Warburg, the first bank to whom he applied for the loan, was not interested (Warburgs subsequently brought R&A to the stock market, acted for GEC in several deals, and employed Weinstock's son Simon in the 1970s). Williams Deacon's general manager Mr King came down from Manchester to see Weinstock, who told him there was no risk in financing the takeover of McMichael because the freehold of its premises was worth more than the loan. The banker responded, 'Why should you sleep in your bed and I lie awake?' pointing out that Radio & Allied had £227,000 on deposit. But he gave them the money anyway, illustrating how persuasive the young Weinstock could be in making a business proposal, as well as showing his ingenuity.

The economic situation in Britain was improving, but it was still uncertain. The economy was beginning to expand as the legacy of war faded and the Conservative government fuelled the 'never had it so good' era. The mid-1950s were uneven times, with a pattern of rising inflation, adverse balance of payments and pressure on the pound which was to be repeated many times over the next three decades. But it saw the beginnings of the consumer boom which was to last until the 1959 election. The pre-election spending spree did not seriously get under way until the end of 1958, but sales of televisions took off in 1954 with the launch of the independent commercial network to rival the BBC. With a combination of innovation and astuteness which pushed Radio & Allied to the forefront of the industry, Weinstock capitalised on the growing demand. Understanding that customers wanted bigger sets at lower prices, he encouraged his engineers to reduce the number of valves used, bringing them down from twenty to twelve per set. And production manager John Banner cut the cost of cabinets by using a new technique developed by a maker of church pews in Scotland. This began an association with Chaim Schreiber, who was contracted to produce the cabinets, which was to last for decades. Schreiber subsequently went on to use his know-how in his kitchen furniture business, which was brought into the GEC net for a time in the 1980s.

Weinstock was happy for R&A to continue as a private company, but he recognised the urgent need to diversify away from televisions before the bubble burst. By 1957 there were twenty-nine competitors making televisions, but demand was bound to peak soon. On top of that, televisions were greatly affected by the government's techniques for controlling consumer spending, the main weapons of which were hire-purchase controls and varying the rate of purchase tax (the forerunner of VAT). Diversification would be easier if R&A had a stock market quotation, which would allow it to issue shares to buy companies rather than paying in cash. Michael Sobell insisted on going for a stock market flotation as soon as R&A had achieved the minimum three-year financial record required by the stock exchange. It reached that stage in 1958, a good time to come to the stock market: business was still booming, and optimism was growing as the economy accelerated in what the 1957 Chancellor Peter Thorneycroft described as 'controlled expansion'.

Despite its brief history, Radio & Allied was able to report that profits had breached the £1 million barrier for the first time in

1957, partly aided by the inclusion of McMichael, which was almost double the figure for its first year. The prospectus for its stock market flotation in June 1958 promised conservatively that the average of its first three years (£828,000) could be relied upon, and with a price low enough to offset any worries about the company or the economy, the bankers S.G. Warburg, just beginning their own aggressive drive through the ranks of the City Establishment, received 5.5 million share applications, although only 1.35 million were on offer.

*The Times* commented favourably on the issue, but was clearly surprised at the size of the over-subscription: 'The success of the offer in the face of uncertain markets seems to be due to three factors. First, there have been very few offers of equity shares recently; second, the shares give an attractive yield of 8.3 per cent; and third, the company's radio and television products were well known in many households.'[7]

Subsequent events suggested that the caution had been over-done. Chancellor Derick Heathcoat-Amory relaxed hire-purchase restrictions in November 1958, and Radio & Allied, along with the rest of the consumer-goods industry, saw its sales surge ahead. Profits in its first year as a public company reached £1.2 million as consumers finally began to reach for the American dream. But this was also the era which coined the term 'stop-go' – a period of tight financial control by the government, clamping down on inflation by curbing economic activity, followed by a relaxation of policy which resulted in a spurt in economic growth fed by consumer spending. With the 1959 general election over, it was time for an end to the easy money which Heathcoat-Amory had unleashed. To combat the resulting inflationary pressures the government clamped down on credit, which was a heavy blow to the television-manufacturing industry. Production peaked at 2.9 million sets in 1959, but by 1961 it had fallen to just 1.25 million.

After Radio & Allied's stock market flotation Sobell and Wein-stock had become paper millionaires overnight, and they quickly moved to consolidate their position. The company was valued at more than £2 million on flotation, and this quickly increased. The shares were first offered for nine shillings each (45p), but reached a peak of 36s.6d (182p) during 1960. The Sobell family owned

two-thirds of the shares, so their fortune was tied to the performance of the company, which was bound to be volatile in its present
state of reliance on one narrow product area which was highly
vulnerable to changes in government policy. They therefore set
about trying to protect their position by seeking diversification or
merger into a larger group. In the eighteen months following flotation they attempted to buy the appliance company Ekco, but lost
out to Pye. They also looked at another manufacturer of domestic
appliances, Morphy Richards, but that was bought by EMI, and had
the first of what would be an occasional series of discussions with
Jules Thorn, another Jewish immigrant who was the energetic
founder of his own electrical empire.

In the end the unlikely partner was the General Electric Company
(GEC). Unlikely because GEC was a giant by comparison with Radio
& Allied, whose 1960 sales were only about 5 per cent of GEC's
£117 million. Indeed, the £9 million increase in GEC's sales in 1960
was more than R&A's total. GEC's diverse interests ranged from
wholesaling electrical products in the UK to nuclear power stations
in Japan. The consumer products business was far outweighed in
importance by heavy engineering, telecommunications and electronics. GEC was a vast international empire, but it had been struggling with poor performance and mounting debts, and a group of
key directors had concluded that its main problem was a lack of
quality management. They were looking for a top manager, and
believed they had found him in Arnold Weinstock.

In the 1950s, GEC was a giant which had lost its way. The company
had been dominated for forty years by its founder, Lord Hirst, until
he died in 1943. From beginnings as a distributor and wholesaler
it had grown to be one of the big three in the electrical industry
(along with AEI and English Electric) by pursuing Hirst's target
of making 'everything electrical'. After his death the group was
sustained by the post-war boom in power and rail equipment, but
when demand suddenly dropped in the 1950s its weakness, especially its lack of direction from the top, was cruelly exposed.

Hirst's history was not dissimilar to Weinstock's, although unlike
Weinstock he was a first-generation Jewish immigrant and an out-
going, almost flamboyant personality. But like Weinstock he was

a self-confident young man who stood no nonsense from his colleagues, resigning on two occasions early in his career when he felt he was not being offered enough money or given enough power by his employer. He eventually became sole managing director of GEC at the age of forty-three, just a few years older than Weinstock would be when he took over fifty-seven years later.

Hirst also shared Weinstock's advantage in not being an engineer. He was essentially a salesman. GEC's rivals were run by engineers and technicians who looked down on consumer products and light electrical goods. They were interested in the prestige of heavy electrical engineering and the technical challenge of generating and transmitting electricity, not in its uses in the home. A significant contrast to the Weinstock era was the presence of a strong number two who was allowed to take over a large part of Hirst's responsibilities. He was Max Railing, another German immigrant who had married Hirst's sister-in-law. Hirst and Railing were an ideal combination of flair and control. Tom Kerr, who as a GEC director in the 1960s would be instrumental in manoeuvring Weinstock into the top job, said: 'GEC without Hirst would have stayed a small electrical shop, but GEC without Max Railing would have gone bust.'[8]

Unlike Weinstock, Hirst stepped back from the business when he reached his sixties, and left Railing virtually in charge while he busied himself with politics and wider industrial affairs from the 1920s on. But there was one crucial similarity between the two men: while Hirst was happy to leave Railing holding the fort, neither he nor Weinstock managed to prepare for their eventual succession, relying instead on an unsatisfactory family dynasty. The problem was magnified for Hirst because both his son and his grandson died in world wars. When Railing and Hirst died within a year of each other towards the end of the Second World War, power passed to Railing's brother Sir Harry and Hirst's son-in-law Leslie Gamage (knighted in 1958), the son of the Gamage's department store owner, who had married Muriel Hirst.

Gamage and Harry Railing were the wrong men at the wrong time. Their age and background did not position them to carry out the necessary shake-up of the faltering empire – Railing was sixty-three when he took over in 1943, and Gamage seventy when he succeeded him in 1957. Their period at GEC had been relatively easy – rapid expansion even in the 1930s slump as the use of electricity spread, with profits held up by a cartel in lightbulbs which kept prices artificially high and excluded competition. And they had always served under the two big bosses, so they had no experience of real power or responsibility.

They took over at a time of expansion, but also of change. Electricity supply was nationalised in 1947, and for a few years there was an abundance of orders from the new Central Electricity Generating Board. But in the 1950s the capacity created to satisfy those orders became excessive. Nuclear power was emerging, but it ate up capital and produced no profits. GEC decided in 1954 to go into this business as an offshoot of its already low-profit heavy-engineering side. It won the contracts for the nuclear plant at Hunterston in Scotland and for another in Japan, but both produced enormous losses for years. Technology was also changing other areas of the group's business, as electronics advanced into telecommunications, military equipment and computers. Making matters even more difficult for British manufacturers in this as well as other fields, industry on the Continent, especially in Germany, had recovered from the destruction of the war and had begun to expand beyond its domestic borders. And the lightbulb cartel, which had earned the electrical giants so much money, was breaking up under the Conservative government's attack on anti-competitive practices.

Meanwhile, GEC's original branch network, which stemmed from its origins as a wholesaler of 'everything electrical', remained in place, with huge stocks but a separation from the manufacturing side, which did not help it to compete with the new electricity showrooms and dedicated wholesalers. When consultants finally began to crawl over the branches at the end of the 1950s, they discovered, among other things, a stack of bedwarmers which filled half a floor of a Birmingham warehouse. Kenneth Bond remembered that the stock from the chain of Magnet House branches around the country was brought to an empty factory in Perivale. 'It ended up with hundreds of thousands of square feet of rubbish. We had enough lightning conductors to meet the requirements of the whole world for about twenty-five years.'[9]

Despite all this, GEC went on in grand fashion, especially under the rather flamboyant Gamage, and his wife. Lady Gamage gave extravagant dinners at Claridge's for 'the ladies and friends of the overseas GEC' which were reported on *The Times*'s Court pages.[10] But the effect of complacency, confusion and poor management – endemic in British industry at the time – could be seen in GEC's financial results. Despite a continued rise in sales, profits at first stagnated and then fell throughout the second half of the 1950s. In his penultimate speech as chairman at the annual general meeting in September 1956, Sir Harry Railing blamed governments at home and abroad, and stressed the importance of the company's costly investments for its long-term growth. His remarks have been echoed by many business leaders down the years, with little practical response from governments:

> Industrial investment and expansion require long-term forward planning and allocation of resources. Changes in government policy – and there have been several changes in the past five years – can unfortunately upset the most carefully laid investment plans . . . In our rapidly developing technological age, the need for an adequate number of properly trained scientists, technologists and administrators must be met. The scientific turmoil of the mid-century has shown up our inadequacies in skilled manpower, and the shortage of teachers is accompanied by lack of adequate schools in which to teach.

Like much of British industry at the time, Railing seemed content to blame the government rather than acting to deal with its decisions. He made only passing reference to the fact that the company's profits had fallen by £1 million from the previous year's peak of £7.5 million, and that cash resources were shrinking. He could clearly give shareholders no inkling of what the board planned to do about the situation, since the board had no plans. By the time he retired the following October, GEC had been forced to issue more shares to raise capital, but found itself unable to maintain the level of dividend on the expanded number of shares. In his last statement as chairman, Railing commented:

> The further outlook depends on greater stability in the country's economic position, the necessity for which has

been clearly pointed out in the Chancellor's recent statements. It is difficult at present to foresee an immediate relief from the pressure on profit margins in view of the overall effects of the further wage advances which have taken place. We also have to face further considerable development expenditure in connection with the new fields in which we are engaged, such as atomic energy and electronics. It is for these reasons that the directors think it prudent to recommend a reduction in the rate of dividend for the year.

Little improvement was seen under Railing's successor Leslie Gamage. Sales continued to set new records each year, exceeding £100 million in 1958. But profits continued to slide, falling below £4 million in 1961 after a brief recovery the previous year – Gamage's last. Gamage ended on the optimistic note characteristic of company chairmen, opening his review in the 1959–60 annual report: 'I am glad to report that the company's trading results show a satisfactory improvement on the previous year and confirm the confidence I have felt and endeavoured to convey in my previous reviews.' But his confidence was barely skin-deep. When it came to the company's prospects he was forced to confess: 'I must frankly admit I am disappointed – without being unduly pessimistic . . . I can offer no forecast, but I hope and believe that by our strenuous efforts to cut expenditure and increase sales we shall be able to maintain – if not to improve on – the results of last year.'

The doubts, rather than the confidence, came through most strongly. The *Times* City Editor commented: 'The GEC report is not an encouraging document.'[11] Others were of the same opinion, concerned in particular at the continued rise in debts and their associated interest cost. A small group of non-executive directors, led by new directors Lord Catto and Sir Toby Low (later Lord Aldington), concluded that radical action must be taken quickly to avoid collapse. One of the group recalled: 'We felt we were teetering on the brink.'[12]

The feeling was crystallised by the mighty Prudential, the country's largest insurance company and a substantial shareholder in GEC. It was as conventional as it was cautious, and probably the least likely City institution to break ranks. But when GEC needed to raise a loan to repay £8 million of loan stock issued shortly after the war, the Pru baulked, and would only contribute half its share. Even today such a move would be a substantial vote of no confidence in the management of one of Britain's leading companies. At the time it would have sent shock waves through the financial and industrial community if it had been made public, which it was not. Instead, the matter was dealt with in classic City fashion, during discreet chats in the panelled meeting rooms of GEC's bankers. But it emphasised the scale of the crisis the company was facing.

At one meeting in 1959 Gamage was persuaded that it would be a good idea to call in management consultants. They came up with the obvious conclusion – although it had not been obvious within the company – that the network of thirty-five Magnet House depots should be scrapped, and this was duly set in train, although not without fierce opposition from the sales people whose empire it was. Other changes were also set afoot. Arnold Lindley, an engineer with an impeccable background in GEC, became vice chairman and managing director in 1959. In moves which were subsequently often attributed to Weinstock, who followed them up, Lindley attacked the bloated bureaucracy at the centre of the group, the most potent symbol of which was the headquarters building itself, where two thousand people were employed. Magnet House, completed shortly after the First World War, had been built by Lord Hirst to demonstrate that GEC had arrived among the first rank of industrial companies. It was the kind of solid, respectable building typical of its time, and stood, significantly, on Kingsway, in London's commercial heart between the City and the West End, and just a few hundred yards from the headquarters of AEI and English Electric.

The end of Magnet House was not just symbolic for GEC, but also of the times, which saw the beginnings of a shift from manufacturing industry to finance and finance-related ventures such as property development. The building was sold to property magnate Harry Hyams, subsequently famous for erecting Centre Point, the towering office block at the end of Oxford Street which stood empty and attracted fierce political controversy in the 1970s. He demolished Magnet House and built what was then a futuristic circular block named Space House, which was later occupied by the Civil Aviation Authority.

Lindley also set in train several other useful moves. But they were not enough, and were not pursued vigorously enough, to pacify increasingly anxious investors. Lord Catto took responsibility for telling Gamage that it was time to go. Even though Gamage was now seventy-three, the message was not well received, especially when it was confirmed by Lindley. But in an aside to the 1960 results the company announced that Gamage would step down at the end of the year.

Lindley's reign was to be even briefer, even though he was not yet sixty. It was clear to him and to the non-executive directors who had encouraged his elevation that GEC lacked management ability. Under Hirst and Max Railing there had been little need for managers who could use their initiative. Now there was a desperate need, but GEC's inbred culture, with a resistance to recruiting from outside, had left an enormous gap. One answer might have been a merger, and there were rumours around the City during the summer of 1960 that both EMI and English Electric were preparing to make a takeover bid.

EMI, then casting around for a strategy to build on its success in recorded music and electronics, decided not to get involved. But formal talks between GEC and English Electric (EE) were announced in September. The attraction was clear for EE – which would have acquired a competitor at a knockdown price – and its chairman Lord Nelson, a dominant figure equivalent to Lord Hirst, but not for GEC. EE's management was not obviously much better than GEC's, and as *The Times* pointed out on 28 September, the industrial logic was not compelling. Despite the prospect of reducing over-capacity, it was clear that size alone was not the solution to the industry's problems: 'Already the companies have been wrestling with the problem of co-ordinating their own different manufacturing divisions. A complete merger of English Electric and GEC would not necessarily make their problems any easier. Not one of the big three in this whole industry has shown that size by itself is synonymous with efficiency.'

GEC's directors evidently came to the same conclusion. Talks were abandoned at the end of November, leaving GEC looking elsewhere to solve its management problems. The company was so poorly regarded at the time that English Electric would probably have been able to win a hostile takeover bid. But contested takeovers were rare in those days, and Lord Nelson did not contemplate such a move, preferring to walk away having failed to persuade GEC's directors to reach agreement

The solution was provided by Sir Harry Moore of the small merchant bank Philip Hill, Higginson (subsequently part of Hill Samuel, which was behind many of the aggressive takeovers of the 1980s). Moore had acted for Radio & Allied in its abortive attempt to buy Ekco and in its recent talks with EMI and others. Now he took Arnold Weinstock and Kenneth Bond to see GEC.

The objective was not entirely clear to the pair of rather new industrialists. They had been talking to Charles Richards, half of the Morphy Richards partnership, who had fallen out with Morphy after they sold the business to EMI. Richards was interested in GEC's consumer products business, which would have expanded Morphy Richards' range without taking it into completely new fields. For GEC the focus was on management, not products. Lindley had just taken over from Gamage as chairman, as well as being managing director. Despite being a career GEC man, like all the executives, he was acutely aware of the paucity of management talent in the company's rambling hierarchy. Like so much of British industry at the time, GEC had relied on cosy trade arrangements which held up profits, especially in the absence of Continental competition in the aftermath of war. Senior managers were either salesmen or engineers, quite ignorant about financial matters, and while the board was not short of financiers, they were bankers, not financial managers. New ideas about cost accounting and management information were beginning to reach Britain from the United States, but they had as yet made little impact at GEC or most other large companies.

To Lindley, and others in the electrical industry, Radio & Allied was an astounding success. It had come from nowhere to reach profits of more than £1 million in just five years. That was almost a third of the entire pre-tax profits of the whole GEC group, and put the performance of its own radio and television business, which

76

was making losses at the time, into sharp perspective. Everybody in the industry had to sit up and take notice, but GEC, uncharacteristically, decided to act.

Rumours of the impending takeover spread through the stock market during February 1961, and the news was formally released on the evening of 28 February. GEC was to offer a straightforward share exchange – one of its shares for each share in Radio & Allied – plus two shillings (10p) per share in cash. It was an astonishingly generous offer, valuing Radio & Allied at £8.6 million, or 33s.6d (167p) per share. That was one third higher than the R&A share price before the rumours began to spread. This was not an unusually high premium to entice shareholders, and the takeover price would be partly offset by £1.7 million of cash held by R&A. But prospects for the business had already started to worsen as the re-elected Conservative government began to tighten the economic screw. The company had been forced to warn in September that the results for 1960–61 were unlikely to match the record £1.3 million profit delivered in the previous year, as GEC also did in January.

The offer also had the remarkable effect of leaving the Sobell/ Weinstock families with 3.25 million GEC shares, which represented 14 per cent of the entire share capital, making them by far the largest shareholders in the company. Their stake was worth over £5 million, more than doubling their fortune since floating Radio & Allied, but also making it even more dependent on the success of the business. Weinstock has often joked that it was a great mistake to take shares instead of cash, since that meant he could not walk away from the company – although in fact GEC would not have been able to raise the money to pay for Radio & Allied in cash, even if Weinstock had tried to insist on it, and there seems little chance of his ever having wanted to walk away from it.

For the GEC directors, who feared they had little time to effect the company's recovery, the price was almost irrelevant. They were buying Arnold Weinstock, and it proved to be a bargain, especially as they also acquired Kenneth Bond, who subsequently turned out to be almost equally important. As part of the deal, Sobell and Weinstock joined the GEC board as soon as the takeover was completed, and Weinstock was to assume command of the combined consumer products business, jointly with Charles Richards (who died in 1964). 'The directors of both companies are confident that the new arrangements will result in the efficient deployment of their combined resources and will provide the basis for an expanding trade in both Home and Export markets,' said the official statement announcing the takeover.

Weinstock was appalled by the mess he discovered at GEC, which opened his eyes to the way that big business was run. The top directors seemed to do little other than attend board meetings, spend a couple of weeks writing the minutes and then another couple of weeks preparing papers for the next one. 'Even then the minutes bore little resemblance to what went on,' Weinstock remembered. Worst of all, there were no proper figures. Weinstock had only ever worked in small, fairly simple businesses in which he knew precisely what was going on all the time, cash was carefully conserved and costs were kept to the bone. GEC, on the other hand, as the consumer business which he was responsible for demonstrated, was a tangled empire with confused lines of responsibility, poor control and very little financial information. The emphasis had been on investment rather than on returns. For example, GEC's television sets were made at a factory in Coventry where large sums had been spent on mechanisation. This was important because the Midlands workers were paid more than £12 a week, half as much again as the Radio & Allied employees in Hirwaun. The investment enabled the factory to produce five thousand television sets a week, and the company proudly presented its achievement to the press in July 1960. Yet even as it did so it had to admit that the factory was working only to half its capacity because there was insufficient demand for its products.[13]

Weinstock discovered that this was typical of much of GEC's operations. As a member of the new management committee which was another of Arnold Lindley's innovations, he found that decisions were being taken to spend substantial sums on capital investment on the basis of what he regarded as insufficient information. Never a collegiate type, nor terribly interested in other people's opinions, he found the meetings an irritating waste of time. In disgust, he stopped attending, staying at Radio & Allied's offices at Langley Park in Slough to concentrate on his job of producing profits from the combined appliance business, leaving others to run the rest of the group. He even refused to report his cash figures to head office because he and Kenneth Bond were worried that the money would be whipped away and wasted on some grand project.

Lindley had recognised the problem of financial information and had brought in an accountant from Courtaulds, E.H. Davison (father of Ian Hay Davison, who headed accountancy firm Arthur Andersen in the 1970s before moving to top jobs at Lloyd's insurance market and the Storehouse retail group). But Davison was an old-fashioned chief accountant rather than a modern financial director, and he was not able to play the part in the shake-up of the moribund GEC organisation which Lindley needed. 'He used to say he was "disappointed" at the results all the time, but he didn't seem to know what to do about it,' Weinstock recalled. The need for action became more obvious as Weinstock and Bond got to grips with their part of the group. They transferred production from Coventry to South Wales. Bond set up systems which worked simply and quickly to reveal a clear financial picture, and introduced the notion of cash controls – crucial in the kind of small business they had been running, but completely alien to the GEC men despite the company's dangerously rising overdraft.

The non-executive directors were impressed, and Tom Kerr, Lindley's able and selfless deputy, was despatched to Langley Park to offer Weinstock the position of group managing director. Assertive as ever, Weinstock named his terms. He would only accept if Bond was finance director, and if there was to be no interference. The board had little option but to agree. Bond was quickly moved to head office, and Davison left in September 1962. Weinstock was effectively in control from that point, and took over officially on 1 January 1963, beginning a thirty-three-year reign which transformed the company and had an immense impact on British manufacturing industry.

The takeover was not smooth, but Weinstock brooked no opposition. Just as he had made it perfectly clear to his father-in-law who was in charge, so he stood for no nonsense from the old guard at GEC. Lindley briefly maintained the fiction that he was still in control, but also revealed how much he had underestimated the scale of change needed at GEC as he told journalists: 'When I took over the joint position as chairman and managing director I made it clear that I did not intend to carry on the dual role indefinitely. Now that the major part of our reorganisation programme is complete we can strengthen the board by bringing on the younger men of outstanding ability . . . I remain chief executive and have at my elbow the support and advice of one of the most able (and I think one of the youngest) groups of men in the electrical industry.'[14]

It did not take long for Lindley to be persuaded, probably by Kerr, that he should go. Before the end of 1963 it was announced that he would step down as chairman, with Lord Aldington, who had been one of the prime movers in promoting Weinstock, taking over as non-executive chairman. But this did not happen before Lindley had undergone a certain amount of humiliation. Weinstock and Bond made sure that he had no involvement in the business, and nothing went across his desk any longer. But it was the small things which hurt most. With his usual eye for detail, Weinstock carried a cost-cutting regime to extremes, cancelling the orders for the directors' newspapers and magazines – in Lindley's case, the *Financial Times* and *Yachting and Motor Boat Weekly*. Curiously, this was the one move which really rankled with Lindley, who accosted Weinstock one morning, saying: 'You stopped me getting them.' Weinstock said: 'No, I stopped the company paying for it.' That was the end of Lindley. In November 1963 Weinstock cemented his position by bringing in David Lewis, Sobell's lawyer, who had advised on both family and commercial matters. Lewis was just as bright and hard as Weinstock, several years his senior, and, as a colleague put it, '101 per cent straight'. He completed a powerful trio which was to work closely together for almost twenty years.

Weinstock brought a completely new approach to the business of running GEC. The company's complacency had already been under attack from Lindley, but now there was a much greater sense of urgency. Weinstock, Lewis and Bond knew what they wanted, and were not too concerned about upsetting people in the process. One early colleague recalled that GEC's managers, used to flabby direction from Magnet House, were often minded to ignore Weinstock's instructions. They soon found that they had little choice in the matter. That had been Weinstock's great attraction to the GEC board. One contemporary member said: 'Arnold was one of the awkward squad, but that was why he was there. Bond was an angel from heaven – an accountant who could see things broadly.'[15]

What Weinstock, Lewis and Bond wanted most of all was accountability – for every manager to know exactly what he was responsible for. There were no more fat consultancy fees from GEC. Weinstock and Bond spread their message of control and account-ability through the empire. Amorphous divisions were broken up into distinct units with specific products so that individuals could be given clear responsibility for smaller operations. 'The first thing we did was to make sure that each business ran a product, with its own managing director totally responsible for everything,' recalled Kenneth Bond. 'He didn't have to buy anything in. There were no alibis. If something wasn't right it was clearly the responsibility of the person in charge. He couldn't blame someone else.'[16]

Each business then had to be introduced to the routine of annual budget meetings and monthly reporting which was to be the man-aging director's key tool of control. The system was simple, appro-priate to Weinstock's small-business background, the lack of financial sophistication among GEC's managers, his horror of bureaucracy and the wide spread of businesses within the GEC group. Weinstock wanted managers to make their own decisions and to stand or fall by them. Responsibility for results meant an end to the usual rosy forecasts. Every manager now knew that if he failed to meet his budget, he would be in trouble, and possibly out on his ear.

It was a revolution which was only possible because of conditions inside the company, but which was also in tune with the spirit of the times. The complacency of cartels had been fuelled by the Allies' victory in the war, which also had the effect of maintaining the focus beyond Britain of most industrialists on the Commonwealth rather than on the European continent. But now British industry was beginning to lose out to better-organised competition from Germany, Japan and the United States. A new generation of man-agers was emerging whose views were not formed by war, pre-war economic chaos and insularity, and who were not constrained by the supercilious distaste for the nitty-gritty of commerce which hampered many of the well-connected directors of leading companies. As Anthony Sampson noted:

> Any British outfit, given half a chance, will settle down into behaving like an Oxford college or a country estate. But in the last few years that illusion has been harder to maintain. In industry, the competition from America and Europe, and the end of the fat years of a seller's market, has at last produced a new competitiveness in which the word 'profits' is mentioned without shame . . . New chairmen have generated a new ruthlessness and (as a leading management consultant put it) 'We are at last coming back to accepting that the job of management is to manage. We are trying to jump over a generation, and to put into senior management young men who have been conditioned since the war to the new world.[17]

(Ironically, in view of what was to come, Sampson included AEI, English Electric and GEC as examples of this new ruthlessness).

These developments were matched in the broader political and cultural world outside Britain's boardrooms. In 1963 Harold Wilson was leading the Labour Party in a final assault on Macmillan's ailing Conservative government, under the 'white heat of technology' banner, with an appeal to modernity and efficiency which could have been modelled on the contrast between the old and the new GEC. On television, *That Was The Week That Was* satirised the Establishment, ripping apart the veil of respectability and infallibility which had helped perpetuate the British system of deference and class. The Beatles stormed on to the music scene, boosting the burgeoning youth culture which was to dominate the 1960s. These social developments hit the headlines and characterised the age, but the arrival of Arnold Weinstock and his henchmen at the top of GEC was far more important for the development of British industry during that tumultuous decade.

In nine years Weinstock had come from the obscurity of the London property world to the top of one of the country's largest industrial combines. The series of deals which had taken him there would not be unusual in the 1990s, as it has become almost commonplace for managers to buy out their subsidiary from a large conglomerate, float it on the stock market a few years later and subsequently cash in their fortunes by being taken over by another conglomerate. But the speed of Weinstock's rise was unique in the 1950s, when the world of big business was much more staid and closed to outsiders such as Sobell and Weinstock. His dramatic rise was due partly to the good fortune of his father-in-law's business being in the right place at the right time, just as GEC's desperate state provided an opening which might not have existed either earlier or later. But it was also due to his own powers and personality, his ability to understand and analyse detailed business matters, his willingness to upset people in the cause of what he believed to be right, and a self-confidence which offset his lack of years, experience and knowledge. Those qualities were to stand him in good stead for the next thirty years at the top of GEC, and particularly in the traumatic period after the arrival of Harold Wilson's first Labour government in 1964.

## CHAPTER FOUR

# *White Heat*

ARNOLD WEINSTOCK became managing director of GEC just forty-four days before Harold Wilson was elected leader of the Labour Party on 14 February 1963, replacing Hugh Gaitskell who had died a few weeks earlier. Weinstock and Wilson were both statisticians by training, but otherwise there was little similarity in their characters, backgrounds, upbringings or career paths, except that they shared a desire to see industry become more competitive and were instrumental in transforming the British industrial scene over the rest of the decade. Both were eventually to be seen as relics of a corporatist past, but in the mid-1960s they were instruments of profound change, symbols of the meritocratic, managerial Britain which was emerging from the post-war upheaval that had seen the country cast off its imperial heritage and some of its elitist conventions. Wilson's leadership of the Labour Party, especially its industrial and economic policies in government, had a dramatic impact on Weinstock and his leadership of GEC. The company became a tool in Labour's drive to modernise British industry, to shake companies from what Wilson saw as widespread complacency and insularity, and to build British businesses big enough to compete on the world stage, run by competent managers rather than titled or moneyed amateurs.

Wilson's surprise victory over Gaitskell's deputy George Brown in the leadership election of February 1963 was a victory for the left wing of the Labour Party over the right, which had supported Gaitskell's defence of nuclear weapons and his attack on the party's historic commitment to workers' power, as enshrined in Clause 4 of its constitution. Wilson had been instrumental in the development of Labour's policy of intervention in the key industries which had not been nationalised – a policy which was soon to touch Weinstock and GEC. In terms which show similarities to the late-1990s stakeholder debate, he argued that private industry had responsibilities beyond those to its shareholders, even though it had no element of state ownership. The private sector still represented by far the greater part of the economy; yet, Wilson argued, 'very little fundamental thinking has been done on the ways in which the government can influence its actions'. He maintained that there existed 'a duty on private industry, no less than on socialised industries, to conform to the national interest', but that the existing structure of private firms meant that 'patriotism and exhortation' alone were insufficient to ensure that the national interest was served.[1]

Wilson's views were far less radical than those which were eventually to be espoused by Tony Benn in the 1970s, and which, as we shall see, provoked Weinstock into public opposition. And they were quite widely shared well away from the left wing of the Labour Party, including by Weinstock. In the early 1960s Britain had entered a period of self-analysis and self-criticism of a type which was to become familiar over the years but which, as subsequently, failed to reach a consensus on the action needed to overcome easily recognised problems. The clear problem was one of relative decline against international competitors. Britain's share of world trade was shrinking at an accelerating rate. There were persistent problems of inflation and trade deficits. But technology seemed to promise a way out. This was the era of the development of Concorde, of factory automation and the spread of computers into commercial and government activity. There was a feeling that technology could liberate people from repetitive and tedious activities, could boost productivity and raise Britain's competitiveness, but that this could only be done with the active involvement of a government committed to those causes, sceptical about industry's ability to manage the technological transition on its own.

Wilson set out his ideas for a meritocratic, technological revolution in the famous 'white heat' speech at the 1963 Labour Party Conference which contained many portents for Weinstock and GEC, but which are also sadly familiar thirty-five years later. It called for intervention to ensure that the benefits of technology were spread evenly, included an attack on defence-dominated research, and talked of a revolution based on new social and economic attitudes: 'The Britain that is going to be forged in the white heat of this revolution will be no place for restrictive practices or for outdated methods on either side of industry.' And it talked of people like Weinstock taking over from the amateurs like Gamage and Railing:

> For the commanding heights of British industry to be controlled today by men whose only claim is their aristocratic connection or the power of inherited wealth or speculative finance is as irrelevant to the twentieth century as would be the continued purchase of commissions in the armed forces by lordly amateurs. At the very time that even the MCC has abolished the distinction between amateurs and professionals, in science and industry we are content to remain a nation of Gentlemen in a world of Players.[2]

Revolutionising 'the commanding heights of the economy' also involved an attack on the commanding heights of economic policy-making – the Treasury. Wilson believed, as many still do, that the Treasury exerted too strong a hold over economic management. The Treasury was mainly preoccupied with macro-economic issues such as the level of sterling, interest rates and the size of government borrowing, and Wilson argued that the needs of industry, and hence of people dependent on industrial success, were given too little consideration. The solution would be the creation of a new Department of Economic Affairs, to wrest some powers from the Treasury and to have particular responsibility for economic planning, taking account of the government's broad objectives and not just the immediate demands of public borrowing or the exchange rate. There would also be a Ministry of Technology to try to ensure that British business adopted the most modern techniques, placing Britain at the forefront of Wilson's technological revolution, which had become roughly translated by the media as 'the white heat of technology'. Both these new government departments would have a crucial role in the future of Arnold Weinstock and GEC.

Labour won the general election in October 1964, defeating a

Conservative government dispirited by scandals such as the Pro-
fumo affair, weakened by the resignation of Harold Macmillan in
October of the previous year, exhausted after thirteen years in
power and out of tune with an electorate eager for 1960s modernity
rather than the past embodied in Macmillan's uncomfortable successor Sir Alec Douglas-Home. Once elected, Wilson set about
implementing his interventionist approach. The Department of
Economic Affairs was established, with George Brown at its head,
and it set about constructing the first National Plan as well as the
major tool of direct intervention, the Industrial Reorganisation Corporation (IRC). The National Plan set out the government's hopes
for the economy – based on consultation with trade unions and
business leaders – for the next five years. It predicted growth of 25
per cent in gross national product between 1964 and 1970, a figure
which it became clear was wildly optimistic soon after its adoption
in September 1965. As the tripartite National Economic Development Council (NEDC) observed after it had accepted the target, it
could only be achieved with a dramatic rise in exports to eliminate
the balance of payments deficit. But the plan also called for higher
productivity, greater investment, a prices and incomes policy to
control inflation, and regional policies to spread the benefits of
growth.

The Plan recognised the 'key importance' of the electrical engineering industry in achieving balance of payments and investment
objectives. Exports of electrical engineering products were forecast
to grow by 6 per cent a year, but that required international stan-
dardisation, something Weinstock and others would be calling for
years later in relation to telecommunications equipment. Exports
of electronics were seen as even more promising, with growth of
10 per cent a year predicted. But the Plan noted that the sector's
performance was dependent on the ordering programme of the
Post Office (then in charge of what is now British Telecom). The
Plan was also prescient on restructuring in the electrical industry:

> In heavy plant the complexities of achieving further con-
> centration have been greater and progress slower [than in
> lighter products]: arrangements for consolidation have,
> however, recently been proposed which would reduce the

number of manufacturers of large turbo-generating equipment from four to three. The significance of such moves is clear in face of the growth in size and complexity of the equipment, and the consolidation of manufacturing in the European Economic Community through mergers of companies and arrangements for rationalisation between the major groups. In view of the increasing scale of manufacturing operations on the continent, the process of major structural change towards consolidation in the British industry can by no means be considered complete.[3]

The Plan did not survive the next disastrous couple of years of Labour power, which saw ballooning trade deficits, culminating in the devaluation of the pound in November 1967. But the government's broader economic and industrial policies did survive, in particular the IRC, which was to have a dramatic impact on the future of GEC.

Weinstock was sympathetic to Labour's interventionist style. He had no time for the overmanning which was widespread throughout British industry, and showed no compunction about adding to unemployment. But he believed then, and continued to do so, that government and industry should work together to improve competitiveness, especially on new technological developments.

When Weinstock took over at GEC at the start of 1963 he wasted no time sitting around waiting for a change of government. He could not afford to, because the company's financial state demanded urgent action. He immediately set about his part in remodelling British industry, reconstructing the GEC empire in a form appropriate to the conditions of the 1960s. He completed the dismantling of the Magnet House warehouse network, and the move from the grand Kingsway head office. His base for the remainder of his time as managing director was to be 1 Stanhope Gate, a distinctly plain glass-and-concrete block just off Park Lane which stands out among the decorous Georgian townhouses around it. It could almost be a symbol of the way in which Weinstock himself has stood out from the conventional big business crowd.

Weinstock's changes were not universally accepted within GEC, and he needed all his conviction and directness to overcome resistance from senior managers who saw their empires being cut away. Deadlines for closing the Magnet House distribution centres were repeatedly missed. In the end Weinstock was forced to tell those in charge that at the end of the year he would lock the doors and throw any stock which was left into the sea. The lawyer David Lewis recalled: 'Early on he found many people were ignoring his instructions. He would say: "Either you do it my way or you go."'[4]

A young technician who worked in one of GEC's labs at the time remembered the breath of fresh air which Weinstock brought to the company. 'All of a sudden here was somebody who knew what he was talking about and cared what we were bloody doing. We used to have people who came round and gazed at the technical excellence, but this wasn't a gee-whizz exercise. He looked at one or two of our proposals and he seemed quite interested. He got rid of a lot of pomposity. He was a very bright guy and his business sense was something we had lacked. All of a sudden we had another dimension – he reoriented us towards the customer and we gradually became more competitive and more oriented towards selling.'[5]

Weinstock's reorganisation of the operating units brought together the various consumer activities in a single consumer products division. Previously, after a number of structural changes since the mid-1950s, Home Products had dealt with household equipment, but there was also a Lighting and Equipment operation, dealing mainly with bought-in products, and the Osram lighting business was quite separate. The creation of a Consumer Products division resulted in four divisions which were roughly equal in terms of sales and assets. The largest, but only marginally, was Telecommunications and Electronics, with sales of £40 million in 1962–63. The smallest was a collection of miscellaneous activities (many of which remained part of GEC well into the 1990s) including Express Lifts, the Simplex dairy equipment company, Claudgen illuminated signs and the fan-maker Woods of Colchester, whose brands included Expelair. This grouping had sales of £27 million. In between these two, each with sales of £32 million, were Consumer Products and Engineering, which embraced the production of generators, switchgear and other power equipment, mainly at Erith in

Kent and Witton in Birmingham (GEC's original manufacturing base).

The balance of sales shows that GEC was dominated by light electrical products. Weinstock was intent on increasing this emphasis, and he quickly began pursuing this central strategy, seeking to reduce GEC's involvement in heavy engineering, where there were few orders and it was therefore difficult to make profits. This was a natural direction for Weinstock, given his own background in radio and television manufacture, but it was also driven by the overcapacity at the heavy end of the industry and the likelihood of continued growth in demand for consumer appliances. Greater affluence and the government's slum-clearance programme, which resulted in a rash of new housing estates, was bound to produce a growing market for new cookers, refrigerators and washing machines, while radio and television sales were continuing to expand, with pirate radio stations fuelling the pop music culture and the promise of new television channels as well as colour broadcasting in the offing. Telephones were also spreading fast through the new housing estates, creating demand for new exchanges as well as receivers. There was little thought that the demand for these goods could be satisfied by imports, although there were growing worries about Italian washing machines.

The creation of new divisions was merely tinkering, however. There were more fundamental moves afoot, continuing the ferment in the electrical goods sector as the leading companies attempted to come to terms with overcapacity and the need for larger scale to produce manufacturing economies. In the early 1960s virtually every company in the industry was involved in talks about swapping assets, pooling common interests or even complete merger. AEI's managing director Sir Joseph Latham later recounted how GEC and AEI were involved in numerous discussions with each other and third parties, most of which came to nothing.[6] Following the failure of the English Electric/GEC talks in 1960, and before Weinstock took over, GEC and AEI actually reached agreement in principle on merging their telecoms and lighting interests, but the deal broke down. In 1963, under Weinstock, there were more wideranging discussions about asset swaps, with the idea of AEI taking on all the heavy electrical activities and GEC acquiring AEI's interests in the lighter end. Again, no agreement was reached. GEC then suggested that it and AEI should sell their heavy business to one of the leaders in that field, C.A. Parsons. Talks continued at intervals into 1965, but GEC usually wanted a price for its assets which AEI thought was too high – a characteristic of Weinstock which stayed with him throughout his years in charge.

The big moves were stalled for the time being, but a couple of steps were made to refocus the group. In May 1963 a reorganisation of GEC's nuclear power activities was announced. Nuclear engineering had been an expensive adventure for the company, and would continue for years to be an area of controversy directly involving Weinstock. GEC first entered the industry in 1954, winning contracts for the Hunterston power station in Ayrshire and Tokai Mura in Japan. The company's annual report in 1964 boasted that the first reactor at Hunterston would probably be able to run at 20 per cent above its design output, while the Tokai Mura station was proceeding to plan, and would be producing electricity by April 1965. But the costs of these developments had been enormous, resulting in losses running into millions of pounds, while a dispute with the South of Scotland Electricity Board over payments for Hunterston ended up in the courts.

The next step was Weinstock's first acquisition, an opportunistic move to build the group's consumer products interests by adding Cannon gas cookers. Evidence of the new managing director's enthusiasm for consumer products was seen in November 1965, when GEC revealed ambitious expansion plans. This was despite a disastrous fire at the Hirwaun factory towards the end of October. The building was gutted, causing damage worth £2.5 million, but within half an hour of hearing about the fire, production manager John Banner had arranged an alternative site. GEC moved lock, stock and barrel into an empty building nearby, and production recommenced within a week, in what the chairman of the local council described as 'an industrial miracle'.[7]

In May 1964 Weinstock agreed to pay £4 million for the Cannon business, adding to the company's existing interest in electric cookers and heaters. This was an uncharacteristically generous offer. Before rumours of the takeover had emerged, Cannon's shares had been trading at little more than £5 each, yet Weinstock offered 127s.6d (637p) per share, a premium of almost 30 per cent. It was a knockout blow, as it was intended to be, announcing to the world that GEC was in good shape and eager to grow.

The effects of measures begun by Lindley and continued by Weinstock could already be seen in GEC's results. Profit before tax in 1963–64, including the contribution from Radio & Allied, almost doubled to nearly £12 million. The R&A cash balances also helped in the crucial task of cutting the company's debts, as did the sale of properties and some minor investments, combined with the strict cash controls introduced by Kenneth Bond. GEC's overdraft fell from almost £6 million in March 1963, just after Weinstock took over, to little more than £1 million. At the same time the group built up cash balances of more than £3 million, a total cash turnaround of nearly £8 million. The improvement continued in the following year, with profits rising to £17 million. The cash position remained the same as at the end of the previous year, due partly to the Cannon acquisition, but also to heavy demands for capital from nuclear engineering.

In his first statement as chairman, Lord Aldington commented on the next stage in the strategy of cutting GEC's interest in heavy electricals. In May 1965 the company agreed to sell its turbo-generator business to C.A. Parsons, which left GEC with an 18 per cent share in Parsons. The deal allowed GEC to escape – temporarily, as it turned out – from power generation. Lord Aldington was keen to point out that the group would still have an involvement in transformers and switchgear, and the Erith plant would continue to design and sell mechanical equipment, although in fact Weinstock was busy trying to sell his transformer and switchgear businesses as well. Aldington described 'another year of substantial progress', while pointing to some black spots, such as the domestic equipment business. He also set the tone for the future, illustrating the no-nonsense stance of the new regime. As so often over subsequent years, he reported that the poor profit performance of domestic equipment (despite higher sales) had resulted in a change of management. This was a feature of the Weinstock era which came as a shock not only to GEC's managers but also to those outside. It helped to banish complacency and instil the profit responsibility which had been alien to many within the company.

Lord Aldington made it clear that there were no jobs for life in the new GEC in a homily on the effects of change in technology, taste and competition which also set out the new GEC philosophy of what in the 1990s would come to be called 'lean management' and 'flat organisation':

> Change will often lead to men and women becoming redundant in particular activities – although that does not mean there will be no other jobs for them to do; and it may on occasion lead to factories being closed. In the course of the last two years we have been constantly engaged in rationalising production within the group and in moving components or products to other more suitable locations . . .
>
> I have watched with pleasure how responsibility is decentralised to managing directors of the divisional activities and by them to individual managers. There are no large staffs in the GEC organisation; each man has a clear job to do and there are no personal assistants. To some, this kind of organisation might appear to lack planning and to run counter to canons of organisation practised elsewhere. In fact it does not at all inhibit planning in its proper role; and it has the advantage of getting the best out of men, of saving time, and minimising waste of manpower and money.[8]

This public message had already gone privately to GEC's managers. Confidential memos from the managing director to all subsidiary bosses stressed the need for improved productivity and control of overheads, in terms which Weinstock would repeat many times over the following thirty years. In a private and confidential memo dated 12 March 1963, he told executives that none of the annual budgets submitted from subsidiaries were acceptable. He acknowledged that GEC's position had improved, but that was only a beginning, and he spelled out his understanding of the capitalist system:

> We have much to do and there is no point in wasting time in setting about it.
>
> We live in a hard and competitive world . . . The survival of the fittest is the law of nature. We can organise to meet its

challenge and in some circumstances shade the harshness of its effects, but we cannot change it.

In modern competition, prices are based on the costs of the most efficient producers. If we are not as efficient as the best, our margins will not be sufficient to pay for our costs, to pay for the things we need to do to stay in business (such as research and development), to provide a reasonable balance out of which we may finance expansion for the future, and to put away a bit for a rainy day.

A word about profits may not be out of place here. In this country we live in a system of something like free enterprise. Under such a system, profitability is the yardstick of performance. In competition such as we meet today, where we (the GEC) have no monopolies and very little in the way of protection, prices cannot be fixed artificially high. The great splurges of expenditure when the country dramatically increased its living standards and its capital expenditure, is over.

In such conditions high profitability is the sure guide to high efficiency, and the ever greater pressure on prices will always prevent our profits from growing beyond a fair economic level.

Weinstock also dismissed speculation about the possible nationalisation of GEC under a Labour government. He said this was irrelevant, since the tasks would be the same: lower costs, higher efficiency and a bigger business.

He was not satisfied, however, with the extent to which his message appeared to have sunk in, despite repeated transmission in memos. On 22 February 1965 he showed his exasperation, as well as his dry humour:

I have this morning read through the general memoranda I have pushed out to managing directors from time to time in the last two years ... I do not believe the instructions and advice contained in those memoranda have been taken sufficiently literally; if, for a short time, they were indeed acted upon, they have soon been forgotten.

In the memorandum of 15 January 1965 I referred to

some suggestions for measuring efficiency. Except in one case, no one has referred to this matter verbally as applied to his own particular unit, or by correspondence, or in draft budgets. If the instructions given from here are not being carried out, or are only being half-heartedly carried out, we can envisage three possibilities:

(a) the instructions are a load of nonsense;

(b) the unit managements are not able to carry them out;

(c) the unit managements do not want to carry them out.

Naturally I reject possibility (a) although you might not do so, and I think that we have not done as much as we should for a combination of the reasons at (b) and (c) . . . It should be clearly understood that we are engaged in industrial warfare . . . We will either gain victories or be vanquished, and in the end it is a question of survival for the company as a whole, for individual units of the company, and for individual managers in the trading units.

There is a wider aspect of this matter. The measures I have been pressing for so long as required of you by the GEC are the same as those which the industry of the UK must universally adopt if the country is to continue as an industrial power with a high standard of living. As in all forms of war, we cannot afford delay, and excuses for lost battles will not regain lost territory.

The message continued to be rammed home over the next couple of years as Weinstock attempted to drive his philosophy of management responsibility down through the organisation. In April 1965 he drew managers' attention to a survey of European electrical companies which showed both GEC and AEI as being profligate with stock levels. 'This state of affairs simply will not do,' he told them, citing Radio & Allied as an example of a company in which 'the top management people [meaning himself] have always taken a direct and pervading interest in questions of stocks and stock control'. That was the model which every GEC manager should follow, making sure that 'their actions must be decisive in the running of the business, as distinct from management being carried along by the current trend, be it good or bad.' A few months later, in a confidential memo dated 20 September, he sought to banish any feelings of complacency, against a backdrop of the government's drive for change, in terms which predated the 1990s discovery of 're-engineering', i.e. radically overhauling a company's approach to the way it does business.

> This is going to be another of those exhortatory memoranda. But I hope you will take it seriously all the same, because if it did not need writing I would not have wasted the time and the paper.
>
> You will no doubt have noticed the increasing reference in national and industrial debate to the need for change. The Chairman referred to it in his speech at the AGM. The First Secretary's National Plan regards it as essential. That is something which we in the GEC recognised some years ago, and we have been striving to bring it about. I suspect, however, that our greatly improved results flatter the success which we have really had in this objective. We have not changed enough for the better, not nearly enough . . . In plain terms there has been, particularly in the last twenty years, a sort of tacit understanding between managers and workers' representatives to keep things as much as possible as they have been; to modify and adapt, to retain comfortable methods and practices, and to avoid at all costs change which is fundamental and drastic – and, for us and the country, absolutely essential.
>
> I have recently seen examples of how, in other countries, production processes have been looked at entirely afresh and labour costs reduced by 50 and 60 per cent; and how overheads by the same *de novo* approach have been cut by hundreds per cent; and I have in the last three years sometimes seen something like this happen, or begin to happen, in parts of the GEC . . . This is a style of approach, a general attitude of mind. We do not ask ourselves nearly enough either –
>
> (a) why we do what we do, or
>
> (b) what other ways might be tried of achieving our aims.
>
> What must be accepted as fundamental is the necessity

Arnold Weinstock (second from right, middle row) at the Stoke Newington Central School before being evacuated to Warwickshire.

Freddie Fogg (fourth from left, second row), the schoolmaster who guided Weinstock to matriculation and the LSE, and who inspired his lifelong love of music.

Weinstock's father-in-law Sir Michael
Sobell, founder of Radio and Allied
Industries.

*Right* Weinstock after GEC's takeover of AEI, 1967.

Workers protest against the closure of AEI's Woolwich plant.

Kenneth Bond, Weinstock and Lord Aldington during the battle for English Electric, July 1968.

Lord Nelson and Weinstock announcing the GEC-English Electric merger, 13 September 1968.

Weinstock and Nelson at the first annual general meeting of GEC-AEI, September 1969.

Weinstock in 1973, characteristically conducting business over the telephone.

of asking questions about ourselves and what we are doing. We need managers and staff who will say 'What did I do today and yesterday?', 'Why did I do it?', 'Why did I do it this way?', 'What other ways were there to deal with the particular issue?', 'Was my decision the best way to achieve the ultimate aim?'

Another vital question to be asked is 'Are my capabilities great enough to enable me to deal with this problem in the best way?' If the honest answer is 'Perhaps not,' then the chap should not be bashful about asking for help from his superiors.

The pace of change was picking up as Weinstock and his inner team settled down. His father-in-law, who had only ever been a non-executive even in Radio & Allied days, finally retired from the GEC board at the annual meeting in 1966. More importantly, GEC welcomed back industrial relations director Jack Scamp from his secondment to George Brown's Department of Economic Affairs, where he had applied his industrial relations skills to the motor industry. Weinstock had opposed Scamp's recruitment under the Lindley regime, arguing against the then-fashionable view that big companies should have a director responsible for industrial relations. He returned to that view in the 1970s, but nevertheless valued Scamp's contribution, especially after Scamp had success-fully carried out a Weinstock mission to cut overheads at the group's Witton plant by £1 million. Scamp liked to describe himself as the half in the three and a half who ran GEC at the time. The three were Weinstock, David Lewis, who had finally joined the board at the end of 1963, and whose influence spread far wider than his official duties as legal adviser, and Kenneth Bond, whose impor-tance was emphasised by his promotion from finance director to deputy managing director in 1966. This team operated as a tightly-knit but informal management committee, operating without meet-ings and minutes, walking in and out of each other's offices as they saw fit, discussing matters as they arose and debating fiercely.

Bond and Lewis were Weinstock's sounding boards, his con-science and his caution. He once described the relationship: 'I get an idea. I talk to Kenneth. If Kenneth thinks there's nothing to the idea I drop it. If Kenneth thinks there might be something to it I'll probably go and talk to David Lewis. If we three think there's something to it we will go out and consult.'[9]

By the end of 1966 the three believed they had GEC in reasonable order, and were keen to move further afield. They had introduced the key financial controls which Weinstock would rely on for the next thirty years to keep a close eye on GEC's growing number of businesses. Bond had rapidly improved financial reporting as soon as he took over as financial director in 1962, but that quick fix was essentially copying the simple controls used by Weinstock and Bond at Radio & Allied. They knew they needed something better for a company the size of GEC, and they knew that American business practice was generally well ahead of Britain in developing management information. So Weinstock sent one of his managers, Derek Powell, to the United States to carry out what would now be termed 'benchmarking'. He investigated the measures in use at the forward-thinking electrical companies Texas Instruments and the US General Electric (GE) (which, despite the similarity of its name, had no connection with GEC).

On the basis of the information Powell brought back, Weinstock and Bond built seven key ratios by which their operating companies would be measured: – return on capital, return on sales, sales as a multiple of capital employed, fixed assets and stocks, as well as sales and profits per employee. This collection of basic performance measures has been criticised as simplistic, but it was designed to be used by and understandable to the engineers who largely ran the business units in GEC.

The ratios were introduced to GEC's managers along with a characteristic Weinstock exhortation to meet the figures the US companies were producing, not merely to calculate the same ratios. In a confidential memo dated 5 September 1966, he wrote:

Just how much we are short of acceptable performance is shown very clearly by some figures which we have as a result of a visit Mr D. Powell made recently to the United States. Comparing the GEC with GE they have four times as many employees as we have, and therefore a much more cumbersome organisation to deal with. Their nett profit as a percentage of sales is comparable to ours, but there all favourable comparison for us comes to an end. GE's ratio of sales to capital employed is double ours, and their percentage of nett profit to capital employed is nearly double ours. Their ratio of sales to stocks is nearly three times ours, and their sales per employee, in money value, is two and a half times ours. Finally, their sales per £1 of fixed assets is one and a half times ours.

Weinstock's close attention to internal matters did not prevent him from looking outside GEC for ways to build the business. His first two transactions – the acquisition of Cannon and the sale of the turbo-generator business to C.A. Parsons – had gone smoothly, but it was to be a case of third time unlucky as he attempted to accelerate the pace of change in GEC's structure and to abandon the agreed approach which he had taken so far. Towards the end of 1966 GEC made its first unwelcome takeover bid – for Telephone Rentals (TR), a company which hired out telephone and other equipment, and whose acquisition would have provided extra business for GEC's struggling telephone equipment arm. The bid was fiercely, and successfully, resisted despite an increase in the original price which left the offer worth more than £24 million. For just a little more money GEC would probably have won. But, in a move which helped build the myth of his meanness, Weinstock decided not to improve the offer, partly because he was mindful of the impact it might have on future bids. He had no intention of stopping at Telephone Rentals, and GEC's directors were concerned that overpaying now might increase the cost of subsequent acquisitions, as targets decided GEC had deep pockets and was prepared to dig into them. A reputation for stinginess, on the other hand, might help depress the cost of the intended acquisition spree.

In the dramatic history of GEC the Telephone Rentals episode seems insignificant, and the sum of £24 million is puny by comparison with what quickly followed. But it was an indicator of what was to come, and of itself had a number of consequences. First, the failure of the bid resulted in Weinstock's traditional response to failure within the company: sacking the offending managers. In this case that meant the merchant bank Morgan Grenfell, which was considered to have been ineffectual in its attempts to persuade Telephone Rentals' shareholders to accept GEC's money. There was no public statement, but GEC decided that that next time it would use a bank with more clout. More significantly, the battle put Weinstock on the map as an aggressive player who had little time for the niceties of business life. Here are the origins of his public image as a cold, arrogant technocrat. His reputation for bluntness was not diminished when he described the TR board as 'a senior bunch' – not the kind of criticism one leading industrialist was supposed to make about others in those courteous days.

*The Times* described the tussle as 'one of the most protracted and acrimonious takeover contests of recent times',[10] and indeed it had lasted most of the winter. It began on 2 December 1966 with a visit by Lord Aldington and Kenneth Bond to the TR chairman Stuart Philcox, at which they revealed their offer of 24s.3d (121p) per share, which was made public five days later. The subsequent battle included a public attack on TR for not giving satisfactory reasons for rejecting GEC's offer. This attack was widely regarded as naive, an accusation that enraged the GEC camp, which felt that its target's shareholders were entitled to more than the customary defence that the price undervalued their company. Weinstock subsequently added an extra two shillings per share at the last moment to reach the final, but still not quite sufficient, offer. For the want of a few extra shillings, Telephone Rentals kept its freedom.

But Weinstock was not put off the takeover trail, in an era when merger mania caught hold in the business world. It was fuelled by a stock market boom which defied the uncertain economic conditions, by a government that looked kindly on mergers which created larger groups with more chance of competing internationally. With the previously rare hostile bid becoming commonplace, the second half of the 1960s saw a rash of takeovers which created many of what remain Britain's largest companies, including the big banking groups. The brewing combine Bass was created at this time, through the acquisition of Mitchell & Butlers and Charrington; Nigel Broakes was buying construction companies to create Trafalgar House; and Jim Slater was setting out on his brief, barnstorming escapade which saw the creation of his Slater Walker financial and industrial empire in just a few years, and its even swifter collapse in the financial crisis of the early 1970s.

Takeovers, of course, were not new, but hostile battles were becoming less unusual. The corporate raiders of the 1950s – often Jewish businessmen such as Charles Clore and Sir Isaac Wolfson – had built up their empires through acquisition, but almost always on a friendly basis. When ICI attacked Courtaulds in 1962, all that changed. ICI, Britain's biggest chemical company, was generally regarded as staid and traditional, with a grand head office on Millbank just along the Thames from the Palace of Westminster. After its attempt to agree a merger with its smaller rival Courtaulds was rejected, ICI uncharacteristically tried to persuade Courtaulds' shareholders with a £200 million offer, which remained for many years the biggest takeover bid ever made. Not quite enough shareholders accepted, and Courtaulds escaped, with Frank Kearton, the main architect of its defence, left in charge of the company as a symbol of a younger, more aggressive generation.

The battle had a dramatic effect on business attitudes, as well as bringing takeovers, which had previously been entirely a matter for the City, into the arena of government policy-making, because of the implications for employment and the economy of a merger between two such giant companies.

But in the early 1960s the takeover battle was still frowned upon in many parts of the old City, as Barclays chairman Anthony Tuke remarked: 'There may be occasions where something more drastic than a gentle kiss on the brow from a Prince Charming is needed to awaken the sleeping beauties. It may even be necessary some-times to tip them right out of bed. But it can seldom be wise to pull down the whole house or even to sell it as it stands to a stranger.'[11]

Nevertheless, the urge to merge became ingrained in British business in the first half of the 1960s, and grew into a passion with the open support of the Labour government. The economic outlook in the mid-sixties was far from positive, but the government's industrial policies, and especially the creation of the Industrial Reorganisation Corporation, offset that. Hampered by the desire to win a second general election, and a refusal to countenance devaluing the pound until it had become unavoidable, the government tightened economic policy steadily, but ineffectively as far as pressure on the pound and the balance of payments was concerned. Even after Labour's re-election with a comfortable majority in March 1966, Chancellor Jim Callaghan stuck to his strategy of defending the pound, at the cost of spending cuts and rising unemployment. In November 1966 unemployment passed the half-million mark – a symbolic point in those days when full employment was a consensual objective – and reached its highest point since 1940 in August of the following year.

At the beginning of January 1966, however, the government unveiled its proposals for the IRC, with George Brown telling the House of Commons that it would search for rationalisation possibilities which would boost exports and accelerate technological development by bringing companies together to enjoy economies of scale. The concept of the IRC was loosely modelled on examples of government industrial intervention abroad, such as in Italy, but was a dramatic departure from the previous British practice of a market economy managed through macro-economic measures and government purchasing power, modified only by the nationalisation of key industries. Its backers in the Labour Party saw it in differing lights, at one extreme taking control of the 'commanding heights' of the economy, at the other merely tinkering to engineer greater industrial efficiency. Its official objective was 'promoting industrial efficiency and profitability and assisting the economy of the United Kingdom' (the words 'and profitability' were inserted as the result of an amendment to the legislation put forward by GEC chairman Lord Aldington). It would have powers to transform the industrial landscape in three ways: putting together companies in the same industry which needed greater scale to compete internationally; putting together companies in different but complementary industries which could benefit from a broader range of activities; and creating 'national champions' out of companies which were perceived as having the greatest chance in their field of international success.

The IRC was to have £150 million initially to put into the ventures which it promoted, and its small team of specialists would be supervised by a panel of part-time board members drawn from the highest ranks of industry. It was chaired by Labour industrialist Frank

Kearton, the man who had saved Courtaulds from ICI in 1962 and remained Courtaulds' chairman. He was a fierce believer in what the IRC stood for, and in the 1970s became chairman of the British National Oil Corporation, set up by James Callaghan's Labour government to capitalise on North Sea oil. Many of the IRC board were less wholeheartedly in favour of government intervention. They included AEI chairman Sir Charles Wheeler, EMI boss Sir Joseph Lockwood and the managing director of Shell, J.P. Berkin. One who turned down George Brown's invitation to join was Arnold Weinstock, on the public grounds that membership would involve too many conflicts of interest, but also in line with his policy of refusing outside involvements.

In addition to the tensions which arose when the conventional capitalist instincts of men such as AEI's Charles Wheeler were confronted with what they saw as government meddling in industry, the man chosen to be managing director of the IRC was fundamentally opposed to the premises on which it had been established. He was Ronald Grierson, a director of the merchant banker S.G. Warburg. As such he had been involved in some of Weinstock and Michael Sobell's early transactions, and he would be associated with GEC for the rest of Weinstock's tenure. In his autobiography Grierson commented:

> From the start I never concealed my deep misgivings about the usefulness of the new organisation and my general scepticism about the concept of government-led restructuring of industry . . . My line was that if at the end of six months we had not done a single deal we should regard this as a quite satisfactory outcome . . . I spent my time giving personal assurances to industry that whatever powers Parliament ultimately gave us we would not use them to force mergers on unwilling parties.[12]

Despite Grierson's misgivings, the fact that he recruited a team of bright young people inevitably meant that the IRC did not sit around doing nothing. His deputy was Roger Brooke, subsequently head of the Candover venture capital business. Sir Christopher Hogg also worked at the IRC before eventually heading Courtaulds and Reuters and taking the chair at Allied Domecq in 1995. And another young Turk was Graham Hearne, who ended up running Enterprise Oil.

One deal whose logic was so compelling that even Ronald Grierson approved of it was the acquisition by English Electric in 1967 of the electronics company Elliott Automation. This was dwarfed, however, by the two mammoth mergers the IRC was involved in during its first two years. They achieved the combining of the big three electrical companies into one, with Arnold Weinstock sitting at the top of the pile, but the process resulted in Grierson's departure from the IRC – and his arrival on GEC's board.

The merger of the big three electrical companies had been waiting to happen for some time, and had indeed been an ambition of the US General Electric in the inter-war years. The logic was obvious: there was too much capacity in the power engineering end of the business, while in telecommunications and electronics the three British companies were small by comparison with international competitors such as Siemens of Germany and Phillips of Holland. Yet the undeniable logic was not strong enough, nor their financial crisis sufficiently acute, to overcome the traditional rivalries and jealousies between the three companies. It needed the impetus that was to be provided by Weinstock and Bond on the one hand, and by the IRC on the other.

Having stabilised GEC's financial position, Weinstock was keen to expand, largely on the grounds that a bigger company could spread its overheads thinner and thus enhance its competitiveness. Unlike his rivals, his vision was unblinkered by convention, by GEC's past, by what passed for 'industrial logic', or indeed by national boundaries. He looked once again at Thorn, the lighting, television and domestic equipment group which he and his father-in-law had been interested in before Radio & Allied was taken over by GEC. But the GEC board was determined that having acquired Weinstock, it was not going to do anything that would result in his control being diluted. Jules Thorn, even in his sixties, would not be interested in being a number two to anybody. Weinstock looked up to Thorn, whom he regarded as a father figure. For his part, Michael Sobell was intensely jealous of Thorn, whose business had enjoyed much greater success than Sobell's. Nevertheless,

Weinstock and Thorn continued to play games with each other, much to the discomfort of some of their staff. For a while following the creation in 1964 of the AEI–Thorn joint venture British Lighting Industries, Thorn and GEC discussed possible further developments in the lighting industry. Thorn's finance director and chief accountant would go to see Weinstock and Bond at Stanhope Gate for sometimes detailed discussions about costs and profit margins: 'These meetings were the occasion for some gentle gamesmanship. By the time the Thorn pair had made the journey of a mile or so back to the Thorn head office, Arnold Weinstock would have briefed Jules Thorn, by telephone, on what had been agreed – an account that usually bore little resemblance to their recollection and which resulted in a sharp rebuke for them from Jules Thorn.'[13]

But any deal between Thorn and GEC was merely a sideshow in comparison to the merger of the three big electrical companies. AEI and English Electric were both larger than GEC, and were quite different companies, but they were influenced by the same factors. In particular they had both suffered from the kind of leadership crisis which had also afflicted GEC after the death of Lord Hirst in 1943. English Electric had been dominated by Lord Nelson, who took over as managing director in 1930 at the age of forty-three, moving from the Metrovick factory in Sheffield (part of what would become AEI). EE was in a bad state, and faced a slump in the heavy electrical industry which was its main activity. Nelson was a tough, austere, hard-working man who lived for the company, building his home in the grounds of its Stafford head office. He was also a great leader, infuriated by laziness or carelessness but (unlike Weinstock) not stinting with praise when appropriate. He tried to treat his workers well, maintaining an apprentice programme and introducing a pension scheme in 1937. After handing over some of his power to his son George in 1956, he remained executive chairman until his death from a heart attack in the corridor outside his office in 1962.

George, who succeeded to the title of Lord Nelson, was nicknamed 'half Nelson' by those who felt he was a pale shadow of his father. In fact he was in many respects just as successful, from his early experience of management at the Napier aero-engine business, where he took over at the tender age of twenty-five. He moved to

EE's head office at Stafford in 1949 as deputy managing director, becoming managing director seven years later. But his father, as executive chairman, was involved in every detail of the business. George was the only other executive director, his fellow board members being selected mainly for their eminence, although some of them, brought in from the civil service and academia, were given quasi-executive responsibilities. The author C.P. Snow, for example (then a physics lecturer), had some responsibility for the recruitment and training of graduates and for other personnel policies. One side-effect of this unusual approach to board selection was that directors were given to showing off their intellectual abilities by scribbling memos to each other in Latin.

The elder Lord Nelson had believed in long-term policies, and was not looking for quick profits. He wanted to build up the company, and spent heavily on research – reportedly £6.25 million in 1951, employing six thousand people in this area alone – and as well as running substantial apprenticeship and training schemes, Nelson built housing to attract workers.

Nelson's long-term vision eventually paid off. EE won the contract for the electrification of British Railways Southern Region, providing the 'third rail' system for carrying the current, which has since been the target of many a commuter's anger because of its vulnerability to snow, leaves and other weather hazards. In pursuit of further railway work he had bought the Vulcan Foundry in Lancashire, whose business included the Robert Stephenson railway works which dated back to Stephenson's *Rocket*. But while Nelson could be described as the inheritor of the Industrial Revolution, he was also aware of the twentieth-century electronic revolution. He bought Marconi from the state-owned Cable & Wireless during the Second World War, beating EMI to the deal. Marconi, establishing a sad tradition which was to persist under GEC's ownership, could not successfully translate its technical skills into consumer products such as televisions. One of the reasons for EE's poor profits in the early 1960s was that Lord Nelson had pursued a commitment to computers.

In an uncanny parallel to Lord Hirst, Lord Chandos at AEI and ultimately Lord Weinstock, Lord Nelson's greatest weakness was his assumption that his son would succeed him. As a result he failed to develop other young managers at EE. But he left the company much stronger than when he joined, the strongest of the three big electrical groups at the start of the 1960s, although struggling under the weight of heavy debts. EE was less profitable than it should have been, but it owned many good businesses. Its main problem was that it was dominated by heavy electrical engineering.

At AEI, the third of the big three electrical companies, Lord Chandos was the equivalent of Lord Nelson at EE and Lord Hirst at GEC. Chandos had been Oliver Lyttelton, a Tory cabinet minister and close confidant of Churchill's during the war. He came from a classic aristocratic background, but he had also earned his spurs in business between the wars as a director of British Metal Corporation and various other companies. He was an educated, sophisticated man, urbane and witty, though also arrogant and snobbish, and has been described as 'a genial tyrant'.[14] When he took over as chairman of AEI in 1945 one of his first moves was to try to improve his surroundings. The company's head office in Kingsway was mundane, to say the least, and Chandos embarked on building a grand new headquarters to fit his and the company's stature. The premises at 33 Grosvenor Place were finally opened in 1958, but by then AEI's grandeur was already a thing of the past.

Chandos left AEI for three years when the Conservatives returned to power in 1951, becoming Colonial Secretary. When he returned in 1954, at the age of sixty-one, he embarked on a ruinous policy of expansion, financed by three big share and debenture issues. He was preoccupied with AEI's organisation, and how to shake it up, for most of his second spell as chairman. His good intentions came to little, however, and when he left AEI at the start of 1964 the company was in bad shape, suffering from a divided legacy which had never been properly addressed.

AEI had been created in 1928 from a merger between the UK subsidiary of US General Electric, the Rugby-based British Thomson-Houston (BT-H), and Metropolitan Vickers, based in Trafford Park. The latter was the successor of the British subsidiary of GE's great American rival Westinghouse. British Westinghouse was rescued, with the indirect aid of GE, in 1919, when the

British armaments company Vickers bought into it. Metrovick, as it became known, had great commercial success in turbines and other heavy electrical engineering, building an outstanding engineering reputation at home and abroad. It was renowned as a training ground, investing heavily in apprentices and research and introducing relatively enlightened labour relations. As a result, many former apprentices made it to the board, but one consequence was that the company was largely run by engineers, who paid little regard to finance. Their technical excellence and reputation also made them remarkably arrogant, which was unhelpful when it came to the merger with BT-H in 1928.

While GE had an indirect interest in Metrovick, BT-H was and always had been its direct subsidiary. It had been the most financially successful British electrical company until the 1920s, due to the profits from its participation in the lamp cartel, and its caution. That caution was thrown to the winds in the 1920s, however, resulting in over-expansion, especially in turbines and other heavy equipment. The subsequent reduction in profits stimulated GE's attempt to bring together all the leading electrical companies, which resulted only in BT-H and Metrovick merging to form Associated Electrical Industries (AEI). In fact there was little attempt to merge the two companies in management or organisational terms. There was a deliberate policy, supported by GE, to use AEI merely as a holding company, and to maintain the separate identities of the two parts. This went to ridiculous extremes, with BT-H and Metrovick bidding against each other for contracts. Each company developed its own jet engine in the run-up to the Second World War (BT-H's team was led by Frank Whittle, the inventor of the jet), and each, also separately, made warplanes – Metrovick in a venture with A.V. Roe to build Lancaster and Manchester bombers at Trafford Park, BT-H with John Brown and Westland. Both companies made great strides in research and development, outstripping all of their competitors. Their efforts did not bring commercial success, however, largely because they remained separate.

After the war AEI embarked on a programme of tremendous expansion under the optimistic direction of Lord Chandos, building an enormous new plant at Larne in Northern Ireland to build large turbines (a BT-H project), and another at Wythenshawe in south

Manchester (apparently a sop to Metrovick). But these plants were white elephants which came on stream just as demand for their products was declining. AEI also never made a success of the consumer end of the business, partly because it continued to operate as two separate companies, and partly because of over-engineering stemming from its high traditions, and the snobbishness with which consumer products were viewed.

AEI went through a series of upheavals from the middle of the 1950s. There were four major reorganisations of the group in nine years, but most of them amounted merely to shuffling the cards, not changing them or the attitudes which underlay the company's poor financial performance. All the effort did not succeed in creating a joint company, or an efficient one. Memoranda were constantly pushed to and fro around the grand headquarters at Grosvenor Place and backwards and forwards from the main operating centres in Rugby, Manchester and Woolwich. Diagnosis followed diagnosis. Much of the self-criticism analysed the problems correctly, but very little action was taken. As one executive said: 'It was a failure not of diagnosis but of will.'[15]

In the early 1960s there were economy drives which, *inter alia*, resulted in the number of liqueurs in the directors' dining room at Grosvenor Place being reduced to just two – brandy and kummel. More significant actions failed to turn the company's finances round, even though they were clearly movements in the right direction. The battles between BT-H and Metrovick were finally addressed, ending the factory-based management and replacing it with product-oriented groups. And a number of disposals or joint ventures were arranged, including a radio valve and tube venture with Thorn, the merger of Hotpoint domestic appliances with EMI's Morphy Richards, and the creation of a joint lighting business, also with Thorn.

Leadership was a key problem. Lord Chandos was by his own admission a great optimist, hence the over-expansion. But he was not a great manager, nor was he succeeded by one when Sir Charles Wheeler took over in 1963. Wheeler was a salesman, who had worked in the steel industry all his life, and had been a director of the great steel company Guest, Keen and Nettlefold, the remnants of which are now known as GKN. He was largely a figurehead chairman – good on bonhomie but weak on detail and action. His right-hand man was Sir Joseph Latham, an accountant from the coal industry. Latham was more action-oriented, but the action came too late. It included the ousting of Wheeler and the elevation of Latham to the position of chief executive at the beginning of 1967 (although, in typically half-hearted fashion, Wheeler was retained as a non-executive chairman).

Latham was clear about the extent of AEI's problems. On 3 January 1967 he addressed a meeting of senior managers in terms which would have appealed to Weinstock. He made it clear that the group's financial performance had been abysmal for the past ten years, and his prescription was fierce: 'What is required is a cold-blooded analysis of each operation and its prospects. We must ensure that the possibilities justify continued investment and effort; if not, we must sell or merge.'[16] During 1967 the workforce was reduced by 4,400. Decisions were taken to sell the grand London headquarters building and to close some factories, and a declaration of the type which would now be called a 'mission statement' was adopted by the management committee. Like Weinstock's, Latham's strategy was remarkably similar to 1990s management practices: to concentrate on a small number of profitable activities where AEI would have major market shares, achieving that by acquisition if necessary. But there was too much dissent among AEI's management, and time was running out, although the breadth of Latham's plans is illustrated by the fact that it was hoped to raise up to £40 million from the sale of assets.

GEC's fight for AEI was to be the bitterest takeover battle London had seen since the ICI–Courtaulds tussle in 1962. The build-up was tortuous; this was no straightforward takeover battle. It was complicated by the involvement of the IRC, the government's explicit support for the kind of move Weinstock was making, and its implicit backing of Weinstock in particular.

In March 1967 the IRC was asked by George Brown's Department of Economic Affairs to investigate the situation in the electrical industry, because of fears about an impending reduction in orders by the Central Electricity Generating Board. The DEA had already looked into the markets for telecommunications equipment, transformers and micro-circuits, so it was familiar with the industry and the people running each company, and was well aware that there was substantial overcapacity in the manufacture of electricity generating and transmission equipment, which might be solved by a merger of two or even three of the big players.

Discussions with the major companies revealed, however, that only GEC was willing to take steps in that direction. The others were too engrossed in their own problems, too proud, or too confident of their ability to prosper on their own. Weinstock, though, had no sentimental attachment to GEC's history; nor did he have any illusions about the future of the industry. There were clearly too many companies, so he regarded consolidation as inevitable. And if there were going to be takeovers, he wanted to come out on top. He, Bond and Lewis were agreed that, having stabilised the company and set it on the path to growth in their first few years at the helm, the takeover of one of GEC's two main rivals was the logical next step. But it was also clear to them that such a move would be very difficult to pull off.

Aware that GEC would face huge opposition to a hostile bid for AEI, Weinstock was keen to get the support of the IRC, and to see that support in hard financial terms. He therefore asked that the IRC back a deal with £15 million of loan stock, which it agreed in principle to do. On 18 April 1967 the merchant bank Hill Samuel (under Sir Kenneth Keith) was asked to draw up a proposal for the merger of AEI and GEC, including the £15 million loan finance from the IRC. The plan, codenamed 'Hedges & Butler', was delivered to Ronald Grierson in the middle of May. Keith asked a friend of his, Lord Renwick, who was a director of AEI, to arrange a dinner at the Institute of Directors on 12 June to sound out the AEI chief executive Sir Joseph Latham (the dinner was held while Charles Wheeler, AEI's non-executive chairman, was away in Australia, because it was thought that Latham would be more amenable). Also present were Frank Kearton and Grierson from the IRC.

Latham claimed subsequently that there was no explicit reference to a GEC takeover of AEI that evening, and he did not tell his board about the dinner, as he believed that it had produced no new developments to add to the discussions which had already taken place over the previous few years. He recalled: 'Throughout the talk there was no specific suggestion that there should be a merger

111

between GEC and AEI, although Keith obviously favoured this possibility. The IRC people said they had talked to Arnold Weinstock, who would be prepared to link with AEI under pressure, but showed no anxiety to do so, particularly as he did not wish to re-enter the heavy electrical industry.'[17]

Latham put forward his own ideas, for specific product-based mergers which would result in just two or three competitors in each major field, rather than a single, broad-based company covering the whole electrical spectrum. He went away correctly believing that the IRC had shelved the plan, in line with Grierson's philosophy that it should not force deals on unwilling participants. Discussions with the IRC continued over the summer about other, less substantial aspects of industry reorganisation, but the issue of merger was not brought up again.

Weinstock was not so easily put off, however, and decided to proceed with an attempt to take over AEI, a bid which would be a turning point both for his own career and for the structure of the country's electrical industry. He knew that acquiring a grand symbol of British industry such as AEI against its board's wishes would not be easy, but he calculated that AEI's poor financial performance, and its record of over-optimistic forecasts and failed promises, had put it within reach. He believed he could win a battle for AEI on his own, but could see that the backing of the IRC might just tilt the balance more easily (and more cheaply) in GEC's favour. He also believed that government support would be helpful following a successful merger, if the administration could be persuaded to help finance research and development through measures such as agreeing to purchase new products when they were created. In the middle of September Weinstock called Grierson while he was on holiday in America, and asked for IRC support for an impending bid. The IRC was also asked to release Lord Keith from his advisory role so that Hill Samuel could act for GEC, replacing its usual banker, Morgan Grenfell, which was out of the reckoning anyway because it worked for AEI. Hill Samuel had acted for Radio & Allied in its takeover by GEC.

Weinstock struck in classic fashion: the worst of AEI's problems had been addressed, but the benefits had not yet begun to emerge. AEI's half-year figures were published on 14 September 1967, and showed a fall in profit from £6.9 million to £3.7 million, but they were accompanied by a surprisingly optimistic statement: 'Although trading conditions are unlikely to improve in the remaining months of the year the Board expect profit to be substantially higher in the second half of the year than in the first half, and in the absence of unforeseen setbacks, profit for the total year should not be less than in 1966.' This optimism was based on higher orders, an expected improvement over the dismal second half of the previous year, and early results from Latham's recovery plan.

But to Weinstock and his colleagues, AEI's confidence looked unfounded. On Monday 25 September, when Grierson returned from America, Weinstock and Lord Aldington went to seek IRC support. The IRC board met (minus Sir Charles Wheeler and Sir Joseph Lockwood of EMI) on the following day and gave its agreement. In typically thorough fashion, Weinstock and his chairman had already laid the groundwork in government circles. They had been to see the Department of Economic Affairs, the Board of Trade and the Ministry of Technology, as well as the CEGB, and had informed EE's Lord Nelson of GEC's plan.

Hill Samuel's Lord Keith called Wheeler immediately and made an appointment for the Friday, without revealing his hand. But on the following day, Wednesday 27 September, AEI's share price jumped, as news of the imminent bid began to leak out, so early on Thursday morning Keith asked for an urgent meeting with AEI, in the company of Lord Aldington. At noon the two men met Wheeler and Latham in their grand Grosvenor Place offices, and handed them a letter and a press release announcing GEC's intention to bid. Wheeler and Latham were surprised by GEC's claim that the bid had the full support of the IRC, since they believed that the IRC had not held any discussions with them about such a proposal. Nevertheless the offer was publicly announced later that day, including the claim that GEC had the support of the IRC. It valued AEI at £120 million, a fifth higher than the value reflected in its share price the previous day.

It was a foregone conclusion that the AEI board, meeting that afternoon, should reject GEC's offer, setting off a battle which resonated throughout industry and shook the City and business establishment. It brought out sentiments normally kept beneath the surface, including an element of anti-Semitism as well as class-based assumptions about the natural right of the great and the good at AEI to resist an assault from an immigrant tailor's son leading a raggle-taggle army of 'traders' who couldn't possibly understand the higher levels of engineering at which their company operated. Weinstock says he did not personally experience any insults, only hearing reports of derogatory references to his race around City luncheon tables. The feelings of superiority about GEC went back many years. In 1921 Morgan Grenfell had counselled GE against contemplating a merger between GEC and BT-H, making it clear that this would have been an upstairs-downstairs marriage: 'Our unanimous opinion is that the standing of GEC is not such as would make it desirable for the BT-H to make an amalgamation or any form of close alliance with GEC . . . in our opinion GEC stands in all respects on so much lower a plane than BT-H.'[18]

That view had persisted among the establishment, for whom GEC remained little more than a grubby wholesaler, quite lacking the grandeur of AEI or English Electric. Weinstock's arrival and the transformation of GEC's finances had done little to improve its downmarket image. Nor had GEC attempted to change the situation. Neither Weinstock nor Aldington had made much effort to cultivate the City, and the Telephone Rentals bid had done nothing to endear them to it. They got on with their business of sorting out the company, and were not too concerned about what the City thought about it. This attitude was to bring Weinstock many enemies and detractors in financial circles throughout his career.

Once the battle for AEI was joined, however, Weinstock's advisers were diligent in promoting him, and in general GEC had a better press than might have been expected. Weinstock had until then been a somewhat shadowy figure, but he represented the new breed of industrialists which was generally welcomed by the media as a means of shaking up the sleepy establishment. When the bid was first announced, most papers were reasonably impressed, although they believed there was scope for GEC to increase its offer. The 'Lex' column in the *Financial Times* observed that there were many alternative destinations for AEI's assets, as well as arguments for GEC increasing the price. 'There is no doubt about the scope to resist; the question is whether it can be realised quickly enough,' the column concluded. *The Times*, an enthusiastic supporter of Weinstock, had to admit that on financial grounds the struggle was evenly balanced: 'At first glance the terms look reasonable but not overwhelmingly attractive.' As the battle wore on, the paper attempted to counter what it described as 'a subtle campaign of denigration of Arnold Weinstock' which had focused on his abrasive manner and his supposedly short-term approach to managing GEC – the first of many occasions over the years when critics would charge him with underspending on research and avoiding difficult industrial sectors in favour of easy profits.

As the arguments raged, the two sides seemed evenly matched. Latham and his colleagues acted with the kind of decisiveness and urgency which would have made GEC's bid impossible had they been applied five years earlier. In a few weeks they achieved a rash of deals, and set up several others. AEI's defence was generally praised when it was published on 20 October. The news that Lord Beeching – an ICI director but more famous for slashing Britain's railway network – was to be the new chairman seized the imagination of many journalists, and briefly appeared to be a trump card. AEI backed up this coup with the revelation that it was talking to STC, the British associate of the US giant ITT, about a merger of telecoms interests, to English Electric about combining the companies' turbine and generator businesses, and to Parsons about transformers. It also announced the sale of its 35 per cent interest in British Lighting Industries to its partner Thorn, for the huge sum of £12 million. Symbolically, the palatial headquarters building on Grosvenor Place, opposite Buckingham Palace Gardens, was being sold, among other properties. Finally, AEI attempted to forestall criticism of its aged, inbred management by stressing the appointment of outsiders and younger men. The *Financial Times* described it as 'a powerful reply'.

The role of the IRC was as critical to GEC's victory as it was controversial. Weinstock and his chairman Lord Aldington were very skilful in the way they managed to engineer IRC support, to the extent that the bid was thought of in many quarters as having been originated by the IRC. Its backing must have been responsible for persuading many shareholders to accept GEC's offer. AEI was well aware from the start that this might be the case, and lobbied strenuously to limit the IRC's support. At first, Wheeler and Latham had some success. They managed to have the original GEC press statement altered to say that the IRC supported 'a merger', rather than 'the proposed merger'.

But that was about as far as they got in detaching the IRC from GEC's side, despite Ronald Grierson's serious misgivings, which eventually led to his resignation. Grierson was keen to ensure the IRC's neutrality if an alternative merger proposal were to arise. He was happy for the IRC to back a merger, but not for it to take sides between rival bidders. He phoned Wheeler on 2 October to make this clear, inviting AEI to make alternative proposals. Frank Kearton, however, had no such qualms. He was convinced that Weinstock was the right man to take on the task of rationalising the electrical industry, and wanted him to get on with it.

On the morning of Saturday 21 October, the day after the publication of the AEI defence document, Latham and his finance director John Barber met Kearton and Grierson to discuss the rationalisation measures they had proposed and to ask for the IRC's support. Latham left feeling that they had made progress, but Kearton was completely committed to the GEC deal. On the Monday evening, following an IRC board meeting, he wrote to Latham puncturing his optimism. Frantic efforts to calm the situation continued over the next few days, but it was too late. Some IRC board members felt that they had been snubbed because AEI had not consulted them before publishing its defence. This omission was rectified on the Tuesday evening, but it was an unfruitful meeting. Latham described the atmosphere as 'unyielding and unsympathetic to the point of hostility', and the IRC agreed to make only two minor amendments to its original letter, which was duly published, with AEI's response, at the end of the week.

The IRC letter made it clear that it was backing GEC, almost willy-nilly:

> In giving this support [to the GEC offer] our Board are
> fully aware that no combination of two businesses is ever
> theoretically perfect in all respects, but have proceeded on
> the strong practical conviction that the huge tasks of reor-

ganisation facing the industry could be more powerfully undertaken by these two companies jointly than by either of them alone ... The GEC board have already given the IRC adequate assurances that they intend, if their bid is successful, to carry out immediate rationalisation steps which would go at least as far as and possibly further than those outlined in your circular.

Latham continued the war of words with Kearton, but to no avail. Kearton's support for GEC went much further than was apparent at the time. He personally visited major AEI shareholders and told them it was their duty to support the GEC bid, as it was in the national interest. The only crumb of comfort for Latham was the resignation from the IRC on 26 October of Grierson and the AEI chairman Charles Wheeler – a final acceptance that his view of the IRC's role could not be squared with its interventionist remit and Kearton's enthusiasm for action.

The battle ebbed and flowed. In the process, GEC's reputation for miserliness proved wide of the mark. The initial offer had been worth 52s.1d (260p) per share. But on 29 October, just a few days before the original closing date, GEC doubled the cash element and included the option of convertible loan stock, which could be exchanged for GEC shares at a later date, instead of cash. When AEI rejected this offer on 3 November, GEC came back on the same day with a further sweetener. Once again the cash element (and the loan stock alternative) was increased, and the closing date was extended to 8 November.

In the final frantic days both sides courted the big institutions who would decide the outcome, dashing around the country to see investment managers in Scotland and the regions of England as well as in the more familiar City haunts. Curiously the mighty Prudential, the largest shareholder in both companies, refused to see the GEC top brass, even though its directors knew Lord Aldington well from his chairmanship of the rival insurance firm Sun Alliance. Under pressure the Pru allowed its investment manager to see a more junior GEC executive. (In the event the Pru chose to stand by the establishment AEI, as did Pearl Assurance, another big shareholder. This prompted a typically cheeky response from

Weinstock, who sent a man in a cloth cap to the next Prudential annual meeting to ask the board why they had backed the loser.)

The offer was now worth 72s.6d (362p), some of the increase being due to a rise in GEC's share price since the battle began. Among the press, only the *Daily Telegraph* stuck by AEI. The rest concluded on balance that GEC's twice-increased offer was enough to overcome AEI's vigorous defence. Even so, the outcome was in doubt until the last moment. Believing he had lost, Weinstock went to *The Marriage of Figaro* at Covent Garden with his wife, leaving his colleagues to chew their fingernails in the office.

Kenneth Bond remembered: 'We didn't think we had got it. Bob Clarke of Hill Samuel had previously said they were still opening acceptances but were only just over 30 per cent. So it didn't look as though we were going to get it. But later on he rang and said: "You've got it." '[19]

AEI still thought they had escaped by a whisker, but frantic buying in the closing hours had edged the decision in GEC's favour. Lord Keith claims that he won the battle for GEC, taking the initiative himself to buy AEI shares on the open market at the last minute on Wednesday evening. It seemed that the insurance company establishment had been defeated by the new mass-market investment vehicles, unit and investment trusts and pension funds, so enabling the meritocratic Weinstock to overwhelm the AEI establishment.

As Weinstock took his seat at Covent Garden for the overture, Hill Samuel announced that it had totted up shareholders' acceptances of the GEC offer amounting to 45 per cent of AEI's shares. By the time of the first interval, Weinstock was told victory was his. He must have enjoyed the rest of the performance rather more than the first act, because, unknown to the outside world to this day, in a drawer in his office at Stanhope Gate was a letter of resignation. As the signs earlier that day had been that AEI might just escape, Weinstock decided that the only honourable course of action would be to offer to resign. 'If we had lost and it was seen as a failure, it was my responsibility. The other side would have crowed like hell,' he explained. He did not expect that the board would have accepted his resignation, but he believed he had to give them the option.

This was the act of a man with a highly developed moral sense, as well as a belief in what he was doing. The fact that he did not expect his resignation to be accepted also illustrates his tremendous self-confidence, and his trust in the faith his board colleagues had in him. This enabled him to take with equanimity a risk which most managers would have found daunting. Had the AEI bid failed and Weinstock's resignation been accepted, he would probably have spent the rest of his working years in small, private ventures, out of the public gaze. That would have suited him in many ways, but it would have deprived British industry of a major force, possibly delaying much essential rationalisation for years.

Initially AEI claimed it had escaped, and even when it became apparent that the morning's count had taken GEC past the crucial 50 per cent mark, Latham still asserted that it was a draw when he called Aldington to suggest a meeting. Over lunch at Hill Samuels' offices Latham and Wheeler attempted to negotiate, but GEC were having none of it. At one point AEI adviser John Baring suggested that GEC could avoid a protracted end-game if AEI finally recommended the bid, which he would do if GEC added another half-crown to the share price. Weinstock promptly pulled half a crown from his pocket and said: 'There you are then, recommend it.'

But AEI were in no position to dictate terms, and eventually they capitulated, allowing GEC to announce victory at 6.30 on the evening of 9 November 1967. A joint statement from the two companies announced that Wheeler, Latham and the finance director John Barber would join the GEC board, and the AEI directors urged shareholders to accept the offer. The only concession they were able to wring from Weinstock was that AEI's redundancy terms would apply. This was important, as they were more generous than GEC's traditionally stingy terms, and in the event there were tens of thousands of job losses, despite Weinstock's optimistic prediction: 'We hope to increase productivity without a lot of people losing their jobs. I hope the rationalisation would not involve much redundancy.'[20]

This optimism was ill-founded, and out of line with Weinstock's habitually honest appraisal of such situations. But there was more than job losses on the horizon. Within a year Weinstock would not only be sitting at the head of a GEC–AEI combination, but the third of the great electrical giants, English Electric, would also be under the command of this man who only ten years previously had brought his father-in-law's little television and radio assembly company to the stock market.

This final stage (for the time being) in the consolidation of the electrical industry would also be heavily influenced by the government's industrial strategy and by the activities of the IRC. It would be less acrimonious than the battle for AEI, although it would leave Weinstock with a lifelong enemy in the form of Sir John Clark, the boss of the telecoms company Plessey.

Plessey's background was remarkably similar to that of Radio & Allied. It was essentially a family business which had gone public and grown swiftly, but was still run by the family. It had been founded as a small manufacturer in Holloway, just a few miles across north London from Weinstock's early homes in Stoke Newington, and was built up by Sir Allen Clark as a maker of components for the radio industry and later run by his two sons, John and Michael. From radios Clark moved into television parts, then telephone equipment and other electrical and electronic parts. Clark was successful but extremely autocratic and idiosyncratic. He is said to have handled redundancies by walking into offices and declaring that everyone on his right- (or left-) hand side was fired.

The company was transformed by two major acquisitions in 1962, the last year of Clark's life, as his ambitious sons attempted to accelerate its growth and equal their father's success. They bought two telephone equipment manufacturers – Ericsson and Automatic Telephone & Electric – which brought Plessey the orders for about two-fifths of the Post Office's telephone exchange equipment, under the system of preferred suppliers which carved up the market at that time. Other acquisitions added radar and automation interests, but even so, Plessey was still by far the smallest of the big electrical companies. Its sales of £145 million compared with more than £400 million for English Electric, almost £200 million for GEC and £265 million for AEI before the takeover.

But Plessey was also more profitable and more ambitious than its rivals. On 20 August 1968 EE chairman Lord Nelson was trying to catch up with events after a fortnight's holiday in Ireland. Out of the blue he was phoned by Field Marshal Harding, Plessey's chairman and previously Chief of the General Staff, who arranged to come and see him the next day with John Clark. When they arrived they presented Nelson with what they described as 'an approach with a view to merger', but which looked to him remarkably like a takeover bid. He was not enthusiastic, and in a statement rejecting the approach he argued that there was little logic in the two companies combining.

The similarities with Arnold Weinstock's assault on AEI were not lost on the participants. Indeed, Henry Grunfeld, the joint founder and boss of Plessey's aggressive merchant bank adviser S.G. Warburg, likened Clark's record in boosting Plessey's profits to that of Weinstock at GEC.[21] Plessey's formal statement supporting its bid emphasised the need for consolidation in the electrical industry, echoing the IRC stance during the GEC–AEI battle, and claimed that more mergers were necessary following GEC's swallowing of AEI.

There was general agreement on that point, but not on the merits of a merger between Plessey and EE. The government, through Tony Benn's Ministry of Technology ('Mintech') and the IRC, was still working hard to create more powerful, internationally-oriented British companies. Professor Blackett, president of the Royal Society and deputy chairman of Mintech's advisory council on technology, had said in a speech in February that year: 'I still do not understand why industry has not, on its own initiative, brought about a drastic concentration of suitable parts of industry.' Blaming Britain's poor productivity and poor standing in high-value international trade on a lack of qualified engineers and managers, Blackett said: 'In a real sense it is the shortage of both skilled managers and technologists which the deficiencies of our educational system and the structure of our industry have imposed on us, which make the greater concentration of industry so vital and urgent.'[22]

Weinstock had his own line into Mintech, because Tony Benn's deputy there was Harold Lever, the self-made millionaire who was a close friend of Weinstock and, usefully, a trusted adviser to Prime Minister Harold Wilson on financial matters. Weinstock had known Lever for years, because Lever's brother had been with him at the

LSE in Cambridge. Mintech had been instrumental earlier that year in the creation of the computer company ICL, which had brought Plessey and EE into contact. Plessey had broached the possibility of acquiring one of its constituent parts, ICT, whose main shareholders were Vickers and Ferranti but which had been heavily supported with government money over the previous few years. Tony Benn went to see Harding to dissuade him so late one night that the field marshal was in his pyjamas. Under pressure from Mintech, Plessey ended up putting £18 million into a combination of ICT and English Electric's computer business to create ICL as a national champion, of which Plessey and EE each owned 18 per cent.

Unfortunately for Plessey's argument about the industrial logic of a merger, this had taken its most obvious benefit out of the equation. Elsewhere there was little overlap between the two companies' businesses, and where it did exist it was in growth sectors such as electronics rather than telecoms equipment or heavy electrical engineering, which was where the main overcapacity lay. It was Plessey rather than EE which needed the merger, to give it a leg-up in gaining international business opportunities. The Clark family's outsider status and fierce reputation was probably another factor in persuading Lord Nelson and his board not to contemplate a merger, and their preferred course of action showed how far Weinstock had risen in a very short time, from being in the same *enfant terrible* position as the Clarks to the verge of the establishment itself.

Nelson knew GEC and its new acquisition, AEI, very well, because he had worked in the industry all his adult life. He believed that if there was to be further rationalisation it should be with GEC, not Plessey. Indeed, he had talked to GEC before Weinstock's arrival, in 1961, about a possible merger. So when Weinstock returned from holiday on 26 August 1968 Nelson invited him for a private chat. Weinstock said he was keen to bring EE into the GEC–AEI fold, seeing further potential to build businesses of greater scale which could therefore be more powerful in their markets and more efficient in their operations. While Nelson was noncommittal at this stage, he was warming to the idea.

His feelings must have influenced the EE board when it met on Wednesday 4 September, as must the rather downbeat assessment of the company's prospects by Lazards, its bankers. Lazards' chairman was Lord Poole, a friend of Aldington's who was well aware of Weinstock's record at GEC and the company's hunger to continue its charge through the industry. The bank was represented on the EE board by Lord Kindersley, who on this occasion did not give the directors the kind of tough backing they might have expected from their financial adviser. He said that fighting the Plessey attack was one option, but did not seem to share the general view around the City that EE could beat off the unwelcome approach more successfully than AEI had against GEC. He suggested two alternatives: a merger with GEC, or the creation of a second huge grouping, taking in cable company BICC, Thorn, the newly-merged Reyrolle-Parsons in electrical plant, and Plessey. Such a consortium might have made sense on paper, but it was too complex a deal to be put together in the period of a public offer for the company's shares, as Kindersley knew. And, crucially, it lacked the support of the IRC. Initially agnostic about Plessey's approach, the IRC had gradually come round to the idea of a GEC–EE merger, under lobbying from GEC, which was also studiously courting other government departments. EE's directors, lacking confidence in their ability to fight off Plessey, but also mindful that GEC might launch a counter-bid, decided that they must sue for peace, and authorised Lord Nelson to begin talks with Aldington and Weinstock.

One key issue had quietly been settled over the phone before the top men from both sides sat down for their crucial discussions on Friday 6 September. Kenneth Bond had travelled to Rye for a game of golf with Aldington, during which he suggested that the issue of the chairmanship of the new joint company was the only potential stumbling block to a merger. Aldington called Weinstock that afternoon and said that he would be prepared to step down and allow Lord Nelson to take the chair. He had known Nelson since his days at the Ministry of Supply in the early 1950s, and had considerable respect for him, so he had no problem about his taking the top position in the new enterprise. His lack of respect for Sir Charles Wheeler and Sir Joseph Latham, on the other hand, would have prevented his taking the same self-sacrificing stand during the AEI battle.

Aldington and Weinstock met Nelson and his managing director

Sandy Riddell on the morning of 6 September. They issued a joint statement that afternoon saying they were in favour of a complete merger of the two companies, with Lord Nelson as chairman and Weinstock as managing director. Plessey was effectively forced to withdraw as a result of this agreement, although its offer remained on the table in case talks between the two giants broke down.

But there was still plenty to do. Such a merger raised all manner of questions for the government, sufficient to distract the Cabinet even from talks about Rhodesian independence, the continuing economic crisis, the Russian invasion of Czechoslovakia and the latest American involvement in Vietnam. GEC's well-established Whitehall connections were exploited to the full. Weinstock and his board colleagues, as well as Lord Nelson, put their arguments for the deal forcibly. They saw Tony Benn at the Ministry of Technology and Anthony Crosland at the Board of Trade to talk about monopoly implications. Jack Scamp, fresh from his stint at the Department of Economic Affairs, went to see Employment Secretary Barbara Castle to promise sensitivity about redundancies and consultation with trade unions. Castle was not impressed, and provided the stiffest opposition to the deal at the Cabinet steering committee on economic policy which discussed the matter on 12 September. Richard Crossman recorded her fears that simply acceding to the takeover made a nonsense of the government's policy on monopolies: 'But it was really no good. The PM, Roy Jenkins, Tony Crosland and Wedgy Benn were all determined to let this go through without even the pretence of a fight.'[23]

On the morning of Friday 13 September Crosland announced that there would be no referral to the Monopolies Commission, and the IRC issued a statement enthusiastically supporting the merger. No terms had yet been agreed, but the biggest merger transaction in British history had effectively been agreed, creating a company whose sales ranked fourth in the world, just ahead of its major European competitors, Phillips and Siemens.

When the terms of the deal were announced, it was apparent that EE's desire to escape Plessey, together with GEC's higher profitability, had led Lord Nelson to give away his company very cheaply. EE shareholders ended up owning only a third of the new group, despite the fact that their company's sales had been almost as much as the GEC–AEI combination, and that EE employed more capital and virtually as many people. It was one of many examples throughout his career of Weinstock's brilliant deal-making abilities.

The takeover completed an astonishing financial coup for Weinstock. In two years he had spent £16 million in cash and issued new shares which pushed up GEC's share capital from £57 million to £136 million. But that increase of 140 per cent quintupled the company's sales and added almost £400 million to capital employed. How much profit the deals brought was a subject of fierce debate which ricocheted around the City for some time, and eventually helped force the accounting profession to develop standards for financial reporting which attempted to define acceptable practice more closely.

By 1970 GEC was reporting profits of £58 million, compared to £18 million in 1967. But after winning the AEI battle, GEC declared that AEI had made a loss of £4.5 million, rather than the £10 million profit it had forecast as part of its defence. Most of the difference was due to GEC's less optimistic view of stock and contract values, and the common practice of an acquirer giving the dimmest possible impression of its target's state of affairs so as to provide a low base from which to improve. But it was the last straw for former AEI directors, who issued a statement defending their accounting practices and complaining that they had not been given a proper chance to defend their forecast.

It was a sour end to a bitter battle, in sharp contrast to the friendly nature of the EE deal, which actually saw the company name survive briefly in the title of the new group – The General Electric and English Electric Companies. It was obvious that the chosen title was too unwieldy to last long, and the 'English Electric' was dropped after eighteen months, but it had been a sop to EE sensibilities, and had helped smooth the merger.

At the age of only forty-four, Weinstock found himself at the head of 228,000 workers, responsible for annual sales approaching £1 billion even at 1960s prices, and custodian of more than £400 million of shareholder's money. It was an astonishing elevation from ten years previously, when he had first become a public company director, running a group with sales of just £5 million. The rise in his personal fortune had matched that elevation. Weinstock family interests in GEC now amounted to twenty-three million shares, some 6 per cent of the total.

But this was not just a personal success story. Weinstock had become the champion of interventionist government policy and a figurehead for the new breed of 'professional' managers who were supposedly about to transform the performance of British business. Never mind that he hadn't undergone a moment's training in business, finance or any aspect of management, nor that he ran his vast empire in much the same way that he had run the tiny Radio & Allied; Weinstock had come to personify the kind of approach which was widely seen as modern and American, and which would oust the cosy Establishment deals and amateurism that had shackled British industry for decades. The US magazine *Business Week* put its editorial finger on the wider social implications at the start of the Plessey–English Electric battle. After reporting that Weinstock had been vilified on television by one of his workers for pursing efficiency too ruthlessly, the magazine commented: 'Weinstock's methods and reputation for ruthlessness dramatise the conflict in a society slow to change but desperately needing a stronger industrial base.'

Weinstock had become a more public personality, profiled in the press in sympathetic terms. He was projected as a hard man, but fair and with the best interests of his company at heart. In the wake of the AEI victory the *Observer* had described him as 'the archetype of the American-style business executive; one of the first British exemplars of the managerial revolution', and went on to paint what was soon to be a familiar picture of him as a rich boss who used the company's money sparingly. 'Weinstock's personal integrity is absolute. He believes profoundly in the stewardship of time and money. This is why he is nearly always in his office. A manager's first duty is to his company. Weinstock would not dream of junketing with the Institute of Directors like [ICI chairman] Sir Paul Chambers.'[24]

Weinstock gave his first ever television interview to the BBC's *Money Programme* in May 1968. It opened with the interviewer, Graham Turner, pointing out that in all his visits to GEC's Stanhope

Gate headquarters he had never once been offered a cup of tea or coffee. Weinstock apologised, saying it had been selfish of him, but added that he aimed to provide employees with proper rewards 'in a rational way', and said that that meant not doing business on the grouse moors, where many directors of leading British companies habitually spent their summer weekends. Several times he repeated his dedication to logic and rationality, and explained his reputation for ruthlessness in those terms.

He also aired his liberal social views, saying he felt an obligation to carry on doing his best for the sake of the nation: 'One has obligations which are not escapable. I am involved in something which I think important. The whole question of the maintenance of full employment, the provision of social services, education, the roads, pensions, welfare of all sorts, requires, indisputably, I think anyway, prosperous industry, efficient industry. We have not been able to achieve all those things without continual economic crises, and the reason for this is that industry is not efficient as compared with industries in other countries.'[25]

In a *Times* interview in December 1968 he expounded theories about motivation and pay, arguing that many people (presumably including himself) worked because their job fulfilled them, and that a key problem with the British system was that it prevented people from building up capital: 'There are people who are committed to doing a thorough job, not only for reward but for its own sake. Such people will work as effectively whether they are standing at a lathe or running a company. It is not merely job satisfaction but rather the fulfilment they gain from doing their best at a job of work.'[26]

This was the kind of techno-social approach which appealed to the likes of Minister of Technology Tony Benn, who was so enamoured of Weinstock that he suggested him for a knighthood in 1968, two years before it was finally conferred.[27] His admiration did not last long, but in January 1969 he wrote, after dinner at the Weinstocks' Mayfair flat: 'Arnold is a very complex character . . . I find him agreeable, easy to work with, but incredibly primitive politically . . . But certainly I have got good relations with him and I want to build on them.'[28]

Richard Crossman was less impressed by Weinstock. He recorded in rather bemused fashion how he had been invited to lunch at Stanhope Gate on Budget day in 1970:

> It was a very gay lunch. I was given plenty to drink and excellent food while this adventurer Weinstock stimulated me to give a lecture about pensions and teach him life's realities. I am curious to know what Ronnie Grierson thought of it all. He had brought along this donnish member of Cabinet, who was performing like an intellectual sea-lion, balancing balls on his nose in the presence of Weinstock, who was performing too. I suppose I ought to have been slightly ashamed.[29]

By this time the Labour government had, in Harold Wilson's famous phrase, been 'blown off course'. In the summer of 1966 it had created huge tension within the labour and trade union movement by introducing a prices and incomes policy in response to growing inflation. In a government shake-up the following summer Wilson had personally taken control of the DEA, bringing in a young Peter Shore, his former parliamentary secretary, as Secretary for Economic Affairs. But just a couple of weeks after Weinstock's victory over AEI, in November 1967, the Cabinet had finally bowed to the inevitable and accepted the need to devalue the pound. The rate against the dollar was cut from $2.80 to $2.40 and a formal application was made to the International Monetary Fund for standby credits of $1.4 billion. The package of austerity measures included a hike of the bank rate to 8 per cent, tighter hire-purchase rules, government spending cuts and a promise to push corporation tax up to 42.5 per cent in the coming Budget. But there was little improvement in the economic situation during 1968, at the end of which Chancellor Roy Jenkins was still looking for cuts in public spending of up to £500 million in a bid to reduce the government's budget deficit.

The Wilson government had come up trumps for Weinstock, however, enabling him to do two deals which would have seemed impossible at the start of the 1960s. But just as Tony Benn's drift leftwards led him to lose patience with industrialists such as Weinstock, so the GEC managing director lost patience with the drift of the Labour Party, under Benn's influence, towards much more direct involvement in industrial organisation. After the spate of takeovers there was to come a period of turmoil and unrest, both at GEC and in the economy at large, which would see Weinstock take an even higher profile, but this time not in sympathy with Labour's aims.

# CHAPTER FIVE

## *Turmoil*

THE FIRST BOMBSHELL fell on Friday 2 February 1968, but many more were to drop in the coming months and years as Weinstock set about the job of making his empire more efficient, as the government had asked him to do when it backed the takeover of AEI. On that Friday, almost three months after AEI had accepted defeat, 5,500 workers at the company's telecoms factory in Woolwich, South London, were told that they were out of a job. The entire factory was to be closed down and production moved to other plants, thus removing overcapacity which had led AEI to make losses in telecoms equipment.

Woolwich was not the only closure announced that day as Weinstock and Bond set in train the reorganisation which they had sketched out on a few sheets of paper even as the bid battle was at its height. Redundancy notices were also handed out to workers at another South London electronics factory, in Sydenham, and at AEI's research laboratory in Blackheath. The Harlow research site was also to be closed and staff at the old Metrovick headquarters in Trafford Park were told that radar and other defence electronics work was to be transferred to Leicester.

The Woolwich closure was by far the most significant of these announcements. It provoked fury among trade unionists and the local population, and became a national *cause célèbre* as an example of the brutality of big business in general and Arnold Weinstock in particular. Trade unionists claimed it was an affront to the government's industrial and employment policies. It prompted questions in Parliament and leaders in national newspapers. *The Times*, in its opening leader on the main editorial page, emphasising the importance of the affair, commented that the closures were the natural consequence of the merger, but that did not make matters any easier for those affected. It concluded, however, that this was the likely face of industry for some time, and that the government had prepared for it with the Redundancy Payments Act, the stipulation of minimum periods of notice and investment in training schemes. 'This sort of thing has to be done and everybody knows it has to be done. There are more redundancies to come as a result of this particular merger. There will be more redundancies from other mergers; indeed one cannot get sufficient higher productivity without them.'[1]

The Woolwich site had been part of the Siemens Bros electrical business since the nineteenth century, separated from the German company by the First World War and acquired by AEI in 1955, after which it became one of the group's three main manufacturing centres, along with Trafford Park and Rugby. Following one of AEI's many reorganisations in the 1950s the group's activities in telecoms, cables and electronics were concentrated there. The plant was easily the largest employer in the Woolwich area, which already had substantial unemployment and was hoping for more jobs, not fewer, as tenants began to move into a vast new housing estate built on the site of the former arsenal. Whole families, even whole communities, worked at the plant, and had done so for generations.

Trade unionists, led by the up-and-coming Clive Jenkins of the white-collar union ASTMS (the Association of Scientific, Technical and Managerial Staffs), picketed GEC's Stanhope Gate headquarters. Mass meetings were called and a rally was staged in the centre of Woolwich, building local support and attracting national attention to put pressure on GEC. Placards asked such questions as 'Who governs? Wilson or Weinstock?' Apart from the fact of the closure, the unions were particularly angry that the consultation which had been promised to the government during the AEI bid battle had not taken place. Union leaders learned of the affair only when their members were notified of their redundancies, so the only consultation which could take place was on how to manage the closure. Weinstock had kept his commitment to concentrate production in development areas such as Scotland and the northeast of England, and to consult with government departments, but only to the extent of telling them that Woolwich was to close a few days ahead of the event. But Jack Scamp kept his promise to Employment Secretary Barbara Castle to handle the redundancies as sensitively as possible. A labour exchange (as job centres were then called) was set up inside the factory, with facilities for local firms to come in and interview staff on the premises. The closure was phased over two years, with no specific deadline given initially and a commitment to find employees jobs in the group's other factories where possible.

That was little consolation for the thousands of people who were thrown out of work, but the unions knew there was no chance of overturning the decision, which was an inevitable consequence of AEI's decline. Their demonstrations and pickets were essentially tactics to get the best possible terms for their members, and to deal with local emotions, rather than a serious attempt to stop the closure. As one prominent AEI trade unionist of the time said later: 'Everybody knew AEI was going broke. If somebody didn't rescue you the whole thing was going to collapse.'[2] There could be little argument with the figures, which stood as testimony to AEI's rash expansion and poor management. They showed that GEC's telecoms business employed 20 per cent more people in only 80 per cent of the factory space, and produced 75 per cent more output.

The union leaders were impressed by Weinstock when they finally met him. Despite his public image as a ruthless financier, they were surprised to find somebody who would listen, who understood their concerns, and who was willing and able to explain why he had to do what he had done. Even though he had moved far from his background – unique among leading industrialists at the time – as the son of an artisan immigrant, it helped him to relate to the arguments of his opponents, even if he could not accede to their demands. The union leaders found Weinstock quite unlike the City figures who populated many boardrooms, who would stand on their dignity and either refuse to talk to trade unionists or who were clearly not in command of the situation. When one union official argued that Woolwich was making a profit, so it shouldn't be closed down, Weinstock answered: 'My dear chap, I could make a better return by putting the money in the post office.' And most of the union negotiators knew that that was indeed the case.

In the end the unions believed they got not only the best deal possible, but the best, most comprehensive redundancy programme which had ever been negotiated at that time. The redundancy payments were probably higher than Weinstock would have liked because, thanks to Latham's efforts, they were based on AEI's terms, which were more generous than GEC's. But the agreement which was hammered out with Jack Scamp also covered other issues which were important to the workers, such as subsequent notice periods and arrangements for staff who were kept on until the final closure of the site. All that did not prevent Weinstock from being pilloried by the unions as an unfeeling butcher, carving up the carcass of the captured AEI; but it did establish a curious respect for him among leading trade unionists, which was to help GEC struggle through the difficult 1970s.

The Woolwich battle also brought out the litigant in Weinstock. Sensitive to any slight on himself or his company, he was always ready to reach for his lawyers. The first defendant was Peggy Middleton. She represented Greenwich, the ward which included the Woolwich factory, on both the local authority and the Greater London Council, and campaigned hard against the closure. Some of her language, as reported in the *South East London Mercury* and in speeches in Woolwich market square, was a little too vicious for Weinstock, who promptly sued for libel and slander. When the case came to court the newspaper apologised, claiming that it had misquoted Mrs Middleton, and the matter was laid to rest. Weinstock had been hurt by the suggestion that he was only interested in money and cared nothing for people or for the social duties of large employers.

Similar actions followed over the years, against publications including *Private Eye*, the *Guardian* and the *New Statesman*. Weinstock was sensitive not only to criticism of his management or his opinions, but especially to suggestions that he was dishonest or unprincipled – accusations which even his enemies would not go along with. He took pains to dispel these notions, and to explain the logic of the closures to anybody who would listen, although this had little effect on those who regarded him as an unfeeling capitalist. In his 1968 *Money Programme* interview, just after a further 2,500 job cuts had been announced, in Birmingham, he talked at some length about the difficulty, but also the necessity, of sacking people.

> You have to distinguish between responsibility as a manager and your personal feelings. A manager has the responsibility to make the best use of resources which are entrusted to his care, and that does include people. If you have to make a decision that a number of people must be sacked from their jobs you will make that on some sort of objective calculation. You know at the time that there are effects on the people in human terms, and you will be aware of the fact that it is undesirable, if it can be avoided, to do this sort of thing. You will not, in some cases, be able to escape it. Once a decision is made you then have to consider the people as human beings. You don't stomp up and say: 'Everybody out tomorrow.' You must try to arrange these matters to cause the least possible hardship, and even the least possible inconvenience.

Warming to his theme, Weinstock went on to talk about the evil of unemployment and the need for industry to counteract it.

> One has to say a little bit more about redundancy because a lot of things have been said, a lot of emotive words used. The real evil one is dealing with is not redundancy. The real evil is unemployment, and we overlook, when we are talking about some workers in some particular place being made redundant, that we have 650,000 unemployed. Now we either get industry efficient or we will have an awful lot more unemployed, and that seems to me the thing which has got, somehow, to be avoided. Now, if you have two factories, both making the same thing and both half full of work and there are no more orders to be got, the costs of the products which they make are such that neither is competitive, then both of those factories are liable to go out of business, so that both lots of people will lose their jobs. If by closing one you can transfer work to the other you will be able to keep the jobs of the people who work in that factory . . . It's most unpleasant for the people who are made redundant, but it is, when you look over the

134

whole of industry, an absolutely essential process which we have got to go through ... It's absolutely cardinal, to our way of looking at things, to realise that we can give the greatest number of people jobs with the greatest security of employment if we are efficient, and not otherwise.[3]

This was a message Weinstock spread at every opportunity, complaining to the *Daily Express* that everybody wanted greater efficiency, but that as soon as he did something to produce it they were up in arms about it: 'But the situation is inescapable if we really want rising employment.'[4]

While many shopfloor workers suffered from Weinstock's no-nonsense style, life was also far from easy for the AEI and EE managers suddenly confronted with the direct, abrasive personality and the 'no hiding-place' management style which had quadrupled GEC's profits during Weinstock's four years in charge. For the most part their contact with him was through a stream of memos, over the phone or at the annual budget meetings which would become notorious well beyond the confines of Stanhope Gate. Weinstock did not believe in spending much time travelling round his empire. He preferred to avoid 'state visits', which he saw as wasting his time and distracting his staff, instead poring over figures in his fifth-floor office and bouncing ideas back and forwards with his close colleagues. When he did venture out, it was not to be taken on a guided tour, as Kenneth Bond explained: 'If he went into a factory he would never go along the route prescribed for him. He would go off on the side and find some chap doing something, and find that that chap didn't really know what he was doing, and nor did his foreman, and so on. He was a great tugger of loose ends. He used to take the view that if you start pulling something and it starts coming away, you've got to keep pulling to find out what's behind it, and you might find there's nothing.'[5]

In the wake of the AEI takeover, however, Weinstock did make some visits to various sites, with the aim of allowing the new GEC employees to meet their boss, and to see for himself the state of the new acquisition. These excursions were dramatic exercises in conveying the GEC philosophy. One person who witnessed the managing director's first descent on Trafford Park remembers it vividly to this day, thirty years later:

'I've never seen anything like it: he was brilliant. He got the budgets out. He asked for the margins, the overheads. There were provisions littered everywhere. He crossed them out and wrote "losses". He rewrote the accounts so that the pretence disappeared. He'd hammer the points home about overheads, e.g. lavatory cleaning – he'd ask, "What are toilet rolls these days?" and multiply that up. He'd shake people into a realisation that money mattered, that costs mattered, that there was a different regime. And he worked at it. I was really impressed by his work rate. There were whole teams of AEI managers, listening to this *tour de force*. Every now and again he was almost over the top, and Kenneth Bond would calm him down. And it went on and on.

'Then the engineers had provided a tour map to go round the factory. Weinstock said: "I'm not interested in where they make the product, I'm interested in the overhead." He ripped up the map and put it in the bin. He then marched out with this huge tail of managers to do his own tour. And he made for the offices, not for the factory floor. He would come across buggers reading newspapers, because they were off the tour route, so there'd be scenes about that. I remember him entering a room labelled "Turbine Publicity Department". That captivated him no end. He barged in, and said to some sort of startled clerk: "Show me some turbine publicity." So there was a fevered opening of cabinets and a pile of nothingness. And he walked out and said to the managers: "I want the Turbine Publicity Department closing." It went on until at least 8 p.m. And as we were driving away the factory was a blaze of light. Weinstock stopped the car, banged on a side door of the factory until he alerted a security man, and got them to switch the lights off. It shook everybody up; he focused on all the right issues. He didn't attack the workers, it was the layers of unnecessary management he went for.'[6]

Weinstock wasn't finished. After Trafford Park the entourage drove off to the modern transformer factory at Wythenshawe, which had been opened in 1957 as part of AEI's ill-advised expansion. All the managers, who had been standing around twiddling their thumbs for hours as their boss's extended tour of Trafford

Park had wound on, were lined up waiting for a huge meal which was laid out in the dining room. The tables were groaning with food, as the plant wanted to make a good impression on its new managing director. Weinstock was not impressed, but was determined to make an impact on this outpost of his empire. He looked around, and took one apple and a few slices of cheese. Then he slowly peeled the apple and sat staring at the assembled ranks of managers trying to enjoy their steaks. It was a great act of showmanship, although the Wythenshawe managers did not much enjoy it. The message was clear: nobody spends the company's money without thinking carefully about it. The point of being there was to make money, not just transformers, or turbines, or whatever else the product might be.

Managers spared the personal delivery of this message had no excuse for not understanding it. After both the AEI and EE acquisitions, Weinstock took the unusual step of circulating a round robin which explained the GEC philosophy and what would be expected of the individual managing directors of the business units. The message to newcomers from AEI included a deliberate confusion between the management consultants McKinsey and the sexual researcher Kinsey – then famous for his recently published first report – to make it clear that management consultants were not wanted in the new GEC.

Weinstock's message to EE executives in a confidential memo dated 29 November 1968 laid out exactly how the central team worked and how they would be expected to perform. Having explained that the executive directors were 'more or less involved in all company affairs', regardless of their supposed specialisations, and having left no doubt that the managing directors of operating units were responsible directly to him, Weinstock went on with the central message that there would be no room for excuses:

> But the real success of our new company depends on the individual managing directors of our many product units. Our help (or lack of it) from HQ does not relieve you in the least of the responsibility for that part of the business which is in your charge ... Our philosophy of personal responsibility makes it completely unnecessary for you to

spend time at meetings of subsidiary boards or of standing committees. Therefore all standing committees are by this direction disbanded and subsidiary boards will not need to meet again (except, perhaps for statutory purposes once a year). If you wish to confer with colleagues by all means do so; even set up again any committee you and the other members feel you must have for the good of the business. But remember that you will be held personally accountable for any decision taken affecting your operating unit. Incidentally, on this matter of personal responsibility, prior permission from HQ is required for any proposal to employ management consultants.

Nobody receiving such a memorandum could be in any doubt that they had better get their results right, or else they would be in trouble. And there, Weinstock wrote, he should stop – 'But at the risk of being boring I think it desirable that I should add a few general remarks.' Those remarks concerned the primacy of return on capital employed, and therefore the need to cut stocks and debtors as well as overheads, but also, perhaps as a reaction to criticisms which had been made of GEC's style, the 'extreme stupidity' of cutting necessary research and other long-term spending. Finally there was a warning about the folly of resistance or politicking: 'We simply cannot afford avoidable problems such as personality clashes, personal prejudices, divisive, misplaced loyalties. We are now one company, one group, and, heaven only knows, we need each other's help in every way.'

The banning of management consultants (after that memorandum, who would dream of asking head office for permission to use them?) was a consequence of the profligate use of consultants in pre-Weinstock GEC and in AEI. Both companies had needed outside advice, because their managements were inbred and in conflict about solutions to their problems. But the potential benefits of external experience were outweighed by the extent to which consultants were called in so as to avoid taking difficult decisions. Hence the problems at GEC in the 1950s and at AEI in the 1960s were allowed to drag on while more consultancy reports were called for, and managers were allowed to escape their responsibility for poor performance on the grounds either that they were waiting for the outcome of an external investigation, or that they were following the prescription from one. The central tenet of Weinstock's approach was that managers must be responsible, must take difficult decisions early in pursuit of that responsibility, and would be held accountable for those decisions. As with much of his approach to managing the group, banning consultants was probably an effective way of instituting that rigour in the early days, but became an unnecessary totem as time wore on, which unit managers learned to get round, for example by describing consultancy spending as 'training'.

Any managing director who had not yet understood that the cosy days had ended when rosy forecasts could be followed by copious excuses received an unpleasant shock when it came to the annual budget meeting. Most large businesses now use some form of annual budgeting as a means of agreeing targets with their subsidiaries and planning for the whole group's finances, but as in so many areas of management practice, Weinstock and Bond were ahead of their time. They developed what would become known as 'bottom-up planning' (as opposed to dictating targets from the top) and 'management by objectives' well before many other groups. But the GEC budget meetings were about more than agreeing the unit's plan for the coming year. These ritualised sessions were Weinstock's primary form of control – not financial but personal. They were his one guaranteed face-to-face meeting with the people running his operating units, and he used them both as a means of assessing his people and of ramming home his principles of management. He would put on a performance which was intended to test his managers' understanding of their businesses, but which frequently tested their ability to endure vicious personal attacks. Indeed, the budget meetings never amended the figures presented by the visiting managers. That would have been giving them an excuse, taking away their responsibility. Weinstock and Bond challenged their managers fiercely, but never told them what the figures should be.

According to the stories told by those who participated in or witnessed these sessions, Weinstock's behaviour appeared to be aimed as much at domination and intimidation as at any other aspect of management, and would not be tolerated in most walks of life in the 1990s. One manager was so relieved that his torture was over that he fled through the nearest door – straight into a wardrobe. 'He is capable of sustaining invective at a higher level for longer than most people I have ever met. I found the only thing to do was to argue back when I thought I had a case, admit it when I hadn't got a case. The biggest sin was to cover up,' said one 1970s executive who left to become a senior board member elsewhere.[7]

Weinstock used simulated anger and aggression as a management tool. He felt it was necessary for his managers to be put through the fire, that they would become better managers for it. He understood perfectly well that it was unpleasant, but he has never felt the need to be pleasant in his ordinary everyday dealings with people, and certainly would not dream of introducing pleasantness into his business. He believed that managers who could not stand the heat did not deserve to be in the kitchen. The performances were not only aimed at executives who had come in to Stanhope Gate from their fiefdoms for the occasion, but also at members of the Stanhope Gate staff, as one recalled: 'He could make life pretty unpleasant and uncomfortable. He could be very unreasonable about you to others. In the middle of a budget meeting he would call down on the phone and drag me through all sorts of things, showing he was cleverer than me in front of people. What he didn't realise was that the MDs would sympathise with me. They would come down afterwards and say, "Hard luck." Whether he was proving how good he was, or that nobody, but nobody had the grasp he had, I don't know.'[8]

The aggressive atmosphere inside Stanhope Gate was largely attributable to Weinstock's abrasive personality, a habitual lack of civility which was perhaps partly a consequence of his shyness and partly of his intellectual ability, which left most others trailing in his wake. His natural disposition was exacerbated by the company history he inherited at both GEC and AEI, of pomposity at the highest levels, accompanied by a lack of understanding of the finances and an absence of control. But Weinstock's autocratic methods were less unusual in the 1970s than they would be today, when there is more emphasis on teamwork and consensus. It was a decade of industrial unrest unmatched since the 1920s, and a culture of managers fiercely defending their corners against each other as well as against the unions was common in many large companies.

Weinstock was not alone in the use of venom and aggression. Managing directors also had to face Kenneth Bond, who was less volatile but could be more devastating: 'Arnold had that tendency to go off at rather violent tangents from time to time. It was Kenneth who would quietly bring him back. As a duo they were bloody powerful. Bond had an outstanding ability to ask the penetrating question.' He could also be harder, and was much less emotional than his boss: 'If you had a battle with Kenneth you came out bruised. You really knew it. It was not a question of Arnold-type sallies. Kenneth knew his stuff and had a particular style of delivery which made you feel pretty small. He could really bruise anybody. But he was also more able to control Arnold than anybody. He would come out of his office next door when Arnold was ranting and say, "Shut up, Arnold. Just stop that." '[9]

If managers thought they had escaped from Weinstock following their annual budget grilling, they were mistaken. No matter how small the unit, or how tiny the issue, the group managing director could be on the phone at any hour of the day or night. One current director recalls being rung on Christmas Eve, just to answer a routine query on his monthly statement. Weinstock would spend up to half his time poring over the monthly management reports submitted by the units, an astonishing investment of effort in detailed scrutiny for the managing director of a leading group. He would pounce on any figure he didn't like the look of. Sometimes he would call the managing director, sometimes his finance director, sometimes he would go direct to the person concerned, such as the purchasing manager. As often as not he noticed things which they themselves were not aware of, as one victim recalled: 'He was a damn sight smarter than any of my accountants. I used to spend a lot of time trying to understand what he was going to come up with when I sent in my monthly report. We nearly always got it wrong.'[10]

There was also a steady stream of memos from Stanhope Gate which attempted to spread the message of personal responsibility and continuous improvement throughout the group. On 9 January

1969, Weinstock wrote to EE managers in terms which quickly made them familiar with what their new colleagues in GEC were used to:

> The most striking feature of the November reports is their complacency. For a company desperately short of money, up to its ears in debt and earning (if you are not too severe about the accounting) about 6 per cent on capital employed, this really is astonishing. One chap says of an overspend of a large sum against budget that it is all right because it is on the right curve for his five-year plan! In almost every case where things have not gone right, the reports tell us what seem like acts of providence; extra provisions are required because a machine does not work or a contract is coming out badly. There is no explanation, no retribution; only the company suffers. Another £50,000 must be provided – then another, then another. No one, apparently, is at fault, nothing has to be done to prevent a recurrence. Just make a provision, and on to the next duff budget!
>
> This will not do for me, and much pain will be avoided if that is understood thoroughly and quickly. When things go wrong, I want to know why – in detail, and what is being done about it, and who is OK and who is not. Managers are responsible not only for the job but for keeping me informed *frankly* as to what is going on.

GEC suffered its share of strikes and work-to-rules, exacerbated by the continuing stream of closures which saw the UK workforce fall from the 228,000 at the time of the English Electric merger in 1968 to only 170,000 by the time Harold Wilson returned to power in 1974. But GEC as a whole was never on strike, as other large companies such as British Leyland and British Steel frequently were. Weinstock had two great advantages over the leaders of such companies. First, his empire was distributed around the country in many different plants, which were part of separate subsidiary companies that negotiated individually with their own unions. And second, he had Jack Scamp, knighted in 1967 for his various services to the government, including his spell at the DEA.

Scamp was well regarded by most of his trade union foes. 'A real aristocrat. Very, very straight,' as one union leader of the period described him. After the difficult Woolwich affair, Scamp moved remarkably close to assuming a national negotiating position, which must have alarmed Weinstock, with his insistence that individual unit managers must bear responsibility for their costs and their labour relations. But the body Scamp created, the National Joint Consultative Committee (NJCC), stopped short of negotiating pay and conditions. It was set up to deal with difficult situations such as the Woolwich closure, and much to the unions' discomfort it became known colloquially as 'The Sacking Committee' – in keeping with the jibe thrown at GEC by union leader Hugh Scanlon, who described the company as 'Britain's largest unemployer'. The NJCC included officials of all the trade unions represented in GEC. At first it met quarterly with GEC's top management, discussing issues of concern with Weinstock and other key directors such as Scamp.

Weinstock would usually be much nastier to his managers than to the trade unionists. He took particular delight in castigating his industrial relations managers in front of union representatives, saying things like: 'I don't know why I employ you, you just give away all my money. I should pay you in washers.' Once a group of shop stewards from Rugby were brought down to headquarters to try to settle a dispute. One of them asked Weinstock – a notoriously bad tipster – for a racing tip, which several others also backed. The horse, which was second favourite, promptly came nowhere. When Weinstock was told the next day that the shop stewards had collectively lost £50 he pulled the money from his pocket and sent it to them.

He wasn't always so good-humoured, however, and engineering union official Johnnie Foster was particularly adept at getting under his skin. At one meeting Weinstock arrived late because he had been to see his doctor, and was clearly not well. Foster expressed sympathy, but said everyone had problems – his being a bank statement that had arrived that morning showing him overdrawn by 7s.6d (37p). Weinstock immediately dug in his pocket for the coins, which he handed over to Foster, saying: 'There, that'll shut you up then.' On another occasion Foster complained that Weinstock was more interested in horses than human beings. 'Do you know, I think you're right,' Weinstock replied after a moment's reflection.

In between the formal quarterly meetings the committee tramped the country as necessary from one crisis to another, mediating between angry local shop stewards and managers. Officials remember some tough sessions. One mass meeting was convened in Liverpool's covered market, which had been prepared for a boxing match that evening, and the officials used the ring as a makeshift stage. It was not a good idea, since there was no escape route. NJCC secretary Roy Sanderson of the electricians' union said at the start: 'If it gets nasty we're through those ropes and up that bloody aisle as fast as we can go.' It did turn nasty, with shop stewards occupying the stage in protest at the planned closure.

The period of bitter industrial conflict set management and unions at each others' throats in many large companies. The almost daily battle to get supplies from strike-hit factories, or to ensure that the machines kept running in their own plants, fed the siege mentality which affected many executive suites. Matters were not helped by the struggles of a succession of governments to come to terms with the trade union issue. Britain's industrial relations record had long been a source of concern. Throughout the 1960s the number of strikes in British industry had been seen as a handicap, especially in comparison with more successful competitor countries such as Germany. Harold Wilson's first Labour government had – in a style which Weinstock would liken to appointing consultants – set up a Royal Commission under Lord Donovan to consider the legal position of the trade unions. At the beginning of 1969 the left-wing Employment Secretary Barbara Castle published a White Paper, *In Place of Strife*, which proposed legislation limiting the power of trade unions, in ways which were eventually introduced by Margaret Thatcher's Conservative government in the early 1980s. Wilson and Castle were forced to back down in the face of resistance from trade unions and divisions within the Labour Party and Cabinet, and the torrid succession of strikes continued. Castle and others blamed the debacle over *In Place of Strife* for Labour's surprise defeat at the 1970 general election.

That defeat ushered in a Conservative regime under Edward

Heath which was initially determined to wipe out the years of socialist compromise, to roll back the borders of state involvement, and to allow a raw capitalist economy in which people would be encouraged 'to stand on their own two feet', in Heath's famous phrase. To the former socialist Weinstock this was a relief, but it did nothing to improve the atmosphere of conflict or to halt the steady stream of strikes. Heath tried, with the 1971 Industrial Relations Act, to do what Wilson had failed to accomplish, but the legalistic approach fell apart under the concerted opposition of trade unionists. His brief experimentation with the free market forces which Weinstock now approved of also came to a sudden halt in the famous 'U-turn' of 1972, when Heath reverted to interventionist industrial policies, including prices and incomes controls. His government finally fell, however, to the power of the union with the greatest solidarity, the National Union of Mineworkers, whose power was increased by the Opec cartel's oil-price hike in 1973. The oil-price rise threw the world's economies off-beam and fed a rapid surge in inflation, which reached almost 27 per cent in Britain in 1975. Government attempts to hold down inflation by keeping wages pegged inevitably caused widespread industrial unrest as trade unions struggled to keep members' pay in line with rising prices.

The bitterness of the disputes, especially with the miners, is difficult to imagine for those used to the more acquiescent workforces of the 1990s, as is the industrial dislocation which faced managers such as Weinstock. The nadir was reached during the period beginning at the end of 1973, when the Heath government, fearful that the miners' pickets would prevent sufficient coal reaching power stations to maintain electricity supplies, dictated that businesses could receive power supplies on only three days of the week.

Heath attempted to defeat the miners politically by calling a general election for February 1974, in the expectation that his stand against the unions would win widespread support from voters. But the country gave Wilson another chance, although only with a wafer-thin majority, even after a second election that October. Heath's failures led to Margaret Thatcher becoming leader of the Tory Party, and strongly influenced her thinking on industrial relations. The result was a stream of legislation throughout the 1980s which largely destroyed the power of the unions.

Weinstock gained a close insight into the impact of Heath's hard-nosed industrial policy when, in 1971, he was made a part-time board member of Rolls-Royce. The illustrious group had gone into liquidation as a consequence of the huge research costs and poor controls over the development of the RB-211, a new-generation jet engine which subsequently became highly profitable and was to remain the core of the company's range well into the 1990s. Pursuing its free market approach, the Heath government refused to bail out Rolls-Royce, but then had to take it into public ownership. Weinstock was dragooned into joining the nationalised company's board by his old financier, Sir Kenneth Keith, the man who won him AEI. He stayed for slightly longer than his agreed two-year term, long enough to see the luxury motor subsidiary sold to Vickers and the remainder of the business back on the road to solvency. But he did not enjoy the experience, and this remains the only outside directorship Weinstock has ever accepted.

At least the Rolls-Royce board was a club which wanted him, even if he was reluctant to join. The reverse was the case at Brooks's, one of London's grandest gentlemen's clubs. The episode proved that the old establishment was still alive and kicking in some corners of London, even if it was dying out in companies like GEC, and that it was not interested in seeing its havens invaded by one of the modern horde of meritocrats. In May 1973 Weinstock was blackballed after he had been nominated for membership by his deputy chairman Lord Aldington. The affair caused a brief flurry and led to the resignations from the club of Aldington and of Weinstock's seconder Charles Villiers, the banker who had taken over from Ronnie Grierson at the IRC in 1967. Weinstock refused to comment about the affair publicly, and put his rejection down to some former victim taking revenge for a corporate defeat. Members who had supported his application played down suggestions of anti-Semitism, pointing out that the club did have Jewish members. One suggested that the opposition to Weinstock stemmed from a mistaken, but widely held, view of his personality: 'I could only think it was somebody who doesn't know him very well and has got in his mind a picture of an autocratic, ruthless tycoon, which of course is what perhaps Arnold is regarded as by the British public.'[11] Others saw the snub as the establishment taking a rare chance to get its own back on somebody who upset its cosy way of doing business.

Weinstock had never been a self-publicist in the style of others in the new generation of businessmen. Unless it was necessary, for example during the AEI bid battle, he kept a low profile outside the group, rarely giving interviews and leaving complaints about government policies to his chairmen, either in the House of Lords or in their annual reports and other formal statements. During the early 1970s, however, he became so alarmed at the leftward drift of the Labour Party while in opposition that he briefly broke cover and came out openly against Labour's plans. The party had considered the record of the DEA, the IRC and Mintech in the 1960s, and decided that their failure had been caused by timidity about both the role of state intervention and the involvement of trade unions in their companies. A new twin-pronged policy was developed which alarmed industrialists because it threatened not only the largest and most important companies with nationalisation, but others with having to cede power to the unions. In the event the alarm proved to be false. Labour's National Enterprise Board of the 1970s was little different from the IRC of the 1960s, and became more concerned with saving companies from collapse than with shaking up industry. And plans for worker participation were stalled by the Bullock Commission, whose recommendations for the formal involvement of trade union representatives on company boards were so controversial that they were never acted on.

In 1974, as Harold Wilson attempted to win a working majority for a manifesto which included these measures, Weinstock voiced his opposition to them. He was encouraged by friends such as *Times* editor William Rees-Mogg, who believed that his standing as an independent industrialist would give his disquiet more weight than the ritual opposition from the Confederation of British Industry.

In a major interview in the *Daily Telegraph* in June 1974, Weinstock warned vaguely that GEC would not necessarily comply with measures which it did not consider legitimate, and floated ideas about consensus and a national coalition government: 'There is a new situation in which we have a government with no overall majority . . . The country is in a sort of limbo. We do not know with any assurance what the people want. In this situation we will not feel obliged simply to go along with policy ideas which we feel will be bad for us and the country. One isn't thinking in these circumstances of standing back from the fray but fighting against deleterious proposals for which there is no mandate and no adequate legal or moral basis.'[12]

He outlined a managerialist manifesto: the agreement of 'eight or ten aims, the pursuit of which the great majority would accept as good and desirable and would be prepared to work for'. And he argued that industry needed a new voice which could argue the case for capitalism, seemingly putting himself forward as a candidate to lead it: 'I am not a political animal and have not even always voted Conservative. I am just a manager and wouldn't know how to be a politician. But perhaps it is time to start to find out.'

Even Weinstock's friends would agree with all but the last sentence of that statement. While he has had an enduring fascination for the political process and the running of government, he has never been able to come to terms with the need to carry colleagues with him and to develop a broadly accepted position rather than merely imposing what seemed to him to be the correct solution.

Tony Benn, Weinstock's former ally at the Ministry of Technology who had helped, through the IRC, to put him where he was, was to come in for particular attack. Weinstock appeared on television during the October 1974 election campaign to denounce plans for the National Enterprise Board as 'the thin end of the Wedgwood Benn', and described Labour's White Paper proposing the NEB as being based on 'a non-sequitur of the most elementary sort', the equation of greater state ownership with greater investment. Lashing out at the notion of planning agreements between the hundred largest companies and the government, he said that Labour's policy was based on slogans, not analysis. In a *Times* article on 26 September he spelled out the common objectives he had referred to in the *Daily Telegraph* three months previously, which he said could be followed by a coalition government elected under proportional representation to avoid the sterility of two-party antagonism and the domination of the Labour Party by a left-wing minority.

The proposed objectives of such a 'government of good sense and good will' included economic issues like the attack on inflation and the stabilisation of exchange rates, and a number of managerialist items like greater efficiency in government. But they also revealed Weinstock's remaining socialist instincts. He called for equality of opportunity ('so far as can be made practicable') and the acceptance of a 'safety net' to protect the worst-off, as well as an education system which would 'provide for maximum opportunity for self-fulfilment of the individual' as well as for the needs of the economy. These sentiments revealed the deprived boy made good behind the façade of the hard-headed businessman. They reflected Weinstock's own experience of inner-city education and a class system which ensured that most of his childhood contemporaries ended up as tradesmen rather than professionals. His background left him with a deep social awareness which was tempered only by his understanding of business imperatives. The result was concern, but not sentimentality, and a conviction that while the needs of individuals should not be ignored, the need for a vibrant economy should come first.

Given Weinstock's position, it is hardly surprising that when GEC made one of its rare political donations in 1974, it gave £25,000 to the Liberal Party, which had amassed an astonishing six million votes in the February election and threatened a breakthrough in parliamentary seats which would have broken the grip of the two big parties. (Hedging his bets, Weinstock also gave £25,000 to the Tories.) In the event the Liberal threat waned and Labour was returned with an increased majority.

In a BBC radio interview in 1975 Weinstock finally laid to rest the prospect of his going into politics, telling psephologist and political commentator Anthony King that he would probably be a bad politician. In a telling phrase, he admitted: 'I wouldn't like to do something badly.' He also acknowledged that a country could not be run like a company, despite his oft-repeated complaints that government should be more businesslike: 'You can't run a country like that with democratic traditions like Britain – it shouldn't be run by people being told what to do.'[13]

Despite Labour's success in the October 1974 general election, Weinstock was not immediately deterred from his campaign against extremism, as he saw it. In a March 1975 interview with Kenneth Harris in the *Observer* he warned of the worsening economic situation and repeated his calls for what amounted to a government of national unity. This time his suggested programme was more specific, including the abolition of the Price Commission, cutting company and executive taxes but also helping the low-paid, the disabled and pensioners. He made it clear that he was not calling for the complete withdrawal of government from industrial affairs:

> I am not against any measure of government action in industry which is relevant and necessary to deal with a given situation, provided there is a reasonable expectation, based on common sense and experience, that it will succeed and is the best means available . . . Generally speaking it is simply not socially responsible to keep people in employment in plants whose output will forever fetch less in the market than the cost of wages, materials and overheads . . . Government intervention must always be for stated purposes which stand up to the tests of common sense and reasoned judgement . . . Government has not been set up to be a huge investment trust, operating in order to make a commercial profit; there has to be some other objective. When that objective is realised the money should have been well spent. If the money is considered not well spent, the government had the wrong objective in the first place. In that case, you don't nationalise the industry, you fire the minister.[14]

Weinstock told the *Daily Express* on 26 September 1975 about his disappointment with the Liberal Party, which he said appeared to be a mixture of liberal Liberals and Marxist Liberals. But in the same interview he confirmed his Liberal leanings at that time by explaining that GEC was taking steps to encourage its workers to be more involved both in their unions and in the company's operations, although they stopped well short of formal worker participation as the Labour Party understood it.

This theme was picked up in the BBC radio interview, when Weinstock described as 'a crusade' the battle to demonstrate that British capitalism worked and was the best possible system. He again stressed that he had been attempting to build greater dialogue between GEC's management and workers: 'We are trying to expound in a practical way the philosophy of the company: that everyone counts, everyone has a role to play, everyone commands respect, and everybody's view should be known when decisions are taken.'[15]

During these years the relationship between management and workers was being critically examined from a number of perspectives. One impetus came from the government. Industry Secretary Peter Shore had announced on 5 August 1975 the creation of an inquiry into industrial democracy, which became known as the Bullock Commission after its chairman, the academic and historian Sir Alan Bullock. The aim of the inquiry was to consider how, not whether, employees should be represented on company boards.[16] The commission failed to agree on its conclusions, and its divided recommendations fell victim to the growing economic and industrial crisis.

But there were other pressures on businesses to review the nature of their relationship with their staff. Conventional, hierarchical mass-production methods were being challenged by the contention that worker participation in management and alternative ways of working could result in greater efficiency, and thus greater profitability. Western businesses were for the first time beginning to take notice of the consensual approach of Japanese companies, while the Swedish car-maker Volvo's experiment with self-managed work teams received wide publicity.

Weinstock's liberal social views and his meritocrat's belief in the potential of the humblest employee made him sympathetic to some of these new practices, although he was appalled at the prospect of putting trade union representatives on the board, which he saw as entrenching conflict. He told the *Daily Express*:

> I agree with those politicians who say that people in industry feel alienated from the system ... There's too much 'we' and 'they' in industry. There are bound to be conflicts in any system, but we've tended to become obsessed with the differences, not with the common ground ... In GEC we already have quite extensive arrangements for consultation

with employees and their union representatives. We're developing this further to give all our people the opportunity to participate in all affairs related to the business and their working lives. We're not talking of gimmicks such as worker directors and two-tier boards and so on . . . we want our people to know that they really matter and to add a new dimension of dignity to their status in life.[17]

Sir Michael Bett, who succeeded Jack Scamp as GEC's head of industrial relations, recalls that in the 1970s Weinstock 'had a hankering for the legitimacy of a politician. He realised he was there to some extent because he was the son-in-law of his father-in-law. He hadn't got the legitimacy of a democratic election. He explored with me more than once the idea that he should put himself up for election. What he wanted, at a time when there was a lot of criticism, was to prove that the people in the business realised that what was being done, unpleasant though it was, was necessary.'[18]

These may have been idle musings, but Weinstock was keen to tap the energies of workers at lower levels of the hierarchy – again predating 1990s management thinking on 'empowerment' by a couple of decades. In a confidential memo to managers on 28 July 1975, he insisted that they must do better in the endeavour to involve staff. He said that while all sizeable units had some form of joint consultation, few were adequate:

In order to create the environment in which the company can function to maximum efficiency, it is essential that the most effective means possible for discussing with work-people's representatives all the aspects of running the business should exist in every operating unit. All joint consultation arrangements must now be reviewed with the object of making them more profound and more effective. Workpeople and employers must become increasingly involved in the business *together*.

The thrust of this instruction was followed up two months later. In a six-page memorandum dated 18 September Weinstock wrote at length about the importance of employee involvement, this time drawing attention to the threat of worker directors imposed by government action.

> We want to build a participative process right through the operations of the company, involving our employees in matters affecting their jobs and in methods, systems and procedures in the factories and offices. They have knowledge and experience, and they have much to contribute ... Very few working managers would find much with which to agree in the dicta of Mr Wedgwood Benn. But who would dispute his thesis that if the skills, experience and intelligence of workers can be harnessed constructively in the operation of industry, if the attitudes of management and workers can be brought together in effective cooperation, then there would follow a great upsurge in industrial efficiency and a general atmosphere of relative satisfaction.
>
> Unhappily, on that constructive basis is built the destructive proposition that the way to do this is by burying all classes except a 'working class' so defined as to exclude millions of working people. This approach masquerades under the label of 'industrial democracy' but there is not much democracy about it and, in the end, there wouldn't be much industry either. It will be a bad job for the British people if that is the best we can do.
>
> In the course of time, it is possible to foresee the emergence of new working methods. We want to get rid of complicated and messy payment schemes and wage structures. Overtime should become unnecessary, save in the most exceptional circumstances. Our people should be able to earn a good living in a normal week's work, although that normal week should produce more, and better, than at present. We should aim ultimately to create conditions in which it will be possible to enhance remuneration out of profits; and we should think about creating far more satisfaction for people outside their work and in retirement.

This vision seems eventually to have faded away, but GEC did get involved in industrial democracy in a surprising manner when it stepped in to help the Meriden motorcycle factory – one of the trio of worker cooperatives (the others being the *Scottish Daily News* and the Merseyside radiator manufacturer KME) which had been set up under Tony Benn, but whose genesis went back to the Heath era. The factory had been abandoned as part of a reorganisation of the motorcycle industry by Norton Villiers Triumph which had been aided by a grant from the Heath government in 1973. The Meriden workers had refused to accept closure and had occupied the factory, attempting to continue production. They were eventually given further support under the Labour Industry Act, but had great difficulty in achieving financial stability. Their main asset was two thousand completed Triumph Bonneville motorcycles, and in January 1977 Weinstock was persuaded by Kenneth Bond that GEC could help. The group stepped in with an offer to buy the machines for £1 million, thus giving the Meriden workers some working capital and a breathing space in which to turn the factory round. GEC brought in Lord Stokes, the former British Leyland super-salesman, to sell the bikes, and seconded Bill Morgan, the former head of GEC's motors business who had been brought into Stanhope Gate, as a commercial director. But like the other Benn cooperatives, the commercial realities could not be overcome even with the greater commitment of worker managers. The experiment finally collapsed, as did Weinstock's brief flirtation with industrial democracy.

Europe was another key issue for Britain in the 1970s. In January 1973 Prime Minister Edward Heath had finally sealed Britain's entry into the European Union, then known as the European Economic Community (EEC). It seemed briefly that this might end the country's ambivalence towards the Continent after years of wavering, during which Britain had first rejected the opportunity to join the EEC when it was established, and was then rebuffed by French President Charles de Gaulle in 1967. But the controversy was not even briefly laid to rest, as Labour Eurosceptics won a commitment that the party, now in government, would seek to renegotiate the terms of entry, and put the revised terms to a national referendum in June 1975. This produced a clear vote in favour of remaining in the EEC (by a margin of two to one), although events in the 1990s have shown that the matter has not yet been laid to rest.

It was clear to the business world that Britain's economic future would be more closely bound up with Europe than with the Commonwealth, which had previously ranked second only to the United States in most companies' export efforts and overseas investment. Weinstock was too busy dealing with issues in the UK to worry much about joining the rush of British companies seeking to capitalise on EEC membership, but there was a brief flirtation with international diversification, both on the Continent and in the US. In December 1973 GEC had bought a French manufacturer of washing machines and dishwashers – Compagnie des Machines à Laver Lincoln – and had followed this in 1974 with the purchase of two other French companies, one in electronics and the other a maker of diesel engines. Weinstock later explained GEC's bid for international growth: 'In some large markets where our participation is too small or where we are not participating at all, if we are going to grow rapidly, which is what we aim to do, we must do it on an international basis. We may also try joint ventures with local concerns overseas and we will invest some money that way.'[19]

It was a fine theory, but the French experiment came to little. The electronics company was sold three years later, and Laver Lincoln survived in the group for only a few months longer than that. The diesel company, Baudouin, was retained into the 1980s, but never delivered the business or the benefits which had been hoped, and it was finally sold at the end of 1987. This disappointing experience set back GEC's Europeanisation for a decade, until dramatic joint ventures at the end of the 1980s finally began to transform this very British company into something more European.

Diversification in the United States was more successful, but was still disappointing. In 1977, in a bid to step up GEC's American business and to capitalise on the burgeoning microcomputer industry, Weinstock snapped up a young high-flyer who had transformed the fortunes of the British computer company ICL. Geoffrey Cross had resigned after five years as managing director of ICL because his son's health demanded a warmer climate, so GEC appointed him to build up a portfolio of US interests, some of which might become part of the group, others of which might merely be investments. The aim was as much to learn from American technological developments as to buy sales in the US. Weinstock explained at the time: 'We have always intended to hunt for new business which would help us expand our home base, by exporting things from the UK and bringing back new expertise from North America.'[20]

But Cross proved a disappointment, guilty of being, in one of Weinstock's put-down phrases, 'very good with the mouth'. He was responsible for what has probably been GEC's worst ever acquisition, the printing and office equipment company A.B. Dick. It was bought in the spring of 1979, and despite years of management changes and various strategies to deal with the change in technology from its core offset-printing heritage, it remained a problem right to the end of Weinstock's leadership of the group.

GEC instigated a rash of American purchases and other deals in the second half of the 1970s, including a microchip joint venture with Fairchild. But as with the French exercise, there was little to show for them by the end of the 1980s. Some, including the Fairchild deal, had been wound up, others simply disappeared from view. The only exceptions were the Videojet non-impact printing business of A.B. Dick, which has grown substantially, and Picker, a medical electronics business which was acquired in 1981. Critics have argued that Weinstock's legendary tight-fistedness prevented GEC from buying meaningfully in the US, where good companies do not come cheap. On the other hand, his defenders can point to the large number of British companies which have bought badly in the US – including Ferranti, the electronics company which was brought to its knees by the acquisition of International Signal, a deal which GEC sensibly turned down.

The unsuccessful attempts at internationalisation in the 1970s left GEC largely dependent on Britain and the former empire. Until the great European joint ventures of the late 1980s, only about an eighth of GEC's sales went to the Continent. The highest level was 15 per cent for a couple of years in the mid-1970s, while it sank to 10 per cent in the early eighties. The proportion of turnover stemming from the UK dipped a little from the level when GEC, AEI and EE first came together, but the UK still accounted for roughly half of all sales throughout the 1970s and into the 1980s.

In the mid-1970s Weinstock was heavily involved in several political controversies, largely stemming from the Labour government's industrial policies. But in the case of nuclear power, the origins of the conflict lay with Edward Heath's Conservative government, which handed the task of building a British nuclear industry to Weinstock. GEC had inherited a nuclear power capability as part of the generating business of its three constituent parts, but that capability had not been translated into profitable activity. Development costs were huge, and it was difficult to recoup them from the small number of orders received from the UK or abroad.

When the growing power of the Opec oil-producers' cartel increased the pressure for alternative sources of electricity generation in the 1970s, the Heath government decided to boost the nuclear programme, and to try to make the process more efficient by creating a single nuclear power company. After a six-month wrangle this was achieved in spring 1973 when the National Nuclear Power Corporation was created, combining the plant-building capabilities of all the participants. GEC ended up owning half of the organisation (later reduced to 30 per cent), with 15 per cent held by the government, and Weinstock was eventually appointed boss.

This was only agreed after difficult negotiations over the kind of reactor which would be built. Weinstock had been in favour of licensing US technology for what were known as Pressurised Water Reactors (PWR), but the British government was keen to see home-grown technology developed, not only for use in the UK but also for potential exports. Weinstock appeared to have been won round to the British Advanced Gas-Cooled Reactor (AGR), but no sooner was the National Nuclear Power Corporation set up than he changed his mind, much to the chagrin of Energy Secretary Peter Walker and others keen to avoid importing US technology.

In December 1973 Weinstock told the House of Commons Energy Select Committee that his views had changed because of the growing energy crisis, as militant miners threatened the security of coal supplies and oil prices were soaring. Previously he had been prepared to push AGRs, because he thought that ultimately they would work well. But the technology was still unproven, even though the first of this type of power station, Hinckley B, was about to come on stream. Since early security of supply was now a priority, Weinstock had concluded that the American PWR was the only short-term option, even though he felt that AGRs might win in the end.

This judgement brought him into conflict with politicians, trade unionists and some technologists, but in characteristic fashion he patiently attempted to persuade his opponents with what he saw as the objective, rational arguments. He held what amounted to a seminar at Stanhope Gate for trade union officials, which several remember as a *tour de force*, illustrating both his ability to grasp complex technical issues and his willingness to spend hours explaining them to an audience to whom other chief executives might not have given the time of day. One who was at the meeting commented: 'Only Arnold Weinstock would go to those lengths, or could explain in simple language what the issues were and why he believed what he did.' Another said: 'He gave an exposition of the nuclear business, technically, commercially, environmentally, which was so impressive. We came out of the meeting thinking, "If some bastard's got to rescue the nuclear industry, it might as well be that bastard." '[21]

Following the election of the Labour government in February 1974, Weinstock's position brought him up against his old ally from the 1960s, Tony Benn. Their once-warm relationship had already cooled, as Benn's corporatism of the 1960s gave way to more radical socialism. As industry spokesman in opposition, and Industry Secretary in 1974, Benn had been behind the interventionist moves which had so alarmed Weinstock – the threat of nationalisation of the largest companies, and the notion of planning agreements between top companies and the government.

This threat disappeared when Harold Wilson moved Benn to Energy Secretary in June 1975, following his support for a 'no' vote in the Common Market referendum; but the nuclear issue further divided him and Weinstock. The battle was confused by the shifting views on the two systems, and others, of the CEGB, which would be the customer for any British nuclear power station. The matter ended unhappily for Weinstock when his corporate partners in the National Nuclear Power Corporation insisted on opting for the AGR, and in February 1978 he bowed out as Britain's nuclear boss. GEC's annual report stated baldly: 'The company has informed HM Government that, at a time convenient, it wishes to end the contract under which it exercises a supervisory role over the activities of the National Nuclear Corporation.' Weinstock himself explained the affair in typically rational terms to Brian Connell of *The Times*:

> We took on the supervision of the nuclear programme in 1974 because we were interested in the nuclear power industry, which was in a horrible mess, and that was sorted out ... There seemed to be no other way, and no other company sufficiently strong in resources and the capacity to do it ... Some time ago, when we saw things were not going as we thought they should, we did tell the Secretary of State that we need not feel in the least embarrassed about changing the situation in which we exercised control.[22]

Another rumbling political row which began in the mid-1970s was over the nationalisation of the British aircraft industry. The terms on which GEC's interests were bought by the government were seen as 'expropriation' by Weinstock, and generated enormous anger over many years as he attempted to rectify what he saw as a moral outrage. The affair is blamed by some for his subsequent reluctance to get involved with any activity which might subsequently fall into state ownership.

It began with the creation of the British Aircraft Corporation (BAC), the forerunner of British Aerospace, in 1960, which brought together the aerospace interests of English Electric, Vickers and smaller manufacturers. The deal left English Electric, and subsequently GEC, owning 50 per cent of BAC. The Labour manifesto of 1974, which had provoked Weinstock into public opposition, included a pledge to nationalise the industry, and this was eventually achieved through the Aircraft and Shipbuilding Industries Act in 1976. The Act did not confiscate without compensation, as some of the wilder advocates of state ownership had urged, but in Weinstock's view the sums paid did not take account of the accumulated profits which had not been distributed to BAC's owners as dividends in the previous two or three years. 'That the shareholders' legitimate interest in the total profits of BAC earned since 1973 should be so reduced without compensation is, in the view of the directors, a deprivation amounting *pro tanto* to expropriation,' fumed the GEC directors' report in 1976. In his statement, chairman Lord Nelson went further, claiming that the 'appropriation' of GEC's interest in BAC was so much worse than any other nationalisation that it threatened British democracy:

> In this case not only is the intention wrong, but it is exacerbated by the nature of its execution, involving a basis of compensation which is (for the first time in a case of nationalisation) manifestly unfair, and defended (in an equally unprecedented manner) by officials as well as ministers, with specious arguments which cannot be intended to do other than dress up a purely political act ... The government hypocritically maintains that its proposals furnish a fair basis for compensation; if they are allowed to go through there must be the gravest doubt as to the capability of our democratic system to protect the rights and property of private individuals and organisations from arbitrary government action.

The matter dragged on for years, but GEC finally had to capitulate. Weinstock was horrified when he got no more sympathetic a hearing from the Thatcher government when it came to power in 1979 than he had from Labour, but on such a matter of principle he was not prepared to give up. GEC and Vickers took their case to the European Court of Human Rights, which finally considered it in 1985. The Court delivered its judgement on 8 July 1986, but gave no comfort to the aggrieved companies, finding that the nationalisation terms were acceptable.

Weinstock's final political battle of the 1970s was a curious replay of the modern GEC's formation, and illustrated the continuing overcapacity in the power generation business and the political difficulties they caused, especially for a government desperate to maintain friendly relations with the trade unions and to avoid further unemployment. In 1977 Labour's successor to the IRC, the National Enterprise Board, attempted to finish the job the IRC had started and to force a merger between GEC and its old rival in the heavy electrical end of the industry, C.A. Parsons, to whom Weinstock had sold his generator business back in 1966. Weinstock resisted the NEB plan, bringing him into conflict not only with Eric Varley, who had replaced Benn as Industry Secretary, but also with

James Callaghan, who had succeeded Wilson as prime minister. Weinstock would have been prepared to take over Parsons, but Parsons' unions were naturally reluctant to put themselves on the slab for GEC's scalpel. The NEB therefore proposed a merger, with itself taking a share in the joint company. This was unacceptable to Weinstock, who had yet to come round to the notion of joint ventures. He told the *Guardian*:

> Everything proposed so far is blatantly stupid for GEC, and we will not agree to anything which is blatantly stupid. In the natural course of events there will be only one turbine generator manufacturer, because there is only enough business for one. But it appears that some people do not like the natural course of events, and so difficulties arise. We are then in the position of having to decide what is in GEC's interests, and nothing which has been proposed so far would be good for GEC.[23]

Weinstock was summoned to see the Prime Minister at 10 Downing Street, and Callaghan attempted to use the carrot of a £200 million order for GEC for the Drax B power station in Yorkshire, which the government had committed to bring forward so as to help the industry. Weinstock called his bluff, however, telling him that Parsons could have the order and insisting that if GEC was to be involved with Parsons, it must have management control. That was not acceptable to Callaghan, so GEC and Parsons went their separate ways.

The 1970s were turbulent years for Britain and for GEC. The economy was in almost permanent crisis, induced partly by the surges in oil prices in 1973 and 1979, and partly by the mistakes of governments of both parties. Edward Heath's Chancellor Anthony Barber unleashed a disastrous expansion in the money supply in 1972 which led to a brief financial boom, followed swiftly by a crisis among 'fringe' banks and property companies which threatened to engulf the financial sector. Both Tory and Labour governments vainly attempted to stem inflation in the first half of the decade, which reached a peak of almost 27 per cent in 1975. And a succession of sterling crises culminated in the Labour government's finances being rescued by the International Monetary Fund in 1976, the price being heavy cuts in public spending, rising unemployment, and incalculable damage to Britain's economic reputation, both at home and abroad.

Weinstock viewed these events with growing dismay, believing that better management in government, and less politics, would have resulted in a stronger economy and thus a better environment for managers such as himself to operate in, to everybody's benefit. He began the decade as the whizz-kid boss of a newly-merged electrical combine that dominated the industry, a modern business hero who had shaken up the commercial establishment just as much as he had shaken up the established bosses in GEC, AEI and EE. But Weinstock's optimism about British industry, which stemmed from his no-nonsense approach and his commitment to efficient production, echoed in Edward Heath's free enterprise victory in the 1970 election, gradually dissolved in the face of economic and industrial chaos.

While much had changed throughout industry since 1968, when GEC began to close the AEI factories, the 1970s ended with industrial relations problems as the engineering unions staged a series of strikes in support of their attempt to reduce working hours. Weinstock was not happy with the way the Engineering Employers' Federation (EEF) was handling the dispute, and contemplated withdrawing the ninety GEC subsidiaries which were EEF members from the organisation. Indeed, he was seldom happy with that or any other employers' grouping – GEC was the only major British company not to join the Confederation of British Industry, for example. Weinstock's dissatisfaction with the EEF provided the trade unions with an opening, and they attempted to exploit it, suggesting a rift. Weinstock hit back with a biting letter to Terry Duffy, engineering union president, in which he said that GEC's impending split with the EEF did not mean that the company had any sympathy with the unions' 'irresponsible' claim. Warning of the coming recession, he ended with typical sarcasm: 'I hope your members will ponder on the validity of the union proposition that its objectives are at the same time to raise wages and increase jobs. It is a novel concept in economics that you can raise demand by increasing the cost.'

There were disappointments on the business front at home, as well as abroad. Foremost among these for Weinstock was the decline of his old empire Radio & Allied, as the GEC subsidiary was still called. The company recorded its first loss in 1977–78, wilting under the onslaught of Japanese imports. On the basis of 'if you can't beat them, join them,' Weinstock attempted to solve the problem by setting up a joint venture with Hitachi.

On the whole, though, the 1970s ended with GEC in strong shape. Lord Nelson concluded a ten-year review by telling shareholders that the anticipated advantages of putting the three big electrical companies together had largely been realised. He pointed out that while consumer prices had almost doubled during the period, GEC's exports had almost quadrupled, capital expenditure was almost seven times higher than in 1969, the group paid about eight times as much in tax, and the average earnings of employees was two and half times what it had been in the first year of the 'new' GEC. He could have added that the group's sales had risen each year, reaching £2.5 billion in 1978–79, nearly three times sales in his first year as chairman; and that despite all the turmoil, profits had not suffered a single reverse, growing to 6.5 times that first year's level. These were remarkable achievements, even allowing for the distortions of inflation, but already there were concerns about whether Weinstock could be as good at expanding as he had been at cutting back. That would be a growing concern in the 1980s, as GEC's cash built up and its labour force shrank.

Away from business and politics, in 1978 Weinstock was elected to the Jockey Club, the pinnacle of the racing Establishment. The following year, Troy, one of the best horses ever to come from the Sobell–Weinstock stud, won both the Epsom Derby and the Irish Sweepstakes Derby at the Curragh. After the stunning series of victories, partly due to Weinstock's son Simon's mastery of bloodstock breeding, Troy was put out to stud, with the Queen among those taking a share in him.

The 1970s saw the death of three of Weinstock's brothers. The eldest, Samuel, who suffered all his life from motor neurone disease despite Arnold's efforts to find a cure, died in Streatham in 1972, while Jakob died two years later. Weinstock lost his closest brother in 1975. Harry, who had taken him in when he was orphaned, and who had subsequently set him on his path in business by introducing him to Louis Scott, died in 1975, aged sixty-nine. All three brothers had led relatively humble lives in trades such as hairdressing or tailoring, as might be expected of people from their modest background. None showed the intellectual power, the drive or the love of the good life of their younger brother Arnold, although all benefited indirectly from his success and wealth.

Weinstock's son Simon, though, did exhibit the same kind of mental ability and business understanding as his father. After a sparkling academic career which saw him winning a scholarship to Winchester public school and reading Classics at Magdalen College, Oxford, Simon went to work for GEC's merchant bank, S.G. Warburg. On 28 November 1979 he married Laura Helen Legh, the daughter of Major Sir Francis Legh, equerry to the Queen Mother and private secretary to Princess Margaret. The wedding was a grand affair at the Queen's Chapel of St John Baptist in Westminster, followed by a reception at St James's Palace. The spectacular seven-foot wedding cake was decorated in the Sobell–Weinstock racing colours of light-blue and yellow. The only disappointment for Weinstock and Netta was that Laura, whom Simon had met at his father's country home at Bowden in Wiltshire before a hunt ball, was not Jewish. Indeed, Netta declared at the time, 'I don't want to talk about it.'[24] The wedding seemed calculated to cause affront to Weinstock's Jewish relatives and friends since it was held on a Friday evening, the traditional start of the Sabbath.

Although Arnold and Netta may have had mixed feelings about the match, suspecting that they had not imbued Simon with a strong enough sense of his Jewish identity, it represented a substantial social advance for the Sobell–Weinstock clan. In just two generations the offspring of struggling Polish–Jewish immigrants, fleeing persecution in their native land, had not only accumulated a substantial fortune, but had made a leap into the highest levels of British society with a marriage into a family of royal courtiers.

In October 1980, a year after Simon's wedding, his sister Susan also married outside the Jewish faith, to Laurent Lacroix, a schoolmaster, at a much lower-key ceremony at the Kensington register office, followed by a party at the Royal Naval College at Greenwich. Her sister-in-law Laura was a witness.

# CHAPTER SIX

## The Thatcher Years

WEINSTOCK WAS RENOWNED among his colleagues for being the first to change his mind about the new government after every general election, and it did not take him long to fall out with Margaret Thatcher after she swept to power in September 1979. Her regime proved to be no less controversial than the Labour years, as the Conservatives pursued an economic policy targeted at killing inflation, and an industrial policy dedicated to stifling the trade union movement. Weinstock was broadly in sympathy with these goals, which had led him to admire Mrs Thatcher in her years as opposition leader. But while he approved of many of the ends at which the Tories aimed, he did not necessarily subscribe to the means, especially when they resulted in a ridiculously overvalued pound which made life murderous for exporters, and when he saw the hardship caused to many at the lower levels of society by rising unemployment. He also departed from the Thatcher approach on what became the most substantial single theme of her administrations, privatisation, and he fell foul of the government's drive to improve defence procurement and to attract foreign manufacturers to Britain. The clash was detrimental to GEC, which suffered hugely over the embarrassing failure of the Nimrod early-warning aircraft, and saw several corporate moves blocked by the government, including its first attempt to take over Plessey. GEC's standing in the City and the business community fared little better than it did with the government, to the extent that the company became the target of an audacious break-up bid at the end of the 1980s.

Weinstock's own reputation also suffered. For much of the 1970s he had been a hero in the City and a favourite with government and Whitehall for successfully rationalising the electrical industry and transforming its financial position. Tony Benn recalled in 1995 that Weinstock had been regarded in Whitehall 'like the chairman of a nationalised industry'. For a time Weinstock was regarded as having the solution to any industrial problem. Senior civil servants sought his advice, which would generally be influential in their subsequent thinking.

But that huge reservoir of goodwill quickly leaked away in the early 1980s, as Mrs Thatcher ushered in a much less comfortable environment for large suppliers to the government. The new regime embraced policies on issues such as privatisation which Weinstock violently disagreed with, but which were generally popular with City and business people. Many in the City viewed Weinstock's opposition as indicating an outdated approach, which helped to fuel their growing disillusionment with him and with GEC. Criticism of what was perceived as the company's stagnation mounted during the 1980s, and Weinstock came to be seen in government circles too as more of an old-fashioned protector of self-interest than the kind of thrusting entrepreneur who was in tune with the spirit of the decade.

The 1980s was nevertheless a period of dramatic corporate activity for GEC, which culminated in a restructuring of the group through European joint ventures which matched the importance of the acquisitions of AEI and EE. The decade began, however, with a successful lobby of the government which led to a fierce debate between Weinstock and his colleagues, and almost resulted in GEC being broken up. The fashion for building conglomerates was still proceeding apace, with companies such as Hanson and BTR just getting into their stride, but questions were already being asked on both sides of the Atlantic about the performance of many large conglomerates. Breaking up, though, other than through the external agency of a takeover, was hard to do in the UK because of tax laws which would impose a financial penalty on such moves. Weinstock and Kenneth Bond set about persuading the Treasury to alter the rules, so as to ease the demerger which they were contemplating.

The idea of demerger stemmed from GEC's growing cash mountain and the difficulty of finding acquisitions to spend it on. The build-up of cash was already proving controversial, and would become more so as critics claimed that it stemmed from under-investment in research and new projects. In July 1979 the *Daily Express* City Editor Roy Assersohn wrote: 'The company's balances have grown to a level which would almost justify Sir Arnold floating off part of the group as a bank.'[1] The cash had begun to accumulate in the 1970s, partly as a result of GEC's tight financial control but also because of limits on dividend increases which were part of both Tory and Labour governments' prices and incomes policies. The first attempt to do something about the situation came in 1977, when a complex capital reconstruction took place, giving GEC shareholders new capital shares which could be traded for cash. 'The reasons for the issue were that in the opinion of the directors the Company's liquid resources were well in excess of its require-ments,' explained the directors' report. A different scheme with similar objectives was attempted in the following year, but the proposed bonus dividend was prevented by continued legal restraints on the level of dividend permitted. The advent of Mar-garet Thatcher's government saw dividend controls abolished, how-ever, and in 1979 GEC increased its dividend by a whacking 55 per cent. But the company still had £249 million cash in the bank in 1980, and it seemed to Weinstock and Bond that shareholders would be better off having some of that cash, as well as shares in separate companies. A stockbroker's calculation found that the stock market would value a demerged group more highly than the price it currently put on the whole empire, but such calculations are notoriously subjective and uncertain, with different analyses frequently arriving at wildly differing prices.

The demerger issue caused one of the fiercest rows between Weinstock and David Lewis, who was nearing retirement but was still an important member of the triumvirate. He had grown accus-tomed to discouraging what he regarded as Weinstock's wilder schemes, while also urging his colleagues to be more creative and adventurous. He fiercely opposed the whole idea of demerger, first on legal grounds and then, once the legal obstacles had been over-come, as a matter of principle: having put the group together, he believed it was important to keep it together, and that the parts were mutually beneficial.

His arguments were supported from some unlikely directions,

namely the operating company managers and certain key customers – and for the same reason. Managers of many units, from generating equipment to defence electronics, argued that they needed to be able to demonstrate huge financial strength to potential customers, so that they could be confident that their GEC supplier would be around for the many years of the contract. The same point was made forcibly by one of the GEC Power group's most important customers, Lord Kadoorie of China Light and Power, the buyer of some of the company's biggest power station contracts. He told Malcolm Bates, a banker who had joined GEC in 1975 and was made a director in 1979, just as the debate was raging: 'You will never get another order from Hong Kong and China. I can't go into a seven-year project and not feel certain that the company has the strength to be there at the end of it.' As a result of this top-level opposition, and with the support of chairman Lord Nelson, Bates took the unusual step of submitting a paper to the board outlining the potential disadvantages of a demerger. It was not easy to argue against the proposal, as it originated with Kenneth Bond: 'It was the hardest thing I have ever done in my career,' Bates said. But added to the opposition from inside and outside the company, the potential value of the move to shareholders was uncertain, and the plan was eventually dropped. In his 1982 statement, Lord Nelson said: 'Our managers prefer the advantages of being part of a group large enough to be acknowledged internationally as of major importance; for the present, further consideration of any major demerger has been deferred.' It was deferred indefinitely.

The demerger debate over, Weinstock set about building up rather than tearing apart, in what would prove to be a tumultuous decade for mergers and acquisitions for British industry as a whole, as well as for GEC. A long stock-market boom, which began as the recession petered out in 1982, led to a remarkable leap in share prices in 1987. This fed a takeover spree that had already beaten previous records. Predators such as Lord Hanson were at their peak in this period, pulling off coup after coup. Saatchi & Saatchi drove through the 1980s, assaulting the US advertising industry to become the world's largest agency; its hubris even produced thoughts of taking over the Midland Bank. Elsewhere, Guinness acquired Distillers in a bitter battle with the Argyll Group which ended in prosecutions and prison sentences for several participants, while in the retail world Burton bought Debenhams and Sir Terence Conran rocketed in no time at all from his little Habitat chain to the top of the BHS and Mothercare group, Storehouse.

Many of the conglomerates created in this rerun of the 1960s merger mania found the aftermath difficult, if not deadly. Even Hanson has broken up in the 1990s. The folly of the deals done and the prices paid eventually justified Weinstock's refusal to join in the City game – a refusal which saw him branded as an unadventurous stick-in-the-mud at the time. GEC did not sit idly by during this period, however, even though it did not submit to the financially-driven moves which were behind many of the biggest deals. Instead, they undertook a steady stream of takeovers, mostly small by GEC standards, and attempted several others, much more significant, which did not come off. Only towards the end of the 1980s did Weinstock manage to achieve the significant deals which changed the shape of the group, by which time many in the City had given up on him and written off the company as a risk-averse, sleepy monolith.

The 1980s started with GEC embarked on a path of internationalisation. The group also appeared determined to ride the bandwagon of computerisation which was beginning to pick up pace. The rash of American deals in the late 1970s was an attempt to fulfil both aims by buying into the electronics industry in the United States.

Weinstock also came very close to buying AEG, the German electrical group. For a time in early 1983 it looked as though the deal would be done. In private meetings between Weinstock and AEG managing director Heinz Durr, it was agreed that AEG's domestic appliance business would be separated out, and that GEC would spend £175 million (and take on huge debts) on a 40 per cent stake in the rest, in GEC's familiar territory of power engineering, telecoms and defence electronics. AEG was one of Germany's top ten companies, but it had made losses since 1979 and was effectively bankrupt. German businesses, notably Siemens, were not keen to see GEC walk into their back yard, but it seemed that there were no other firm offers. At the last minute, however, Weinstock lost his nerve. He decided that AEG's pension commitments were too onerous, and negotiating the necessary job cuts with the trade unions would be too difficult, to justify even the cheap price he would be getting the business for. He pulled out, losing a golden opportunity to buy a stake in a crucial European market.

At home, Weinstock allowed himself to be outbid for the music to defence electronics group Decca by Ernie Harrison, the young, thrusting, entrepreneurial head of Racal. Racal was often cited by Weinstock's critics as an example of what GEC could have done with greater imagination and less caution. It had been built up from scratch after the Second World War to become a significant player in defence electronics, especially radio communications. Unknown to many in the City, however, Weinstock came close to launching a takeover bid for Racal on several occasions during the mid-1980s.

There were successful acquisitions during the early years of the decade, however. The weighing-machine and petrol-pump company Avery was acquired for almost £100 million in 1980, after the Monopolies and Mergers Commission (MMC) had given the deal the all-clear, and after agonised debate by Avery's trade unions. Avery was a classic case of British management failing to adapt to new technology, and of GEC capitalising on its technological expertise to make a success of the acquisition. It was a long-established business with a tremendous brand name and a deserved reputation for craftsmanship and quality. But it was stuck in the days of brass weights and mechanical devices, had failed to come to terms with electronics and was in danger of going bust. That is what persuaded Avery's trade union representatives that it would be better to risk the fire of GEC than to stay in the frying pan, but they managed to extract from Weinstock a two-year moratorium on redundancies – a substantial bonus given GEC's drive to cut jobs and its parsimony with redundancy payments.

GEC's annual report for 1979–80 said that the acquisition was part of a strategy 'for supplying office and business systems to meet the growing requirements of industry and commerce for automated methods of collecting and processing, storing and communicating a continuous flow of information'. This was an understandable objective for an electronics group at a time when personal computers were beginning to be produced in sufficient volume, and at sufficient quality, to be of interest to businesses. Given the current convergence of computing and telecoms it was also remarkably prescient of GEC to attempt to capitalise on its expertise in both.

But a lack of faith, patience or courage meant that the laudable aim of developing a business computing arm was not achieved. In the early 1980s the group's research labs were working on business computer systems, electronic mail, teletext, videophones and other electronic applications for industry and commerce. The company was able to report in 1981 that GEC Computers had increased sales by 60 per cent, and profits had improved despite higher research and development spending. That year's review of operations commented on the mix of skills which were available in the communications field, where 'important new research' was looking at networks of computers in offices and factories: 'The company's knowledge in telecommunications, office equipment and computers provides the backcloth to this important research area'.

The theme was continued in the following year, when a new subsidiary, GEC Information Systems, was created. This brought GEC Computers together with other units in the fast-growing field of information technology. The aim was 'to provide integrated information networks based on voice and data switching systems, computers, word processors and local area networks'. Admirable aims, but GEC failed to anticipate the dramatic advance of personal computing, a field which it never seriously entered. The drive into business computing petered out, and GEC Information Systems had disappeared within three years. The annual report in 1985 revealed that commercial systems had produced a substantial loss, with familiar consequences: 'Changes have been made in management and organisation.'

This brief flirtation with new fields was followed by a reversion to the familiar territory of defence and telecommunications, but attempts at expansion there were thwarted by a serious worsening of relations between Weinstock and Mrs Thatcher. He had never been one of her most admired business people, being associated with cosy relationships with nationalised industries and the Ministry of Defence. Despite his lowly beginnings as the orphan of parents of meagre means, Weinstock did not fit Thatcher's romantic image of the self-made entrepreneur: his battles against the industrial establishment were now so far in the past that he had himself become part of the establishment. She preferred the newer heroes, such as Lord King of British Airways and Lord Hanson, who had none of Weinstock's social conscience and shared many of her prejudices. As Thatcher's biographer Hugo Young put it: 'He was just the kind of industrialist to whom the great romancer of entrepreneurship was least likely to warm . . . He was yesterday's man, a symptom of times past.'[2] Weinstock had been a valued adviser in her earlier days as leader of the opposition, but she had come to believe he was always looking for government help for GEC. James Prior, one of Margaret Thatcher's ministers who later became chairman of GEC, remembered: 'GEC was always regarded as a company which was after big subsidies or protection and so on. Arnold was regarded as a very formidable man to deal with, but they had all that money, so why did they have to have subsidies? This was the sort of line which came up in Cabinet, led actually by Mrs Thatcher, who had a sort of love-hate relationship with him in the early 1980s.'[3]

Weinstock's directness and honesty were also handicaps in his relationship with the new Prime Minister. Unlike others, he did not play to her prejudices and vanities, as Kenneth Bond recalled: 'He would give her advice she didn't want to receive. He didn't pull his punches.'[4] Another problem was that GEC has always been a haven for what came to be known as Tory 'wets' – old-fashioned 'one-nation' Conservatives who did not share Thatcher's enthusiasm for bashing the unions, and who deplored the huge rise in unemployment that was a consequence of her policies. Lord Aldington, GEC's former chairman who remained on the board until 1984, had been a deputy chairman of the Tory party in the 1950s, and remained on the left of the party in the House of Lords. Sara Morrison, who joined the board in 1980, was a deputy chairman of the party in Ted Heath's day, moving to GEC after Thatcher beat Heath in the leadership contest following his second election defeat in 1974. But the ultimate affront to Mrs Thatcher was the appointment of Jim Prior as GEC's chairman in 1984. He had been one of her least-loved Cabinet ministers, initially in charge of the union-bashing legislation at the Department of Employment, but pursuing it with such a lack of enthusiasm that he was given the poisoned chalice of Northern Ireland.

In the early 1980s the relationship between Weinstock and Thatcher was satisfactory. She had given him a life peerage in the 1980 Queen's Birthday Honours, and was happy to help GEC win contracts overseas, notably in the Middle East. Weinstock's early speeches in the House of Lords were classic crossbench business contributions, including attacks on bad management and on the Treasury, as well as a liberal sprinkling of Weinstockian epithets. In his maiden speech in November 1980, on economic affairs, he observed: 'In the Treasury and the Bank of England we have professional economists who are amateur administrators locked in debate with professional administrators who are amateur economists.'[5] He accused critics of the government's anti-inflation policies of not having any alternatives, and went on to attack inflation accounting and the perils of bureaucracy. He ended with a homily which would have appealed to Thatcher:

> More than twenty-five years in manufacturing industry and even a relatively brief spell before that in the Admiralty has taught me the benefit of keeping things simple. I suggest that it has been a great weakness that in one area after another we have tried to persuade ourselves that we can avoid facing up to reality. If we look straight, we can see that it is only through honest hard work and good products that we can build a strong economy ... My Lords, our people can do as well as any others in the world if they are free from distraction and from false prophets. Let the red tape be cut away, let industry deal with the facts, undoctored by the accountants, uncorrupted by the economists, and it will get on with what has to be done.[6]

Weinstock's second contribution was in the Queen's Speech debate the following year. He sided with Lord Robbins (whom he described as 'my deeply respected friend and mentor') broadly supporting government policy 'even if not agreeing with it in every respect', but his speech contained the first hints of criticism. He made a gentle call for public investment and a more conciliatory attitude to trade unions, as well as an attack on the Treasury's strictly monetarist approach:

> Efficiency in British industry has improved quite a lot in the last few years, and so have the relationships between those who work in it. That improvement now needs a more positive impetus than is to be gained from growing unemployment and increasing pessimism ... If we are unjustified in blaming the government for the greater part of our economic maladies, they deserve no praise for their presentation to the British people of the problems . . . Ministers have been almost entirely negative, depressing and demotivating, in contrast to the country's need of more enterprise, more creativity and more vigour. If we have merited sulphur and brimstone it has been duly administered and perhaps we should be thankful for it. But most people will not place their confidence indefinitely in physicians who offer no prospect of any other diet, and who have increasingly given the impression that they would not know how to concoct one. That these feelings of unease and discontent should be widespread reflects political failure. But it is not failure beyond redemption. Neither is it a failure to be redeemed by resort to other forms of nastiness, such as union-bashing.[7]

These criticisms were followed by a fairly muted attack on the government's strategy of attracting inward investment from foreign companies, especially Japanese ones. Speaking at a special one-day seminar on innovation organised by Mrs Thatcher in September 1983, Weinstock pursued one of his hobby horses, which would bring him into repeated disagreement with the Prime Minister. He argued that inward investment was a short-term solution, and that assembling foreign companies' products did not bring basic technological skills to Britain, and also had the effect of sucking skilled British workers into 'foreign outposts' supported by taxpayers' money. Like all Weinstock's interventions in political debate, this complaint was based on personal experience, and largely directed at the television and radio industry, which was particularly close to his heart.

Radio & Allied had done well in its early years within the GEC stable. It made record profits in 1970–71 as colour broadcasting took off, but the boom was short-lived, thanks partly to the economic malaise which followed the 1973 oil-price hike, and partly to the flood of Japanese products. Several Japanese manufacturers decided to set up plants in Britain as a way of getting around voluntary import limits. Ironically, a number of them were attracted to South Wales in exactly the same way that Michael Sobell had been after the Second World War, by special grants designed to attract investment and provide jobs. Sony set up a plant in Bridgend in 1973, and the following year Matsushita, the JVC company, followed suit in Cardiff. When Hitachi decided to get in on the act, however, British manufacturers complained to the government that it was senseless to pay Japanese companies to enter the UK, where they would put existing British jobs at risk. They persuaded the government to abandon promises of aid.

But the British producers suffered badly, with Radio & Allied reporting its first-ever loss in 1977–78. Weinstock effectively sued for peace, entering a joint venture with Hitachi in 1978, under which the Japanese company would provide the crucial tubes and other key components. But it was a doomed enterprise. Weinstock, believing that GEC was being taken for a ride, sold out to the Japanese in March 1984. It is a move that he has always regretted. The automaton which he has often been painted as would have examined the numbers and concluded coldly that selling was the right thing to do. But Weinstock is a sentimental man, and he did not take the decision lightly to sell off what was his own family heritage.

Later in the 1980s he contemplated re-entering the radio and television market, but was persuaded against it by the head of GEC's domestic equipment division, Jeff Sansom. It was the end of the Sobell business, and a sad comment on the inability of British manufacturers to compete with foreign rivals.

Weinstock remained resolutely opposed to the British government attracting foreign manufacturers. In 1987, in response to comments by Prince Charles, he told the *Daily Express*: 'Prince Charles may welcome the Japanese presence in this country for creating jobs, but I don't. They are setting up over here in subsidised development areas to get round import barriers. They are competing against British industry and British taxpayers are helping to pay for this. I don't think that is very funny or very intelligent. We are playing cricket while the Japanese have gone in for all-in wrestling.'[8]

While these episodes brought Weinstock into conflict with government policy, his criticisms were low-key. That changed, however, when in early 1984 he found the government pushing ahead with the privatisation of British Telecom as a single entity, despite all his advice and lobbying. He was opposed to this on principle (the creation of a private monopoly) and in practice (the likely impact on British companies), and used the seat in the House of Lords which Thatcher had bestowed on him to argue forcefully against it. He only took the unusual step for him of going public with his opposition after repeatedly failing to persuade Industry Secretaries Cecil Parkinson and Norman Tebbit, as well as other ministers, that the plan was mistaken. His pleas were interpreted as special pleading from someone who had made millions of pounds supplying the nationalised telephone service.

To some extent Weinstock's fears were connected to the likely impact of privatisation on GEC's telecoms business. But his concerns about simply transferring a public monopoly to the private sector were shared by many who had no financial or party political interest, and the House of Lords managed to make several significant amendments to the privatisation Bill, aided by the intervention of Weinstock on many detailed points during its passage through the House. In his final speech as the Bill neared the statute book, he acknowledged these improvements, notably the agreement to place the draft licences for BT before Parliament, but he repeated his opposition, in typically forthright style:

I do not like this Bill, and whether or not it is in my best material interests I am bound to say so. I do not speak on behalf of GEC, and my views are certainly not derived from GEC's membership of any 'charmed circle', as was predictably alleged in another place. Neither is it true that I am part of an unholy alliance with the Labour Party and

Baron Weinstock of Bowden at his introduction to the House of Lords,
15 October 1980.

Weinstock with his right-hand man, Sir Kenneth Bond, 1985.

Riccardo Muti, Weinstock's musical hero and devoted friend.

Peter Reynolds, manager of the Ballymacoll Stud in County Meath.

Troy, the pride of the Sobell-Weinstock racing partnership, winning the 1979 Derby with Willie Carson.

Weinstock at the races in 1985.

the trade unions, although if such an alliance had existed it would not necessarily be unholy to share the view of those institutions that the government are mistaken in what they are doing . . . The basic fact remains that this legislation is meant to transfer a national monopoly service to private hands, in the belief that this will further the cause of competition and of a free market in telecommunications services. Several noble Lords referred to this delusion during the second reading and subsequently . . . No responsible body of opinion believes that BT will constitute other than a monopoly or that its monopoly powers can be kept under control by Oftel [the telecoms regulator] through the proposed licence. If, as ministers say, competition and liberalisation are the main aims, there is no reason why those aims could not have been achieved without altering the ownership of BT and by enforcing BT's assistance in the developing needs of potential competitors. No – except for fleeting references to the Public Sector Borrowing Requirement, the reasons your Lordships have been given in support of this Bill do not bear the weight of close examination, and it is no wonder that the Bill seems to command so little enthusiasm among government supporters. What is needed to improve and enhance communications services and to promote competition to that end is a coherent idea of how we can meet our evolving requirements in future years, and to make the best of our national resources. That is not the route the government have chosen . . . In contrast to their substantial achievements in other fields, the government are making a pig's ear of these matters. Ministers have said that once liberalisation is accepted, privatisation of British Telecom inevitably follows. This proposition is nonsensical. The object of privatisation, in a single step and at a proper price, is in blatant conflict with the objective of promoting competition.[9]

Earlier in the Lords debate, Weinstock's attack on the British Telecom privatisation had contained the seeds of a greater assault on the government's economic and industrial policy which was to follow. This was a spirited defence of manufacturing industry in the face of the idea that Britain should become a 'service economy', which had been espoused by Mrs Thatcher and her Chancellor Nigel Lawson. Part of Weinstock's dissatisfaction with the BT Bill had been the lack of consideration for manufacturers of equipment. Now he broadened this concern to manufacturing in general:

> In this country there is a tendency to regard manufacturing industry as something of declining importance. I have forgotten what is the exact percentage said to be now employed in manufacturing industry, but it is of the order of twenty-something per cent. That indicates that seventy-something per cent is employed in other industries, said to be mostly service industries. Servicing what? The insurance companies, the banks, the stockbrokers, the pension funds, are providing services to industry. At the base of all this great service industry activity in which we place so much hope for the future lies manufacturing industry. I fear that if manufacturing industry fails, unless we become merely a country entertaining tourists, the service industries, or a large part of them, will go with it.[10]

This kind of concern was becoming widespread in Britain, especially as 1983 had seen the the country importing more manufactured goods than it exported for the first time in its history. This was a severe shock to a generation of industrialists brought up on the notion of Britain as 'the workshop of the world', and following expressions of alarm by various peers during the winter of 1983–84, the House of Lords set up a Select Committee to investigate. It was chaired by the old GEC hand Lord Aldington, and its members included Lord Kearton, who might be described as the midwife of the modern GEC through his role as chairman of Labour's Industrial Reorganisation Corporation in the 1960s, former Coal Board chairman Lord Ezra, and Lord Beswick, once a Labour industry minister who was the first chairman of British Aerospace. They met thirty-eight times during the winter of 1984 and into the following summer, taking evidence from bodies as diverse as the Chambers of Commerce, the Tobacco Advisory Council and Unilever. Weinstock was one of those interviewed, as was another prominent

178

anti-Thatcherite industrialist, ICI chairman John Harvey-Jones. Chancellor of the Exchequer Nigel Lawson and Norman Tebbit, who was then Trade and Industry Secretary, gave the government's view, but they received short shrift from the committee.

It quickly decided that its remit should be extended to consider manufacturing as a whole, not just the balance of trade question, and proceeded to chart the decline in manufacturing output since 1972, which had accelerated rapidly since Mrs Thatcher came to power. In 1980 and 1981 output had fallen by a seventh, and despite a recovery since 1982, it remained below the 1979 level. Manufacturing had fallen to barely a fifth of gross domestic product in 1983, from 28 per cent ten years earlier when Thatcher's arch-enemy, Ted Heath, had undergone the U-turn which she was determined to avoid. When Nigel Lawson argued that all advanced countries had seen a fall in the share of manufactures as they became more sophisticated economies with a greater share of service industries, the committee retorted that only Britain had seen an absolute fall in manufacturing. They insisted that this mattered, as exported goods were responsible for 40 per cent of Britain's overseas earnings as well as for the collapse in the non-oil balance of payments since 1980. Weinstock's own industry, electrical and electronic engineering, showed a trade deficit in 1984 of £1.4 billion – a plunge since 1978 exceeded only by the stricken motor industry.

Weinstock and Harvey-Jones grabbed the headlines when they gave evidence of the damage their companies had suffered as a result of the government's policies. Weinstock was particularly scathing about the government's faith in service industries. In typically colourful and biting language he asked: 'What will the service industries be servicing when there is no hardware, when no wealth is actually being produced? . . . We will supply the changing of the guard, we will supply the Beefeaters around the Tower of London. We will become a curiosity. I do not think that is what Britain is about. I think that is rubbish.'[11] Harvey-Jones said that ICI's UK sales had fallen by 11 per cent since 1979, and that almost a third of the customers supplied then had folded. The *Guardian* noted in an editorial comment that it was not as easy for Mrs Thatcher to brush aside such protests as it was to dismiss left-leaning policy institutes, and commended Weinstock and Harvey-Jones's bravery: 'It takes a certain courage these days for industrialists, who in terms of personal taxation have been extremely well-treated by this government, to rise above the tide of party politics and speak up for industry.'[12]

Mrs Thatcher was not impressed. Challenged by a Labour Member of Parliament who cited this evidence at Prime Minister's Question Time in the House of Commons, she responded angrily, referring to GEC's profits: 'In fact, as distinct from opinion, manufacturing employment in this country has been falling since 1966. Lord Weinstock is very well aware it is quite possible to have a flourishing manufacturing sector even though it employs fewer people.'[13] Nigel Lawson claimed that the trend which the committee was worried about was both inevitable, because of the impact of North Sea oil on the strength of the pound, and reversible, as the oil surplus would decline towards the end of the 1980s and that impact would cease. But the peers noted drily: 'In the light of the evidence they have received from many other quarters, the Committee take issue with fundamental assumptions on which the Treasury view is founded.'[14] They argued that competitiveness and the exchange rate were important factors in Britain's manufacturing decline, that the exchange rate had been artificially high because of oil and because of the government's financial strategy, and that those factors would not necessarily be affected by falling oil production. They concluded:

> The Committee's view is that the continuing deficit in the balance of trade in manufactures is a symptom of the decline in Britain's manufacturing capacity on the one hand and of poor competitiveness of important areas of manufacturing on the other. Unless the climate is changed so that the manufacturing base is enlarged and steps are taken to ensure that import penetration is combated and that manufactured exports are stimulated, as the oil revenues diminish the country will experience adverse effects which will worsen with time.[15]

While calling for 'a change in national attitude', the report also had several specific policy suggestions, few of which were likely to appeal to Mrs Thatcher and her leading ministers. They included familiar calls for restraint in wage increases, better standards of design and quality, and a higher level of recruits to management. But the committee also demanded action from government of a style which had virtually disappeared with Jim Callaghan's Labour administration in 1979. They wanted the government to consult widely through mechanisms such as the National Economic Development Office (which had been sidelined by Thatcher) to develop consistent economic strategies that favoured manufacturing. It called for government support (anathema to Thatcher) for research, exports, infrastructure and training, a stable exchange rate, low interest rates and government support in its own purchasing for British manufacturers.

Lawson dismissed the report as 'a mixture of special pleading dressed up as analysis and assertion masquerading as evidence',[16] but in his contribution to the House of Lords debate on the report, Weinstock was equally scathing about the Chancellor and his policies. He began by refuting Lawson's contention that a decline in manufacturing was a long-term trend in all industrialised countries, quoting figures which showed that only in Britain had manufacturing grown by less than GDP since 1960. He went on to challenge the suggestion that a manufacturing deficit was an arithmetical result of the oil surplus, and argued that the government could save money by buying British, which would lead to higher employment and consequent tax benefits:

> It is important to see what has happened for what it is – not an arithmetical necessity, but the result of a political decision to give overriding, indeed exclusive, priority to reducing the rate of inflation; and that has had the consequences of restricting output and raising unemployment ... When the government and the great national utilities buy from UK industry instead of from foreign sources, jobs are created, or at least preserved, without any additional cost to the Exchequer ... There must be competition to prevent feather-bedding. But national immolation in the name of a non-existent free market is surely carrying things too far.[17]

This was Weinstock's last major speech in the House of Lords. His rare contributions since then have been on subjects of more personal interest, notably horse-racing and the problems of the betting or breeding industries. But it was not the end of his troubles with Mrs Thatcher, because his comments on the need for the government to buy British were not merely generalised arguments, but were based on GEC's own recent experience. Throughout the period when he had been battling in the House of Lords he had also been engaged in a tussle with the Ministry of Defence which had much more serious immediate consequences for GEC – although he always suspected that his difficulties with defence contracts were not unrelated to his challenge to the government's economic polices.

There were huge problems with a major GEC contract to develop an airborne early-warning system, known as Nimrod, with electronics from the GEC-owned Marconi which could detect submarines. Nimrod had first gone into service with the Royal Air Force in 1970, replacing ageing turbo-prop Shackletons and successfully using the airframe of the Hawker Siddeley Comet – the first jet airliner. GEC's nightmare began in the mid-1970s when a decision was taken, under intense political and industrial pressure, to adapt this aircraft for the task of spotting low-flying Soviet bombers which could escape conventional ground radar. The Callaghan government had previously decided to go along with the rest of the NATO alliance in ordering US planes based on the Boeing 707 and known as AWACS – airborne early warning and control system, but heavy lobbying from British contractors and trade unions attempted to reverse its decision. The British consortium, including GEC and Hawker Siddeley, did not claim that the updated Nimrod would be a match for AWACS, but offered it on the basis that it would be cheaper and would provide more jobs in the UK – an important consideration at a time when unemployment was creeping up and the government was facing a mounting economic crisis.

As so often when such decisions had to be made, GEC actually had a foot in both camps: it would have been a sub-contractor for the AWACS radar, but would have a greater involvement as prime contractor on Nimrod. Weinstock lobbied hard for the UK solution. The challenge to get the new Nimrod in the air in just four years seemed insurmountable, however, especially considering that the US AWACS had taken fifteen years to develop.

A prototype of the odd-looking aircraft, with bulging radar pods at nose and tail, made its first public appearance at Hawker's factory in Woodford, Cheshire, on 1 March 1977, and the final battle over the decision raged for the next few weeks. Defence Secretary Fred Mulley was told that only five hundred jobs would come with the AWACS project, while Nimrod would provide employment for seven thousand. Boeing challenged these figures, but could only promise a thousand jobs in the UK. There seemed little doubt that Nimrod would be cheaper because existing aircraft would be converted, rather than building new airframes: there just happened to be eleven spare airframes lying around, largely as a consequence of earlier government support for their manufacture in a bid to save jobs in Cheshire.

Fred Mulley was said to favour the US option, which was apparently the choice of the RAF, and consistent with its demand that it must have the aircraft in service by 1981. But NATO ministers could not agree on the project because of reluctance by West Germany to commit funds to it. Eventually the jobs argument won the day. On 31 March Mulley announced that instead of paying £260 million as its contribution to NATO's AWACS force, Britain would spend the cash on eleven Nimrod aircraft, the first of which would go into service with the RAF in 1982.

The first aircraft made its maiden flight in July 1980, but the complex electronics was still sitting in Marconi's factory in Hertfordshire. And it soon became apparent that the 1982 deadline was not going to be met, while the projected £20 million cost for each plane was wildly optimistic. The scheduled delivery date was put back to 1984, but when the first plane was delivered in December that year, the radar systems were still not working properly, while the cost had risen to £90 million per plane. Early in 1985 the RAF was predicting that it would be another two and a half years before the aircraft were fully operational. Announcing this latest delay to the House of Commons Defence Select Committee, Air Chief Marshal Sir John Rogers warned that the total cost of the eleven planes would now be more than £1 billion, compared to around £250 million when they were first ordered in 1977.

The argument for abandoning the whole project was growing stronger. Under severe pressure from Defence Secretary Michael Heseltine, GEC made a belated attempt at setting out how it might be rescued. In November 1985, as the original contract neared its end and the last of the competing AWACS aircraft were delivered to other NATO countries, the company told him it would cost another £250 million on top of the £1 billion already spent to finish the job, which would take another three years. Heseltine met Weinstock and his chairman, Lord Prior, and they thrashed out a deal that represented a last chance for GEC, which had clearly only hung on to the contract by the skin of its teeth, even though Defence Procurement Minister Norman Lamont acknowledged all the blame should not fall on the company: 'The government have sought in these negotiations to give them every opportunity to recover a most unsatisfactory position which reflects, in part, wider shortcomings in the management of defence procurement.'[18] GEC would have six months to come up with a firm price and deadline for delivering the radar, but would shoulder all the costs during that period, and in that time the government would examine other options, such as reverting to the original choice of AWACS.

It was six months of hell, not only for the Marconi engineers desperately trying to create a viable ending to the mess, but also for Weinstock, the politicians involved and other companies offering competing solutions. One of those was GEC's old rival Plessey, which joined forces with the US group Westinghouse in supporting the Boeing AWACS option. Another, bizarrely, was Airship Industries, which suggested using dirigibles rather than aircraft on which to mount the radar.

GEC took the six-month reprieve to mean that it was still in with a good chance of retaining the contract, but as the period drew to a close it became increasingly apparent that it faced a Herculean task, partly because of opposition from Mrs Thatcher. In late 1985 Weinstock queered his pitch yet again over the Westland Helicopters affair, in which Michael Heseltine, in the face of opposition from Mrs Thatcher and most of the cabinet, had attempted to stitch together a European consortium to save the British company. Under pressure from British Aerospace, which would have had a leading role in the European alternative, and the MoD, which reminded Weinstock forcefully that the Nimrod decision was still outstanding, GEC joined the Heseltine camp. Unfortunately, they lost the fight. Heseltine stormed out of the government on 9 January 1986, losing Weinstock a potential ally in the Nimrod battle, and Weinstock and GEC were further alienated from the Prime Minister.

As the final decision on Nimrod drew near, Jim Prior abandoned the normally subdued, behind-the-scenes lobbying process and went public in October 1986, arguing firstly that Nimrod's technical problems were largely behind it, and secondly that GEC was suffering political opposition. He admitted that GEC had not performed brilliantly in the early years of the contract, but added: 'The fight is now moving into a political phase. There are many in government who don't like GEC for one reason or another, and believe that we have done too well out of the Ministry of Defence over the past twenty-five years.'[19] He won a brief extension, but not the argument. The MoD announced that a final decision would be taken by the end of the year, and that it would be between Nimrod and AWACS, ruling out the other options.

As Boeing stepped up its offensive, drawing Racal as well as Plessey into its consortium and promising that fifty thousand British jobs would result, Prior launched a last-ditch delaying tactic with the politician's suggestion of an independent inquiry, but that was brushed aside by the new Defence Secretary, George Younger. There was a growing feeling that Mrs Thatcher had already chosen in Boeing's favour, as a form of revenge against Weinstock, as the *Guardian* columnist Hugo Young noted: 'It would also be one in the eye for Weinstock, a valued counsellor when the Tories were in opposition but now, after crimes ranging from his attacks on the privatisation of British Telecom to his part in the House of Lords' slating of the government's industrial record, firmly located on the list of the damned. All this makes it tempting to see the Prime Minister's interfering hand behind a bad decision.'[20] The row became more acrimonious as decision day approached. GEC and the RAF openly attacked each other, with the Air Force taking the unusual step of publicly denying GEC's claim that its tests had not been objective. Weinstock arranged a private meeting with Mrs Thatcher, but she refused to countenance further delay or to overturn her decision to back AWACS, which was awaiting a rubber stamp from the Cabinet.

Despite the fact that GEC had managed to drum up support from seventy backbench Tory MPs as well as the Labour and Liberal opposition, it lost the battle. On 18 December 1986, almost ten years since his Labour predecessor had given the go-ahead, Younger announced that Nimrod was being abandoned and that Britain would, after all, buy AWACS. Driving home the attack on GEC, he said that the decision rested on whether the company could be relied on finally to deliver a system that worked to specification:

> The question I have had to consider is whether, taking into account the work done since February, and in particular of recent flight trials, together with our knowledge of the results they have achieved over the last nine years, I can have confidence that they could deliver aircraft with the levels of performance in the timescales they have offered. I am sorry to say that the conclusion I have reached after the most careful consideration is that I cannot have that confidence.[21]

Weinstock was furious, and blamed the MoD. He had already told the *Daily Telegraph*: 'I think the treatment by the Ministry of Defence in this matter doesn't live up to the standards one expects from the public service in this country. There does appear to be something wrong here and we don't think it is Nimrod.'[22] He wrote a long article in *The Times* arguing for an independent assessment of the whole process:

> Surely we should now be given the opportunity of putting forward our critique of the whole assessment before some mutually agreed independent party capable of making a judgement as to whether the conclusions of the assessment are justified. If that assessment is right we will be very grateful to have been saved the loss and ignominy which failure on our part to fulfil the contract would involve. If not, the government would want to reconsider. Because of the importance and significance of this matter for Britain, in terms of defence, avionics, jobs, export earnings and national pride, the decision should not be allowed to be

taken against such a background of seeming confusion and disorder.[23]

He might have included GEC's and his own reputation in the list of subjects which would be affected, as had already been noted in the *Telegraph*: 'The loss of the Nimrod contract will not be a serious financial blow for GEC, but its credibility and reputation will be badly dented – as well as that of its managing director, Lord Weinstock.'[24] There were even suggestions that this might be the beginning of the end for the long-serving GEC boss. *Guardian* Financial Editor Hamish McRae suggested that investors had three choices, one of which was 'to get together informally or more formally to help the company rebuild its top management. This would be by far the best solution for GEC. Change is in any case soon to take place. GEC chairman James Prior very much regards his role as seeing through the succession to Lord Weinstock, for he is now approaching retirement.'[25] The feeling in the City was that Weinstock and GEC had been badly damaged by the affair – a view shared by Weinstock himself.

It is clear that Weinstock and GEC were not entirely to blame for the Nimrod fiasco. The whole thing was a political mess from beginning to end, and GEC suffered from bad management by the MoD as well as from various operational difficulties which were not of its own making: the Comet airframe was really too small to be adapted to its new purpose; the MoD made thousands of changes to the specification, resulting in a requirement which was virtually impossible to meet; and, unusually, there was no prime contractor to keep a grip on the project. Nevertheless, critics argued that GEC's failure was at least partly a reflection of the culture which Weinstock had instilled: a culture of fear in middle management, combined with the dominance of finance, which meant that as long as the MoD kept paying, nobody in Marconi was too concerned that the supposedly sophisticated early-warning system could not tell the difference between an enemy helicopter and a double-decker bus.

This last issue of 'cost-plus' contracts – in which the government pays a profit margin on top of agreed costs – was one of the most significant to come out of the Nimrod affair, both for the MoD and for GEC. It had been the standard method of doing business for years, justified by the uncertainties that usually existed when contracts were being signed, because of technological developments which most defence work involved, and allowed contractors to agree costs as the project proceeded and technical issues became clearer. The MoD had to be persuaded that extra costs were justified, but GEC, with Weinstock's insistence on clarity about costs, became absolutely expert at managing this relationship. While the system made some sense, though, it left the MoD lumbered with virtually the entire risk on the contract. Suppliers like GEC knew that they would not only be compensated for all reasonable costs, but would also get a profit margin on top. It was a gravy train, and when the new head of defence procurement, Peter Levene, set about putting an end to it in the early 1980s, the only surprise was that the fixed-price contracts he introduced had not arrived earlier.

Cost-plus habits were so ingrained at Marconi, however, that it took several years, and new management, to begin changing the culture. Weinstock did not seem to understand the dramatic impact the new regime would have on the company, and it would not be until 1995, when Peter Gershon took over, that Marconi seriously began to reassess the way it set about defence contracting. Gershon rammed home the message that the balance of risk had now shifted sharply against the company. Fixed-price contracts meant broadly that any cost overruns came out of the company's profit, rather than adding to it. To Weinstock that merely meant even greater emphasis on cost control and project management, but to Gershon the answer was for Marconi to take less risk in the first place – to identify its key skills and to concentrate on them, buying in more from outside and so laying off risk on those sub-contractors. Weinstock's failure to understand this message in the late 1980s was perhaps an indication that he was beginning to fail to adapt to new conditions, and that his total dominance over the company was preventing new ideas from coming forward.

While he was embroiled in these political battles, Weinstock did not forsake his usual corporate activities; but his political differences with the government again stood in his way. Even as he was struggling in the House of Lords to amend the BT privatisations Bill, he was setting out again on the acquisition trail. GEC had come through the early-1980s recession smaller, but nevertheless fit. The purges of the immediate post-merger period at the end of the sixties had left the company's total British workforce at about 170,000. This had slipped further, but levelled out at around 155,000 in the latter part of the 1970s. By 1984, however, the number of UK employees had dropped to 132,000. Sales and profits had continued to rise each year to 1983, however, driven by the addition of the US businesses and continued growth in the electronics operations. The cash hoard also continued to grow, reaching £1.5 billion by the mid-1980s from only £100 million in 1976, and the company was under increasing pressure to spend the money in one way or another. A relatively small sum (£82 million) was repaid to shareholders as a special dividend in 1982, but Weinstock had better ideas about what to do with the money.

Only a month after revealing that he wanted to make acquisitions, GEC announced in June 1984 that it was having talks with British Aerospace (BAe), the partly-privatised successor to the British Aircraft Corporation, the nationalisation of which had been such a sore point with Weinstock that he was still pursuing his claim for compensation through the European Court. Weinstock had been provoked into action by Thorn-EMI, the combination of the manufacturing business built up by Jules Thorn with Sobell's old music and electrical equipment partner. The group approached British Aerospace in early April 1984 and had friendly discussions for several weeks with its board, as well as sounding out the Ministry of Defence and the Department of Trade and Industry about a merger. Eventually BAe insisted that an announcement about the talks must be made through the stock exchange, which was done on the day of its annual meeting, 15 May. While 'the world at large reacted with some astonishment',[26] Weinstock reacted by joining in the fun. On 1 June it was announced that GEC was also talking to British Aerospace. BAe broke off talks with Thorn-EMI on 12 June, and did the same with GEC a month later, arguing – reasonably enough – that its suitors had had enough time to make up their minds, and should either make an offer or go away. Both declined to make an offer, in GEC's case spurning the chance to squash doubts about its management and strategy which had been rising in the City. As Guy de Jonquieres commented in the *Financial Times*: 'A bid for BAe could reassure those doubters in the City who have recently questioned how sure GEC is about its own future direction. As well as quelling speculation about the fate of its £1.5 billion cash mountain, a takeover would provide GEC with a major new opportunity to prove that its judgement and management talent are as acute as ever.'[27]

The converse was also true: the lack of a bid helped to fuel those doubts, despite GEC's claim that the deal would probably have been blocked by the Ministry of Defence, which wanted to maintain competition among defence suppliers. For many in the City, though, such excuses didn't wash. What came over was a growing lack of nerve, a loss of confidence.

Few in the City know, even to this day, how close GEC came to pulling off more than one dramatic acquisition in this period which would have restored City confidence. On more than one occasion during the mid-1980s, GEC seriously considered mounting a bid for Racal, the smaller electronics company run by Sir Ernest Harrison, with defence interests but also a growing communications arm which eventually became Vodafone. GEC believed it would not have been allowed to make a simple acquisition of the company, since competition policy would have intervened to prevent a powerful single supplier. The merger of Racal's defence business with that of GEC would probably have been acceptable to the MMC, even if the Ministry of Defence could be expected to object to the reduction of competition. But GEC could not see itself being allowed to acquire the communications side of Racal, given its involvement in supplying telecoms equipment.

While a straightforward takeover seemed out of the question, a joint approach with another company might stand a better chance of success. There were two possible partners. STC, which had unwisely bought computer company ICL and had lured Marconi boss Arthur Walsh from GEC to be its chief executive, was keen on the idea of making a joint deal with GEC, but when they approached Weinstock they discovered he was already talking to Cable & Wireless, whose interests include the Mercury telephone network.

A joint bid from GEC and Cable & Wireless came within a whisker of being launched in April 1988. The details of the plan had been agreed between the two partners after four months of negotiations. GEC would have ended up with the industrial electronics and defence businesses and 25 per cent of Vodafone. But at the last minute C&W's advisers, the stockbrokers Cazenove, had to tell them it would not be possible to raise the money necessary to contribute their share of the bid price. GEC's huge cash pile meant it could have financed the bid entirely, even lending C&W the necessary funds, but that would have looked remarkably odd, and was not seriously pursued. Second thoughts were not possible, because Ernest Harrison got wind of the impending attack and announced immediately that 80 per cent of Vodafone would be spun off to give Racal shareholders a bonus investment in this new mobile-phone company. After that, Racal was both less vulnerable and less attractive to a predator.

Racal was not the only target in Weinstock's sights as he tried to spend GEC's cash pile – not to satisfy the critics, whom he largely ignored, but to consolidate the company's market positions and add useful technology. Ironically, one target was Cable & Wireless, with which he had come closest to launching the Racal deal. As with Racal, Weinstock concluded that a joint bid would be essential to win round the MMC, and this time GEC's partner was Siemens. The German electrical giant was keen to enter the UK telecoms market, but nervous of the reception a German bidder would receive. GEC's discussions with Siemens did not get far, but this was another serious acquisition move of which the company's City critics were mostly ignorant. The failure to mount these attacks helped to perpetuate the view of GEC and Weinstock as fading heroes whose time had passed – until further drama intervened. It began with a bid for the old rival Plessey at the end of 1985, but was not consummated until the end of the decade.

In June 1985 a junior industry minister, Lord Lucas, had offered his opinion that GEC and Plessey should merge. In comments which shocked Labour peers, he argued: 'It is necessary to do at least £1 billion turnover to stay in this game. They should be amalgamating or collaborating with other companies to secure export markets.

191

They will not survive at their present turnover on UK-only purchasing.'[28] Nobody outside the House of Lords took much notice, but Lucas was merely giving vent publicly to what seemed obvious to many privately. Plessey, under Sir John and Michael Clark, had seemed to be successful following its defeat by GEC for the hand of English Electric in 1968. The Clark brothers had been criticised by some, including Weinstock, for failing to build on their father's success in creating the company, although they had invested heavily in modern plant and product development and diversified through acquisition. But several of the acquisitions had not proved successful, notably the US telecoms business Stromberg-Carlson, bought in 1982 but a loss-maker ever since, vindicating Weinstock's repeated refusal to buy it. Plessey remained primarily a telecoms company, and its profits stemmed largely from telephone exchanges sold to British Telecom. Profits were clearly going to be much harder to come by with a privatised BT, and Plessey's new electronic exchange, known as 'System X', had already proved problematic.

The development of System X was a classic case of poor government–industry relations, the telecoms equivalent of Nimrod, with government blaming industry for delays and cost overruns, and industrialists such as Weinstock complaining that BT's specification made it impossible to sell the equipment abroad and thus recoup development spending. The idea was born in the mid-1960s, and a joint body was set up in 1968 bringing together the manufacturers and the Post Office, which was then responsible for telecoms. But it took five years to evolve the concept of System X, and another four years of lengthy negotiations before the first contracts were placed, with the work split 40:40:20 between GEC, Plessey and STC. Echoing the Nimrod story, major design changes were introduced in April 1980, three years after the first contracts were placed. The first exchange went into service in July 1981, but the loose-knit consortium was riven by disagreement and hampered by lack of clear leadership, just as with the Nimrod fiasco. BT finally lost patience and warned the manufacturers that it would buy from abroad if they could not sort out their differences, and proposed that the way to do that was to give just one company overall responsibility. The ensuing squabble was sorted out only by the intervention of Mrs Thatcher's industrial troubleshooter, the head of P&O Jeffrey Sterling. His efforts resulted in GEC being left only as a sub-contractor on the main development project, despite Weinstock's direct appeal to the Prime Minister, and Plessey having overall responsibility. STC dropped out.

Despite Plessey having won the senior role in System X, the logic of putting its telecom activities together with those of GEC was compelling even to Sir John Clark, and had been discussed inconclusively between the two companies several times since 1983.[29] A merger would give Plessey the scale it lacked, boost GEC's telecoms business, and create a UK telecoms player large enough to compete globally.

The Clarks did not want to be subsumed within GEC, however, and as GEC neared the end of its vain battle to retain the Nimrod contract, Sir John made new overtures to Weinstock about buying GEC's share of the System X business. Weinstock responded by making a tentative approach on 3 December 1985, suggesting he might be interested in buying Plessey for £1.2 billion. It did not take the Clarks long to tell him they were not interested, and instead they made a firm offer to buy GEC's interest in System X. On 23 December GEC made a formal takeover offer, but the battle was interrupted by an almost inevitable reference to the MMC, ironically the very body whose intervention, had it been sanctioned by the Labour government in 1968, might have delivered English Electric to Plessey.

The MMC concluded, after six months' deliberation, that the benefits of merger for System X were outweighed by the loss of competition in other fields, notably defence electronics, where Plessey was particularly strong in radar. The Ministry of Defence had spoken, and its voice was loud enough to stop GEC's bid. Only one member of the MMC team accepted the Weinstock line that the dangers of monopoly were balanced by the monopolist purchasers, BT and the MoD. Weinstock was blocked, but at least he had acted, and it would not be long before his acquisitive instincts were satisfied, at least in part.

The Plessey episode once more brought out the litigant in Weinstock. Takeover battles typically involve strong language, but Plessey's outspokenness on GEC's technological record went too far for him. On 19 January 1986 GEC sued Plessey for libel over statements in its defence document which Weinstock, in typically colourful language, said 'would have done credit to Dr Goebbels'. GEC's Chairman Jim Prior said Plessey's defence painted a caricature of the company and 'a fanciful idealisation of Plessey'. GEC complained initially to the Takeover Panel, the voluntary City body which rules on such disputes, but the panel was unable to get the combatants to agree, and an outraged Weinstock insisted on taking the matter to the courts. GEC also issued a circular to Plessey shareholders, superfluous because of the bid's reference to the MMC, but necessary in Weinstock's view to protect GEC's reputation against Sir John Clark's allegations. The circular told the Plessey investors: 'The Plessey directors have presented an image of GEC so unreal as to call into question their own credibility – even on matters affecting Plessey itself.' It contained an almost word-by-word rebuttal of Plessey's arguments, as well as answering the more substantial criticisms of its research spending, its internationalisation and even its financial record. The writ was finally settled almost three years later, with Plessey paying undisclosed damages and costs and apologising. But the doubts about Weinstock's regime lingered, and were to be heard many times during his remaining years in charge, with critics accusing him particularly of failing to spend on research and development.

During the Plessey affair Weinstock also launched a furious battle with Professor John Stopford, an academic at London Business School who had written disparagingly about GEC and whose criticisms of Weinstock's management style had been used in the Plessey defence document which had so enraged him. Stopford was astonished to find himself on the receiving end of what he described as 'hate faxes' as Weinstock bombarded him with invective. A writ followed, but Stopford responded by counter-suing Weinstock, as well as by launching his own barrage of faxes. Eventually he suggested that they meet at Stanhope Gate.

When they met, Weinstock, who was accompanied by technical director Derek Roberts, assailed Stopford with a tirade which included accusations of an anti-Semitic campaign. Stopford, however, had taken advice from colleagues who knew Weinstock well. He had been told that if he kept his temper and survived the opening attack he would be able to continue to a more reasonable discussion. And so it proved. Having weathered the initial storm, he began to argue his case, which was essentially that GEC had not invested enough to ensure its long-term development. Unsurprisingly, the two men failed to agree, but the meeting ended on more or less level terms, after Weinstock had asserted that he would never turn down a decent investment proposal. Stopford retorted by asking how many of GEC's managers would believe that. After some muted consultation with Roberts, Weinstock replied: 'About half – and they are the good ones.'

Weinstock used the defeats over Plessey and Nimrod as a lever to try to energise his managers. In a confidential memorandum written on New Year's Eve 1986, he set out a manifesto for British industry as well as a call to arms to transform GEC. He began by acknowledging that 1986 had been a bad year, encompassing the rejection of the bid for Plessey as well as the Nimrod affair, but set out a robust defence of the group's performance. Profits had been stable, he pointed out, and produced a return on equity of 17.5 per cent over three years. GEC's older businesses had seen profits decline by a total of £250 million, but that had been replaced by new business. 'Not bad for a slumbering giant,' he noted. Research and development spending had also been increased, without which profits would have increased by £120 million, although the long-term well-being of the company would have been damaged. And there was a defence of the 'cash mountain', which, Weinstock pointed out, was lent to the government in the form of gilt-edged stock, or to industry through the banking system. 'It will stay like that until suitable opportunities are identified for its redeployment,' he stated defiantly.

The bulk of this year-end message centred on the Plessey affair, and the role of competition. Weinstock argued that taking over Plessey would have reduced costs, and so benefited Britain.

> There is a basic disagreement between those who believe that what is best for Britain is the mindless pursuit of competition for its own sake, and those who think, as I do, that competition policy must reflect the facts that:
> (I) it is Great Britain which is the real competitor against

other countries, so that British firms must not be put in a worse position by the British government than their foreign rivals,

(II) where competition at home is superficial, or apparent rather than real, it costs the nation nothing to 'reduce' it in order to increase international competitiveness, provided there are adequate safeguards against exploitation,

(III) a measure of trust and co-operation between government and major firms is necessary to enable British industry to hold its place in world markets and to provide the technology and training without which British industry will suffer.

In my belief the decision to stop us from buying Plessey was wrong and so was the decision to abandon Nimrod . . . That said, we should not seek to escape our portion of the blame, not least for not refusing to continue with a task which we must, or should, have know was underfunded and could not be brought to a successful conclusion without a major change of direction . . .

I would like to see in 1987 an end to the carping comment we have suffered recently, the year in which GEC is again generally recognised for what it is, a progressive national asset of inestimable value. To re-establish that recognition we must demonstrate more clearly that we are on the offensive to exploit our opportunities.

Weinstock wasted little time in following up this message. In another memo on 30 January 1987 he set out an ambitious growth target and made it absolutely clear to his executives that GEC was ready to make acquisitions:

We need to do more to expand into areas related to our existing businesses and to increase GEC's presence in territories where we have not been as strong as we would have wished, particularly in the United States and certain European countries . . . operating units should be more active in seeking out acquisition opportunities and should not be diffident about bringing them to Stanhope Gate.

The target at which the company should aim is to double

by the year ending 31 March 1990 the level of profits achieved in the current year. Acquisitions and joint ventures could make an important contribution.

Plessey was still the prime acquisition target, but a new GEC offensive was delayed by a peace initiative from the other side: following the blocked bid in 1986, Sir John Clark was soon back with a merger proposal. The logic of combining the telecom operations was still overwhelming, and in the autumn of 1987 he approached GEC. At first Weinstock assumed Clark wanted merely to put together the public switching operations which System X was central to, but to his surprise Plessey was talking about a complete merger of both companies' telecoms operations. The result was the creation, in March 1988, of GEC Plessey Telecommunications (GPT). The new company, owned 50 per cent by Plessey and 50 per cent by GEC, with board representation similarly split between the two former rivals, was a more substantial player than the separate interests of either participant. It achieved the objective of a single, major UK telecoms company that had been pursued by Weinstock for several years, although it was still relatively small by the standards of the increasingly global market.

This was by no means the end of what was seen by many as a feud between Weinstock and Clark, which erupted into full-scale war before long. The board of GPT was at odds almost from the start, as Plessey's Stephen Walls revealed during the ensuing battle.[30] And no sooner had the company been formed than Weinstock was talking to Siemens about a joint takeover of Plessey. Weinstock's new-found love of joint ventures was based on the difficulty of GEC being allowed to do anything on its own, which also saw Weinstock in talks during this period with both American GE and the French electrical company Alsthom. GEC and Siemens were no strangers to each other. They had had close dealings when Weinstock wanted to rescue AEG in 1983, and subsequently they had talked about the possibility of mounting a joint bid for Cable & Wireless.

Within eight months of GPT's birth, GEC and Siemens struck. On 16 November 1988 they announced that they had created GEC

Siemens, a jointly held company, which would buy Plessey for £1.7 billion and break it up between the two partners. This was a neat attempt to circumvent the objections which had prevented GEC's previous bid for Plessey from proceeding, and it also satisfied the strategic objectives of both GEC and Siemens for international expansion. Siemens had long wanted to get into the British market, while the two companies' agreement would include GEC acquiring a half share in Siemens' defence business. But it was inevitable that the plan would once again be scrutinised by competition authorities, so a long-drawn-out tussle was anticipated from the start.

Sir John Clark had no intention of waiting for the Ministry of Defence or the MMC to save what was still essentially his family company. He immediately attempted to forestall Weinstock by going to court, seeking an injunction to prevent the bid going ahead on two grounds: that GEC had agreed with the government at the time of the previous bid not to buy more than 15 per cent of Plessey, and that the joint bid was contrary to European law. It was a long shot, and only managed to delay the battle. As some observers noted, however, recourse to the courts was unusual in Britain, and possibly reflected the American experience of Stephen Walls, the tough finance director recruited little more than a year earlier and now the heir apparent to Sir John Clark. The *Guardian* observed: 'Do not be too surprised if other tactics familiar on Wall Street are deployed: a management buyout or a bid by Plessey for GEC.'

But first came the traditional cut and thrust of the bid battle, and the by now similarly traditional intervention by the government. Clark responded to the threat of losing his company in characteristically pugnacious fashion. Introducing his defence document in a letter to shareholders on 6 January 1989, he wrote: 'In order to get round the well-founded objections of the Monopolies and Mergers Commission it [GEC] has concocted a bid with Siemens of West Germany, a most appropriate partner: not just a conglomerate but a poorly performing one.' Two days later the bid was referred to the MMC, which began a brief rerun of its investigation three years previously.

In the meantime, on Saturday 7 January, these two routine events were completely overshadowed by an astonishing new development. Plessey's merchant bank, Lazards, announced to a stunned City that it was putting together a consortium to bid more than £7 billion for GEC. This was seen as an example of what had become known as the 'Pacman defence', after the popular computer game in which the victim turns on its prey. The manoeuvre had been used occasionally in the US, but this was the first time it had been tried in Britain. On top of that novelty, Plessey's bid for GEC would be the largest takeover in British history, by a large margin. It put the financial and business world in a frenzy.

In fact the defensive nature of the manoeuvre was opportunistic. Lazards had been toying with the notion of Plessey mounting such an assault for more than a year, believing it could capitalise on City dissatisfaction with GEC and with Weinstock in particular. The deal had merely been waiting for the right moment, and Plessey's plight had provided that. It pipped Rothschilds, which had also been trying to put together a deal involving the American General Electric.

The *Sunday Telegraph* described Lazards' counter-attack as 'an amazingly ambitious plan'. Its sister paper, the *Daily Telegraph*, believed it would be 'the biggest and most explosive takeover battle in the City's history'. The *Independent* called it 'the most spectacular bid ever attempted in the UK'. Weinstock was less extravagant. He told the *Sunday Telegraph*: 'We have heard the mutterings of the medium. Now we must wait to see if any ectoplasm appears.' Using a different metaphor to convey his confidence to the *Sunday Times*, he said: 'We will have to look at the rabbit before we decide how to shoot it.' His chairman, Lord Prior, was no less eloquent in action. He promptly resigned from the board of Barclays Bank (of which Plessey was a customer), on the grounds that it was part of the consortium and was engaged in drumming up £3.5 billion of loan capital to finance the bid.

A company, called Metsun, had been set up to make the bid, code-named 'George', and a chairman with impeccable credentials had been recruited. Sir John Cuckney, reputedly a former intelligence officer, had risen to the highest levels in industry and finance. He was about to retire as chairman of Westland, the helicopter company which had been at the centre of the political storm that saw Michael Heseltine leave the government. He was also chairman of Royal Insurance and of the venture capital group 3i, and was well known in many boardrooms around the business world. He also had no love for Weinstock, whom he despised for his rudeness. Cuckney had once walked out of a private lunch with the GEC boss because he regarded his brusque behaviour as unacceptable.

When Lazards broke cover with its Metsun plan, it was not to announce the takeover bid but only to reveal that the company had been set up 'to formulate a proposal which may or may not lead to an offer'. Behind the City jargon was an admission that the consortium was short of firm commitments from heavy hitters. Plessey was obviously a member, but while other electronics companies were mentioned, none had signed on the dotted line. One potential partner was STC, chaired by the man who claimed credit for winning AEI, Lord Keith, and run by Arthur Walsh, a long-serving Marconi executive who had left GEC on bad terms with Weinstock shortly after being promoted to the board. Another was the French electronics company Thomson-CSF, and there were suggestions that the US giant General Electric, once the hidden hand behind much of the UK electrical industry, might also get involved. Lazards did not have much time to win commitments, however, and as the week wore on following the bank's amazing announcement, it became clear that making the bid would be more difficult than announcing it.

Weinstock and his colleagues at Stanhope Gate were fairly calm in the face of this threatened reversal of roles. They were confident they could fight off Lazards, and Weinstock concluded that even if they could not, they would at least get a good price for their shareholders. But it was a tense time for those who were less able than Weinstock to distance themselves from the consequences of a takeover. For a few days it seemed that GEC would be on the receiving end of a deadly blow. GE's revered boss, 'Neutron Jack' Welch, flew in from America, and the streets around GEC's Stanhope Gate headquarters, where many of London's top hotels are situated, were briefly buzzing with activity as the negotiations wound on. The unsightly GEC building is within a prospectus' throw of the Dorchester, Grosvenor House, the Intercontinental and the Four Seasons, where representatives of GE, Thomson and other potential bidders met to try to put a deal together. Participants rushed from one hotel to another, almost within earshot of Lord Weinstock.

But they were not the only ones negotiating, and Friday 13 January turned out to be unlucky for Plessey and its Metsun partners. On that day Weinstock announced that he had lured the most powerful potential member of the consortium, GE, into a deal. The two companies would merge their domestic appliance operations in Europe – essentially meaning the UK – and their medical electronics activities, and GE would also participate in GEC's planned joint venture with Alsthom of France in power generation. It was a master-stroke, which effectively killed off the Metsun consortium in an instant. Without GE it was little more than a Plessey defence team, and a pretty weak one. Metsun and Lazards put a brave face on it, but by Thursday of the following week they had to admit that the brave plan was stillborn. Indeed, it had been ill-conceived, as the *Daily Telegraph* cruelly explained, while noting that even the victorious Lord Weinstock had not escaped entirely scot-free:

> An extraordinary fairy tale – GEC and the bid that never was – ended predictably enough in farce yesterday. Metsun, the £2 off-the-shelf company which planned to bid £7 billion for the group, put out an absurd press release saying it had decided not to proceed with its offer. This time the notepaper read Barings rather than Lazards, but it is impressive that both banks have managed to keep a straight face right through the performance.
>
> Playing the Brian Rix role, Lazards has lost the financial equivalent of its trousers . . . Lazards should have known that it takes more than a good idea to make a £7 billion takeover bid work . . . As for Lord Weinstock, the affair has given him a new lease of life and he will doubtless carry on with renewed vigour. Yet as a shareholder suggested at yesterday's extraordinary general meeting to approve the Plessey bid, it is time that GEC coped with the management succession in the measured way that world-class companies such as ICI and Shell do.[31]

Weinstock had out-manoeuvred his enemies to escape the bungled attack from Metsun which also saw off others, such as Rothschild, who might have contemplated taking GEC on. In September 1989 the MMC duly reported on GEC's bid for Plessey. They found that this time, subject to certain conditions, the competition questions had been answered satisfactorily, leaving Plessey defence-less. GEC duly completed a trio of joint ventures in power systems, domestic appliances and telecoms, giving it new footholds on the Continent and effectively barring any future attempt to break up the group, which would be bound to fail without the approval of its joint-venture partners. This defensive aspect, however, prevented GEC's spurt of dramatic action from silencing its critics, for whom the series of deals might otherwise have been an answer to their pleas for action. There were still plenty of people in the City and elsewhere in industry, including in GEC, who bemoaned Wein-stock's apparent lack of adventure, courage and vision, and the consequent failure to use the cash which had so concerned Mrs Thatcher.

Weinstock never managed to heal the rift between himself and the Prime Minister, despite a peace-offering in the form of one of GEC's rare corporate donations to the Conservative Party in 1987 and a lengthy article supporting the government in the run-up to that year's general election. As a peer he did not have a vote, but he made it absolutely clear where he would have put his cross if he had:

> If I had to vote in 1987 it wouldn't take long to decide to opt for Mrs Thatcher, and another Conservative govern-ment ... There ought to be positive reasons for sending Mrs Thatcher back to Downing Street for a third term. There are, and I believe that to be so notwithstanding painful disagreements in the past few years with the present government on quite substantial issues. Whatever it has got wrong, the government has got a lot of things right, and many of those things are fundamental for the country's future well-being.[32]

He went on to show his usual lack of political judgement, pre-dicting that Liberal–SDP Alliance leader David Owen would eventually emerge as the best alternative to Thatcher, as well as tempering his enthusiasm for modern Conservatism with praise for the post-war Labour government of Clement Attlee and predicting a unifying influence from Mrs Thatcher's third term:

Mrs Thatcher has been an authoritative leader of government for eight years. Even if you don't like everything she has done, it is difficult to deny that she has successfully challenged harmful national assumptions, predominant in Britain since the war, about the structure of society, and has swept away some important obstacles to progress. The character of her administration has been more decisively different from a grey average than any since the Attlee government of 1945 ... It is true that Mrs Thatcher has moved the centre around quite a bit, but I believe and expect that her next government will turn out to be far more of a force for national unity than many middle-wayers imagine.

In the event Margaret Thatcher departed in 1990, having fallen foul of the European question which Weinstock had negotiated successfully in his own field. He would continue at the head of GEC for many more years, but with every year that passed the question of the succession, as the *Daily Telegraph* had pointed out, became more and more pressing.

It had grown in significance with the arrival at GEC of Weinstock's son Simon, which led to a widely held view that Weinstock was intent on creating a dynasty. Simon was highly regarded at S.G. Warburg, and enjoyed his corporate finance work there, but his father constantly tried to persuade him to join what he – perhaps subconsciously – regarded as the family business. Simon eventually caved in and joined Weinstock at Stanhope Gate in 1983.

If Simon was ever to qualify to step into his father's shoes he should have moved out of head office and run one of the group's operating units. But Weinstock kept him at his side, at the same time harbouring the ambition that he would nevertheless take over one day. To that end, Simon became commercial director in 1987, but his appointment to the board at the age of thirty-five, with no operating experience, dismayed many within GEC. His role as heir apparent was to cause continuing disquiet among investing institutions, and became a running sore during the final years of Weinstock's reign.

Simon's was not the only arrival among the top management

team during this period, as Weinstock maintained his customary carousel in the boardroom, while attempting to satisfy critics of his tight and solitary management style. The early 1980s had seen the arrival on the board of Malcolm Bates, Sara Morrison and Lord Rees-Mogg, all of whom, like Simon, were to be close to him for the rest of his tenure. With the retirement of David Lewis in 1982, the nature of the long-standing top team was substantially changed, although Sir Kenneth Bond did not retire until 1990, and he remained closer and more significant to Weinstock than any other member of the board.

Lord Nelson retired in 1982, giving way briefly to Lord Carrington, an old-style Tory who was another refugee from Mrs Thatcher. He had resigned as Foreign Secretary in 1982 following the Argentinian invasion of the Falkland Islands, and seemed a sensible replacement for the long-serving Nelson. Carrington had no connection with the electrical industry, but he had been in business before his lengthy political career. As a director of the mining company Rio Tinto Zinc he had built up excellent contacts around the world, although mainly in areas such as Africa which were of little use to GEC. But as a minister in every Conservative government since Churchill's last, he had superb connections in Whitehall and Westminster – always a key consideration for Weinstock. As chairman of GEC, however, Carrington was not a success. He did not get on with Weinstock and never settled to the role Weinstock allotted to him, of travelling the world as a sort of super-salesman. He left within two years, and the period was to merit only a couple of lines in his autobiography.[33]

Following Carrington's departure, however, GEC recruited another member of the 'wet' wing of the Conservative Party in Jim, later Lord, Prior. He took over in 1984 and, against most expectations, proved an excellent choice. A bluff farmer with virtually no business experience, Prior also had substantial experience in government, though not as much as Carrington and not in the departments which mattered most to GEC. But after a rocky start he settled into a satisfactory relationship with Weinstock, and was ultimately instrumental in managing the succession in the mid-1990s.

As well as the boardroom comings and goings, Weinstock

attempted to change GEC's management style. The managing directors of his operating companies had long complained about their inability to become involved in the group's management. Each unit was treated separately, each managing director was responsible only for the destiny of that unit, and there was precious little horizontal communication around the group from unit to unit. The rationale for this was quite clear: given the past he inherited at both GEC and AEI, Weinstock was terrified of corporate bureaucracy, and was determined from the start that managers should not be able to blame anybody else for poor results. Secondly, he could see no need for unit managers to look beyond their units. If anybody needed to do that it would be done at Stanhope Gate, primarily by himself and Bond.

But by the mid-1970s, when Weinstock had imposed his methods and taken the group in hand, many managers wanted a further challenge, and part of that challenge was to become more involved in determining the direction of the group as a whole. Some limited attempts had been made to satisfy such demands. Bill Morgan, the former head of GEC's motors business, had been brought into Stanhope Gate, for example, but had found himself neutered and soon left. In the early 1980s several other executives were appointed to the board, but given that the board only met four times a year and was not accustomed to discussing strategic issues, their involvement was barely raised beyond their own immediate areas of responsibility.

In 1985, however, Weinstock bowed to demands for more involvement and a more collegiate style by setting up a Board of Management. No explanation for this was given in the annual report – a list of the twenty-seven members was merely printed alongside the board of directors. They included the executive directors, key corporate executives such as the heads of finance and press and publicity, and the bosses of the main operating subsidiaries. The first meeting of the new Board of Management was a disaster. There were two problems – far too many members, but more substantially, Weinstock as the chairman.

He is not chairman material. His patience is paper-thin unless he is closely interested in a subject. He has no interest in a balanced debate, nor any recognition of the need for people to air their views, and he is uncomfortable in anything other than small meetings. The first item on the agenda of the first meeting was investment in microchip production, a subject dear to the heart of technical director Derek Roberts. Roberts had prepared twenty slides to make his argument for more investment, but Weinstock hates such formal presentations. As one attendee recalled: 'He put the first slide up and Arnold tore into him about the nature of the slide and how many more there were. He spent two hours on the first slide, had a sandwich and went home.'

The meetings did not improve much after that. About the only substantial discussions the board held were on how to celebrate the company's centenary in 1986. Otherwise, as one Stanhope Gate insider described it: 'Weinstock used it as a vehicle to attack, effectively, the man who sat opposite him. He would focus on somebody in trouble, whose accounts he had just read, and in front of all those people he would go through the accounts and absolutely tear this bloke to shreds – so much so that the meeting barely got started. He didn't really want to know what all these bastards thought, anyway.'[34]

The Management Board met every other month for about eighteen months, then fell into disuse and was eventually abandoned before the end of the 1980s. It was the end of any attempt to force change on the way the group was run. There were some specific changes – finance director David Newlands introduced an element of strategic discussion into budget meetings, for example – but after the failure of the Management Board, there was no serious attempt to attack the compartmentalisation which characterised Weinstock's approach. The board's failure reflected a weakness in Weinstock, who was never able to transcend the small-business, total-control approach he had brought with him from Radio & Allied, and which had been so successful in his early years at GEC. But it also reflected weakness among his senior colleagues and non-executive directors, who could have brought about the changes which were widely seen as necessary. The victory over Plessey and the defeat of the Metsun consortium, plus the joint-venture deals, had left Weinstock in an unassailable position within the company.

# CHAPTER SEVEN

# *New World Order*

ARNOLD WEINSTOCK entered the 1990s, his fourth decade at the helm of a public company, in good spirits. He had seen off the marauders, in the shape of the poorly contrived Metsun takeover attempt; forged a series of new business alliances designed to equip GEC better for the emerging globalised marketplace; and had sufficient cash in hand and capital orders on the books of his group to ride out the deep recession ahead with aplomb. At the age of sixty-five he had once again confounded his critics and demonstrated, certainly to his own satisfaction, that he had the energy, foresight and skill to carry on as managing director of Britain's biggest manufacturing enterprise.

Weinstock felt comfortable enough with the world to engage in a rare bout of triumphalism, boasting in a 1990 New Year press interview that the success of his international strategy had exceeded even his own expectations: 'Three years ago, I said I would do three things to expand internationally. The only difference was that I did four.'[1] The four deals, completed in 1989, were the joint takeover of Plessey with Siemens; the creation of the GEC–Alsthom power subsidiary; the link with Jack Welch's General Electric of America to sell consumer products; and a joint satellite venture with Matra of France.

As had been the case some thirty years earlier, when he put together GEC from the remnants of Britain's poorly run electrical engineering industry, Weinstock had seen a global future and had taken action. His hand may have been partly forced by the need for a defensive strategy, but he had come to recognise that in a changing world order national champions were no longer enough. Those companies which insisted on looking inwards for their markets would wither and decline; those which took a long-term, global view of the world would succeed. For much of his time at the head of GEC Weinstock had been happy enough to pursue large-scale government civilian and defence contracts. But the old order was transforming rapidly. The end of the Cold War would mean a dramatic ratcheting-down of the defence budgets of the more mature industrial powers like the United States, Britain and France, which would no longer be involved in an arms race with the Soviet Union. Defence contractors could no longer look to NATO and the Western alliance for their markets.

The contraction of defence spending would also lead to the consolidation of defence industries, a trend highlighted by a series of mega-mergers in the United States. Among the most dramatic of these was the emergence of Lockheed Martin as the world's largest defence contractor. In August 1994 the military aircraft maker Lockheed and the missile manufacturer Martin Marietta would merge. Just a year earlier Martin Marietta had bought GE Aerospace for $3 billion, and at much the same time Lockheed had bought the fighter aircraft interests of General Dynamics. The merged company would make a bid for the New York-based defence electronics and aerospace group Loral, which would create a $30 billion defence giant.[2] On a similar scale, in December 1996 two monoliths of the US aerospace industry, Boeing and McDonnell Douglas, would choose to merge, creating a new aviation powerhouse, under the Boeing banner, with $48 billion of revenues and employing more than two hundred thousand people. These were not the only examples of US military contractors agglomerating so as to meet the circumstances of dramatically lower Pentagon spending after the largesse of the Reagan/Bush years. The concentration of the industry was positively encouraged by the Pentagon, and nodded through by the anti-trust authorities. At a dinner with defence company executives in 1993 which has been called 'the last supper' by Lockheed chairman Norman Augustine, the US Defense Secretary William Perry urged further consolidation on the contractors. Since then there have been no fewer than two dozen mergers and acquisitions among the significant US defence players. There was little alternative. President Clinton's administration, which came to power in 1992 and was re-elected in 1996, saw the Pentagon budget as bloated and a relatively soft target in the effort to lower the federal budget deficit and focus the economy on civilian technologies.

If European companies were to have any prospect of competing in the global arms market with the new American giants, they too would have to consolidate. In Britain the Thatcherite policies of the 1980s, which had sought to bring a measure of price sensitivity to the UK defence industry through competitive bidding, were suddenly looking wrong-headed. Britain needed its national champions if it was to have any prospect of competing with the Americans in the new marketplace, as Weinstock was painfully aware. He had long wanted a takeover of the defence interests of British Aerospace, if only as a means of protecting one of the largest buyers of GEC electronic equipment: 'I would have liked to have put the defence businesses together,' he has said.[3] But there was acute awareness at GEC that the Nimrod fiasco and GEC's alliance with Michael Heseltine during the Westland affair were still sources of rancour inside the Conservative government.

Weinstock knew that even defence companies built around the concept of national champions would not be sufficiently robust to compete in the increasingly global world. GEC would have to make alliances across Europe's boundaries, as well as in Britain itself, if it was to prosper after the end of the Cold War. The international deals of 1989 were an important step in the right direction as far as the company's civilian businesses were concerned, but organising the defence industries for the twenty-first century would become a dominant theme for Weinstock in the 1990s.

This was not an easy task. Defence cooperation in the new Europe was still rudimentary. Moreover, many of the main Continental contractors were state-owned. Those which were not suffered from complex and incestuous share structures which made simple takeovers difficult to achieve. Unscrambling these complications, while not beyond Weinstock's still considerable artistry, was a task which would become more difficult for him as each year passed because of his advancing age and the pressure on him to ease his way out of the executive role at GEC.

The marketplace was also changing. Whereas growth in the industrial economies barely expanded in the 1990s – by 2.5 per cent per annum – the emerging market economies were growing at two or three times that rate. This meant a shift in emphasis from Europe, North America and Japan to up-and-coming areas. By far the most significant development was the opening up to Western commerce of the Asia-Pacific region, including China and the Indian subcontinent, which had an insatiable appetite for Western defence and capital equipment, as well as consumer goods. The end of the Cold War and the resolution of some long-running regional disputes opened up new areas to trade and investment, ranging from Southern Africa, to the transition economies of Eastern Europe, to the Middle East.

Geo-economics increasingly dominated a diplomatic agenda which had in the past been driven by geo-politics alone. The free movement of foreign capital into these countries through the bond markets, the banking system and stock markets would also make it easier for countries previously excluded from the liberalised economic system to benefit from the defence equipment, technologies and power systems available on the global markets. In heavy engineering GEC–Alsthom was able to compete effectively in the supply of power systems to the emerging markets.

In much the same way as Weinstock had over the decades exploited his network of political contacts to assist in securing defence, telecoms and power orders in the domestic market, he now set about using the same kind of networks to gain British exporters access to the prize overseas markets. Figures like his chairman James Prior, who had proved a useful conduit to the British political establishment, were now required to do the same abroad. Prior, and later Richard Needham, a former Trade Minister who joined the GEC board in October 1995 amid controversy over his near-direct move from government to industry, were as likely to be in Beijing, New Delhi or Hong Kong as attending board meetings at Stanhope Gate.

Weinstock himself had little time for global business travel. He was bad-tempered enough when required, for ceremonial purposes, to visit one of his domestic plants, and was positively unpleasant to be with when his services were needed overseas. La Scala and the Salzburg Festival were one thing, but trailing around obscure Texas factories or hobnobbing at the Chinese court were another.

James Prior was philosophical about the job Weinstock had assigned him:

> I had this job of sort of opening doors all around the world, and that was a role that Arnold never wanted to do. He liked to stay here the whole time. So my role was very much to get out. I guess it's how we developed, I think, such a good relationship, because we both had our particular roles to give to the company, and that brought us much closer together in the end. I think chairmen have to chase around the world. The world has changed. Chairmen here were rather grown-up characters, and I think that changes as business changed.
>
> I think both in China and South-East Asia, in particular, and to some extent in the Middle East as well, we were able to unlock doors in the last few years that otherwise couldn't have been opened in any other way. And that has been very beneficial to British industry. Let's face it, although we go out and get the orders, a lot of the work is not done by GEC companies. It's done by many other British companies, so I think it is good for British industry. Arnold is criticised a lot, but he has brought a sort of subjective, objective approach to British industry and a hell of a lot of business.[4]

The reshaped group after the 1989 series of defensive alliances bought Weinstock and GEC time after the criticisms of previous years. In 1990, when many corporations globally were starting to suffer after the boom of the late 1980s, GEC recorded profits of more than a billion pounds for the first time in its history. While several other favoured companies of the 1980s slipped badly, including British Aerospace, GEC sailed on through the recession relatively unruffled. Profits did slip in 1991 and 1992, but that was at a time when it seemed that much of British industry was doomed as a result of high interest rates, the squeeze produced by British membership of the Exchange Rate Mechanism, the collapse of domestic demand and recession in many of the Group of Seven countries. GEC emerged comparatively untarnished, its net cash resources strengthening year by year. The reaction in the financial press was unusually generous, *The Times* declaring in December 1991:

> Lord Weinstock may not be the City's favourite business-man, but the cautious cash-conscious habits of the GEC's long-standing managing director certainly pay off in hard times. The apparently defensive alliances formed with Alcatel-Alsthom and Siemens have spread its market in crucial investment goods at a time when the British economy has come under increasing pressure. The joint venture with its American equivalent (GE) in British domestic appliances has held up well through the introduction of new products and, despite continuing restructuring costs, GEC is generating cash strongly.[5]

However, the commentator, like others, could not resist a side-swipe at GEC's reluctance to resolve the problem of who would follow Weinstock at the helm, and noted that 'management succession remains an unresolved issue'. Although Weinstock had again demonstrated that he could deliver, the financial community remained deeply concerned as to what would follow his era.

This was not based simply on animosity to the Weinstock style, although there was an element of that from some writers and analysts who had over the years felt the sharper end of his tongue. There was a feeling that Weinstock's highly personalised style of management, dependent on a small cadre of advisers and executive directors rather than boardroom government, was out of keeping with the rising interest in corporate governance and the increasing demands by shareholders for more say in how companies ran themselves. Moreover, behind much the unfavourable feeling was the belief that Weinstock intended his son Simon to eventually succeed him as managing director of GEC. This was an ambition which Weinstock would nurture long after it had become clear to his closest colleagues, major shareholders and the City that it should not happen. The succession issue would become the dominant theme of Weinstock's last years at GEC, and would in many respects colour the assessments of his industrial legacy.

\*    \*    \*

The sweeping industrial partnerships which Weinstock put together in 1989 demonstrated that although not a convinced European, he was one of the few British industrialists to recognise that in a global marketplace standing alone – except in some niche sectors – was no longer an option. However, the European defence industry presented a far more difficult challenge for GEC than the power-systems market. In order to provide a credible counterbalance to the fast-consolidating US military contractors, a pan-European defence structure was required. Some civil alliances, like Airbus Industries, have developed, but the degree of integration among the great European aerospace manufacturers has been limited, the level of transparency poor and the emergence of a corporate identity on trans-European lines has proved difficult. In contrast to the purposeful efforts made by many countries to forge a European monetary union, setting aside large elements of national sovereignty in favour of currency, monetary and fiscal policy, the nations of Europe found it difficult to find common ground on foreign policy and defence issues. Individual states, particularly the United Kingdom and France, jealously guarded their role on the geo-political stage, and this national determinism has expressed itself in countries' determination to maintain control over their own defence manufacturers.

The cultural bias against defence cooperation was compounded by the fact that many defence contractors, particularly in France, were still owned by the state. It would be necessary to disentangle them from state control, introduce free-market efficiencies and integrate them with overseas counterparts all at once if Europe was not to find itself overwhelmed by the new breed of American mega-contractors.

An opportunity for Weinstock to demonstrate his command of the new European defence realities was to come in January 1990. One of the few trans-European defence projects was the European Fighter Aircraft (EFA). But the production of the plane, a potential successor to the highly successful British Aerospace Tornado fighter and a rival to the range of fighters coming off US production lines, was by no means a certainty. Although the UK was keen on such a project, which would spread the development costs among the defence industries of its European partners, the Germans were less than convinced. Their defence minister Gerhard Stoltenberg expressed fears that uncertainty over the financial future of Ferranti, the British firm with the best radar technology, could damage confidence in and planning for the fighter. Ferranti, which had never enjoyed the strongest financial controls, ran into serious difficulties in the autumn of 1989 when it was discovered that its takeover of International Signal & Control (ISC), a Washington DC-based defence group founded by the wayward entrepreneur James Guerin, was a chimera, ISC's accounts concealing widespread fraud and malfeasance. Before long a gaping hole of £215 million had opened up in Ferranti's accounts, threatening its survival as an independent company.

None of this came as any great surprise to Weinstock and his colleagues in GEC's inner cabinet. Before landing Ferranti as a parent, Guerin had first approached GEC as a potential partner. The deal was examined by Weinstock's number two, the deputy managing director Malcolm Bates, who had the good sense to send Guerin packing after he failed to disclose details of ISC's main customers.

Ferranti's troubles could not have come at a worse time for the British government. The Germans threatened that unless the contract, worth an estimated £2 billion, was transferred to Ferranti's German rival Daimler-Benz, the British-led ECR 90 radar option would be replaced by the German MSD 2000 system. The Ministry of Defence needed to act swiftly.

Weinstock had been offered the chance of buying a stake in Ferranti before, but had demurred: 'In this business you're operating like a radar scanner all the time. Ferranti is something that appeared periodically on the screen.'[6] In late 1989 the stockbrokers Smith New Court had asked him whether he would be interested in paying a premium for the thirty million shares controlled by the disgraced James Guerin, then being sued for fraud by Ferranti and later gaoled on the same charges. But Weinstock had never been much interested in paying premiums for anything.

Now, from his office at Stanhope Gate he observed the manoeuvrings, in effect awaiting the call from the Ministry of Defence. The initial favourite to buy Ferranti, the state-owned French group Thomson-CSF, backed out of the deal on 18 January 1990 after failing to win a guarantee that it would gain the radar contract. With the backing of Defence Procurement Minister Alan Clark at the Ministry of Defence, the stage was now set for Weinstock's public entry into the battle. Clark wrote in his diary on Friday, 19 January:

> Today I *dominated* the department. Repeatedly I sent for Quinlan [Sir Michael, Permanent Secretary at the MoD], Spiers [Donald Spiers, Controller Aircraft], John Colston [Assistant Secretary]. Periodically I talked to Arnold Weinstock. By sheer energy and clarity of thought I put together the deal that saved Ferranti, and its Radar, and thus EFA in time for it to outface Stoltenberg on Monday when the German delegation come over. John Colston took notes, and tried to keep TK [Tom King, the Defence Secretary] in touch.[7]

Much of the preparatory work had already been done. Ten days earlier Simon Weinstock, as the commercial director with special responsibility for GEC's defence interests, had, with other GEC officials, held talks with Ferranti's chairman Sir Derek Alun-Jones. The talks were considered useful enough for Ferranti executives to visit GEC factories, and there was a suggestion from GEC's advisers Hambros that a joint venture might be appropriate. But Sir Derek rejected this idea on the grounds that it would make no sense for Ferranti to put its prize assets, its defence business, into a joint venture which it would not control.

The pressure was now on. The German government's delegation was due in London, and larger interests were at stake than Ferranti's future: failure to resolve the radar issue could ruin the most ambitious trans-European defence project, the EFA. As the demands from the Ministry of Defence grew, Weinstock prepared for a tough bargaining session. Fully aware that he held all the cards – political support for the deal, a cash hoard and time – he was reluctant to pay the £310 million the Ferranti board had been asking for. He sat back and waited.

Late in the afternoon of 19 January Sir Derek was on the telephone. Ferranti still wanted £310 million, but was prepared to throw in a half-share of Ferranti's Italian business, in which GEC had long been interested. It was a done deal, although there was an element of gamble in Weinstock's decision to go ahead. There was no guarantee that the German government, which had never been enthusiastic for the EFA, would not find an excuse to back away, leaving GEC-Marconi with overcapacity. Nevertheless, the deal showed that when the chips were down, Weinstock, despite his differences with the Conservative government over Nimrod and Westland, could be relied upon to support a deal which was in the British national interest, and which was symbolic of the need for Europe to cooperate more closely in its defence contracting if it was to have a big stake in the integration of European defence industries and procurement.

The Ferranti transaction, coming after the absorption of Plessey's defence businesses, consolidated GEC-Marconi's position as a major defence contractor. It also confirmed defence/electronics as providing the largest chunk of GEC's turnover, with sales of £3 billion a year. But it is conceded inside GEC that the division still operates well below its full potential. Plessey has taken an extraordinarily long time to pay its way, and the Ferranti purchase still remains vulnerable to vacillations in Germany and elsewhere over the EFA project. But the two purchases were important for GEC. After struggling for a decade with Mrs Thatcher's drive for competition among defence contractors, the company had emerged in the 1990s as the only significant player in defence electronics free from the threat of domestic competition which might shrink its generous margins.

The purchases had also broadened GEC's reach beyond British shores. GEC Marconi Electronic Systems in New Jersey controlled the technology for US Air Force Joint Tactical Information Distribution System (JTIDS), an alternative to radar for fighter aircraft seeking to identify targets. The relationship with Thomson-CSF in France has also blossomed through the Matra partnership in space systems and Ferranti-Thomson Sonar, providing submarine technologies. GEC-Marconi can also claim to be a powerhouse in advanced electronics and technology. Despite criticism of Weinstock for stockpiling funds and failing to invest in industry, the group's research and development has never been short of cash. The research centres at Caswell near Milton Keynes and Great Baddow near Chelmsford are highly regarded in a range of technologies. GEC-Marconi's technological and electronic supremacy have made it a world-class company with a global market, some 50 per cent of its sales being outside the UK.

While Weinstock was to gain control of Britain's sea-going defence platform through the 1995 purchase of VSEL, the Barrow-in-Furness yard which makes the Trident submarine, he was repeatedly frustrated in his efforts to gain a grip on the flagship defence aircraft manufacturer controlled by British Aerospace. The logic of a tie-up between GEC and BAe, the two main British defence contractors, had been obvious for some time. As the provider of much of the avionics for BAe's aircraft, GEC saw a merger as a necessary move to protect its market through a degree of vertical integration and the creation of a defence company which, with the correct alliances in Europe, could successfully take on the US military contractors. Moreover, fixed in Weinstock's mind was a belief that BAe, or at least part of it, should have been part of GEC. This view, recalls Dick Evans, chief executive of BAe, dated back to the nationalisation of the British Aircraft Corporation by the Labour government in 1976: 'Arnold said to me on a number of occasions that there had been an understanding between himself and the government on compensation. I always felt that he was associated with the dynamics business, the electronics sort of businesses of Hawker Siddeley and British Aircraft Corporation. And I rather felt that Arnold believed that as part of the deal, through nationalisation, at least some of those businesses would come into GEC. And that, of course, never happened.'[8]

In Weinstock's view it made no sense at all to link the civilian aircraft businesses with military equipment under a single national-ised umbrella. 'It was rubbish,' he says with some bitterness.[9] He felt that the best solution would have been to put the defence business together under GEC's control.

The 1990s were to see GEC and BAe circling each other in search of a possible combination. The logic of creating a vertically in-tegrated British defence giant, with sales of £8 billion, had clear appeal. GEC first declared its interest publicly in 1992, at a time when it was beginning to look as if BAe, far from becoming a defence champion, might not even survive. Under the chairman-ship of Professor Roland Smith BAe had expanded into a series of new businesses at the end of the 1980s, taking over first Royal Ordnance and then the Rover group from the government. Later it would also take on the property company Arlington and the construction firm Balast Needham. The only explanation for this diversification into a range of businesses which BAe knew little about and which required heavy capital input was that given the end of the Cold War, the company could no longer rely on defence for its financial returns. Nevertheless, any deal – like the Rover transaction – which took a problem off the government's hands was bound to be seen as a favour which would be returned in the future. Such considerations are always important if a company is part of the military-industrial complex.

But the 1990s would demonstrate that BAe would have been better advised to have focused on improving its core aerospace businesses, rather than stretching its management. In 1991 the company's pre-tax profits slumped, and some £329 million of cash drained away. The crisis was so deep that Roland Smith was forced off the board in a ruthless exercise of corporate governance by the big institutional shareholders. That was not the end of BAe's troubles. After a bungled £432 million rights issue in 1991, the new chairman John Cahill was obliged to announce a half-year loss of £129 million and a write-off of £1 billion, the heaviest deficit ever declared by a British manufacturer. Cahill was also removed fairly swiftly.

Weinstock was reluctant to stand by and watch one of GEC's biggest customers go to rack and ruin. He had nothing but disdain for BAe's poor financial management, which was draining cash at an unacceptable rate, but he was determined to secure the company's future and GEC's own customer base, as he noted in October 1991: 'We have considerable concern for British Aerospace. It makes the carriers for a lot of our equipment and so we desire it should survive intact, and should not fall into foreign hands. We want to work even closer with them. We cannot do that if they are weak. We have said we want to do whatever is possible to keep them strong.'[10] He added that BAe's problems were of its own making: 'The way it has managed its affairs, the sudden departure of the chairman. We do not want to do anything they do not want us to do, anything that would threaten them.'

In early 1992 rumours of a GEC bid were rife on the stock market, and BAe's share price climbed strongly, despite the company's deep-seated problems. GEC's finance director David Newlands sought to cool the speculation: 'We have no shareholding in British Aerospace, we have no hostile intentions towards them. We wish them well.'[11] But, fuelled by Weinstock himself, the speculation refused to go away. At the results announcement for the first six months of 1992 in July, Weinstock made no secret of his strategic view, stating: 'In several of the more sophisticated systems there is no room for two prime contractors.'[12] As one of the main players in the defence industry, Weinstock felt personally frustrated by the failure of GEC to become a prime contractor.

In particular GEC was anxious to pursue tie-ups with BAe and other defence contractors in a range of areas, including missiles and torpedoes as well as the warship and aircraft systems. Weinstock's determination to press ahead with UK and Continental alliances was partly galvanised by the conduct of the Germans over the EFA contract and the need for GEC to find more reliable customers for its electronic systems. He insisted that the EFA would go ahead whatever happened, noting, however, that if it did not it would not be catastrophic for GEC-Marconi, even though it had already won £500 million of contracts.

As part of his effort to keep the £22 billion EFA project going, Weinstock suggested again that a management alliance between BAe and GEC could deliver the same plane to customers in Britain, Italy and Spain if Germany dropped out. This, he said, might provide a cheaper solution than a European joint venture, with a degree of private-sector risk for the prime contractor. GEC would be the favourite to undertake that role, because of its proven ability to adjust to lower defence spending and control costs.

Despite Weinstock's accurate reading of the situation in Europe's defence industry, few in government or in the City appeared to be listening. In an appearance before the Commons Trade and Industry Select Committee in April 1993, Weinstock – who generally preferred to conduct his business with government behind closed doors – publicly expressed his frustration. He charged John Major's government with pursuing a *laissez-faire* attitude towards the British defence sector, while competitors supported their defence industries. There was too much competition, he complained. While competition was never wrong, it made little sense when there was only one serious customer, the British government: 'A free market in defence equipment is more ephemeral than real,' he insisted.[13] It was a prophetic comment, given the full-blooded support the Pentagon would give the big US contractors in their series of agreed mergers, which would be nodded through by the competition authorities.

The frustrations Weinstock was experiencing in the political sphere were also being felt in the commercial area. The on-off proposals for a merger of defence interests with BAe or for greater cooperation on the EFA project continued throughout 1993, but went nowhere.

In the summer Weinstock went shopping again, this time in the hope of ensnaring the defence business of Thorn-EMI. With its interest in the Rosyth Royal Dockyard, its stake in Babcock Thorn, and its expertise in electronic warfare, battlefield and aircraft radar, electro-optics and fuses for ordinance, Thorn's defence interests would have been a good fit for GEC. But at Thorn-EMI Weinstock was no longer dealing with the old campaigner Sir Jules Thorn, who three decades earlier had joined him in what was essentially a carve-up of the UK lighting industry. The relationship between Thorn and Weinstock later cooled, when Sir Jules bought out AEI's lighting assets from under GEC's nose during the course of its takeover of the company. But the two men still liked each other.

Thorn had retired in 1979, and in 1993 Weinstock found himself dealing with the blunt, self-made figure of Sir Colin Southgate, who was less than impressed with GEC's initial offer of £160 million. In particular he was concerned that Thorn-EMI would have to make a writedown of goodwill in its accounts. Weinstock was, however, not prepared to pay more, and ordered a due diligence investigation to establish whether the company was worth what he was prepared to pay. This led him to conclude that the numbers were very tight, and that Southgate was demanding too much money. Weinstock's main goal remained getting his hands on a platform which offered him a prime contractorship, but the Thorn deal did not meet this test either. Despite his determination to bring together the remnants of the UK's defence industry, Weinstock characteristically was not prepared to pay a premium for the privilege, and the deal fell through.

By the end of 1993 Weinstock was on the prowl again. Several months of talks between Thomson-CSF and the Texan chairman of the Ferranti rump, Eugene Anderson, had come to nothing, and once again Weinstock found himself as the buyer of the last resort for the remaining morsels of Britain's defence and electronics industry. After the damage inflicted by the Guerin scandal, Ferranti was a shadow of the company which after the 1988 takeover of ISC had sales of £1.3 billion and a workforce of twenty-three thousand. Anderson, who took the helm at Ferranti in 1990, inherited £700 million of debt against £200 million of assets, and would be forced to make a further £300 million write-off. His period as chairman had been a long fight against the inevitable: almost every asset had been mortgaged, efforts to reach a deal with Thomson-CSF, the partner in its sonar business, had failed and the order book was shrinking. Hopes of securing a $100 million air defence contract from Bahrain, which could have kept the company's remaining three thousand employees occupied, were shrinking. Anderson's last hope of preserving what was left of Ferranti was GEC. Weinstock's initial offer of one penny per share, or £10.1 million for the equity capital, made on 29 October 1993, looked mean, although when the £140 million of debt was added, the real price was close to £150 million. From GEC's point of view the wreckage of Ferranti was perhaps worth salvaging for its £100 million of potential tax losses and access, perhaps, to some of the £106 million pension surplus. Even more important was the opportunity to gain control of Ferranti's defence systems, simulation and training businesses and keep them away from other potential buyers.

If Weinstock had hoped for a relatively trouble-free passage for his offer, he was disappointed. A small shareholders' campaign against the penny per share bid was launched by a private investment analyst, John Katz, who insisted that if the business went into administration it would produce a better deal for shareholders than acceptance of the offer from GEC. In the event Katz's vocal criticism proved irrelevant. After a GEC team of fifty experts including accountants and lawyers had crawled over the carcass of

Ferranti, they concluded that even the one penny bid – with the requirement that the debt be taken on – was too generous. GEC took the unusual step of applying to the Takeover Panel for permission to withdraw its bid because of material changes discovered as the result of the due diligence exercise. In Weinstock's view there was simply no value there. The offer was abandoned, but GEC left the door open to purchase parts of the company from the receivers Arthur Andersen.

The withdrawal produced adverse comment, reviving the criticism of GEC for failing to use its cash resources in a responsible way. As *The Times* commented: 'The collapse of the Ferranti bid may be a bitter blow for Britain's defence industry, but in GEC's terms it hardly rates a tremor. The great cash machine rumbles on; it could have bought Ferranti more than twice, debt and all, out of the cash generated in the last year. But GEC's latest withdrawal must reawaken doubts that the group can adapt to a world with low inflation and low interest rates. This is the third time that GEC has tried and failed to land a deal since the spring.'[14]

It was not until May of the next year, 1994, that GEC finally swooped upon the remaining Ferranti assets, buying the defence integration systems, training and simulation businesses from the receiver and saving 1110 jobs for a price in the order of £60 million, without any debt. A month later Marconi acquired further Ferranti assets, including the munitions guided support business. By September it had added Ferranti's satellite communications and microwave components and the instrumental test ranges activities. Finally, Weinstock made his move on the separately traded 50 per cent stake in the Ferranti-Thomson Sonar Systems, whose order book included components for the Sting Ray torpedo recovery and instrumentation sections, the final sonar order for the Trident submarines and work on the EH101 Merlin and anti-submarine helicopter. Weinstock saw the Ferranti-Thomson purchase as a means of forging a new link with Thomson's wholly-owned Thomson Sintra Activités Sous-Marines, thus bringing together a £400 million European sonar business which would have sufficient size and resource to challenge the US defence contractors.

Weinstock's passage to the control of the Ferranti fragments was eased by the support of Whitehall, with the Ministry of Defence increasingly coming around to the GEC view that in the new geo-political climate what was needed were UK defence champions, which could also keep jobs and technology in Britain. This was a dramatic reversal of the government's position less than a decade earlier.

Despite the scepticism of his critics in the financial community, who were always willing to spend GEC's cash pile on the company's behalf, Weinstock and his colleagues played a waiting game and won the defence parts of Ferranti at far lower cost than when it had launched the much-maligned one penny per share bid. With the Ferranti businesses safe in his hands, Weinstock now had bigger targets in view.

In 1992, with British Aerospace on its financial uppers the company's chairman John Cahill suggested to Weinstock that the two companies once again explore a defensive alliance. However, talks on such a deal would have to be postponed until the government had secured the second stage of the 1988 Al-Yamamah arms deal with Saudi Arabia, the biggest export transaction in Britain's history. The Prime Minister John Major and King Fahd of Saudi Arabia reached agreement to go ahead with the second stage of the deal in January 1993, although it would not be until June that the detailed package was put together. Under the outline deal Saudi Arabia would buy forty-eight Tornado fighters, of the kind which had shown their muscle in the Gulf War of 1991, at a cost of £5 billion. BAe would provide the airframes and much of the electronic gear, and avionics including inertial navigators and laser rangers would be provided by GEC-Marconi.

With the delicate business of securing the Saudi orders out of the way, Weinstock and his opposite number Dick Evans, the burly chief executive of BAe, who several years earlier had turned down an offer from Weinstock to take up a position as GEC's marketing director, were able to take the merger talks forward. GEC held almost all of the cards: its market capitalisation at the time was four times that of BAe; it had a war chest of some £1.4 billion in cash; and BAe was still haemorrhaging cash. Both sides had mixed feelings about an alliance. Weinstock was uneasy about having anything to do with BAe's civil aviation interests. Evans was less convinced of the strategic arguments for a British national cham-

223

pion than Weinstock, but believes that despite the problems a deal was possible:

> Well, I thought at the time we could have done it. It would have been the right thing to have done. Bear in mind that we were looking at the time at a completely different situation in terms of this industry. We hadn't got to the point where huge mergers were taking place in the United States. There were always absolutely major questions, even if the dialogue was in tune, whether it would have got anywhere. The absolutely fundamental question is how could British Aerospace have existed if it had merged its defence interests with another company? All the liabilities of this company [BAe] would have a lot to do with civil aircraft, which is precisely why Arnold didn't have an interest in this part of the business.[15]

Despite this potentially fatal difficulty, Evans found Weinstock 'very positive' in their face-to-face talks: 'Arnold has always been positive. There's never ever been any difficulty putting the British Aerospace defence business with GEC. The question was, how did the rest of the company survive?'

In the event the talks failed after the broad outlines of the possible deal were leaked to the *Sunday Times*, breaching the confidentiality agreement between the companies. Weinstock believed the details were passed to the press by opponents inside BAe, with the intention of scuppering the deal. Dick Evans, though, was less certain: 'I am not apportioning blame on any side. I genuinely don't know where the leak came from. Where and why it came from, it was inevitable that it would stop the thing dead. And it did.'[16] It was immediately clear to both sides that, with prominent overseas contracts potentially at risk, the talks could not be conducted in the public arena.

Although BAe had tentatively initiated the talks, it was concerned about domination by GEC and the possibility that its rival might obtain confidential business information. Evans now concedes – with the benefit of hindsight – that a deal would have been in both the national interest and in the interests of GEC and BAe: 'The likelihood was that we would actually get more out of the business together than we were getting out of it independently, of the individual parts.' However, in order for this to have happened the two sides would have had to resolve the thorny problem of the contingent liabilities of BAe's civil aviation. In the end it was as much the caution of Weinstock and his immediate GEC colleagues, and his unwillingness to become involved in the risk which had almost sunk BAe, as the public disclosure that killed the deal.

This was almost certainly the last chance for GEC to swoop in and buy BAe on the cheap. As the 1990s progressed British Aerospace carried out a restructuring of its business and balance sheets which would transform the way the company was perceived by investors and make it far less vulnerable to absorption by its more powerful rival.

The catalyst for GEC's next major move to consolidate its position as the UK's premier defence contractor was the opportunist bid by British Aerospace for the Trident submarine shipyard VSEL in October 1994, which would provoke an aggressive counter-bid from Weinstock. In some respects the BAe bid was out of keeping with its broader defence strategy. Unlike GEC, which had been concentrating on mopping up Britain's defence interests into one mega-contractor, BAe had been focusing on forging European links as its way of maintaining a strong position in defence systems as well as military and civil aviation. To this end it began to flirt with developing a closer relationship with its French counterparts Dassault and Aerospatiale. However, the paper offer by BAe for VSEL, which made large surface ships, howitzers and naval guns as well as submarines, was as much financially as defence driven. Dick Evans saw the company as part of BAe's longer-range strategy to rebuild its strained balance sheet. The contentious sale of Britain's last mass-market motor manufacturer Rover to BMW in early 1994 had removed a cash-hungry car-maker from BAe's books. Although the sale only netted £529 million in cash, it effectively removed £1 billion of debt and the need to raise more money by borrowing to invest in new models.

The VSEL offer would continue BAe's process of restoration. In effect it was a kind of rights issue, designed as it was to raise extra resources. It would boost BAe's net assets, bring net cash of £288 million onto its books and also tax gains worth £100 million. In effect the deal would recapitalise BAe.

The ensuing battle between GEC and BAe for control of VSEL had much in common with previous conflicts between the two titans of the UK defence industry. Ten years earlier, when GEC bought the Clydeside naval shipyard Yarrow, Weinstock had wanted to do the deal jointly with British Aerospace, but was turned down by the BAe board. He had wanted to take advantage of BAe's experience as a prime contractor, and was also interested in the group's missilery and knowledge of aircraft sub-systems. 'There had always been a position where Arnold had wanted to work with British Aerospace on the radar systems side,' Dick Evans says. Thus when VSEL approached BAe about making a bid, there was a belief that the two companies – BAe and GEC – might divide the spoils. Essentially, BAe would concentrate on the surface ships and GEC would take on the submarine fleet. The last thing BAe expected was a hostile response from Weinstock.

Moving aggressively, GEC launched a dawn raid against VSEL on the stock market, capturing a 13.7 per cent share. This immediately placed BAe on the defensive. At the same time GEC launched a full bid for VSEL at £14 per share, valuing the company at £531.7 million and instantly putting it on the back foot. Weinstock had spent enough time playing with BAe. This time he was determined to win whatever the cost, and saw that he could use a successful bid for VSEL as a lever for a hostile tilt at BAe itself, now that it was rid of Rover and had secured the second stage of the Saudi Arabian contract. Having established that GEC could act as a prime defence contractor at Yarrow, Weinstock was determined that this was one bid which would not get away. He set about an active lobbying campaign among influential journalists, using his favoured instruments the telephone and personal persuasion to convince them and the wider public, including the Ministry of Defence, of the good sense in the deal. He saw VSEL cementing GEC-Marconi's lead as the UK's prime sea-going contractor, preparing the way for its taking control of the air-going platform too.

BAe came back with a counter-offer for VSEL, but had no chance against a GEC willing to open its coffers if necessary and convinced of the longer-term need to run its Yarrow yard, building smaller ships such as frigates, in conjunction with VSEL. GEC came back with a knockout bid of £980 million after the Monopolies Commission nodded the deal through. Unusually Weinstock, who traditionally assessed takeover bids on the basis of value and assets alone, took what he calls 'the wider view' on this occasion. The affair caused some bitterness between Weinstock and Dick Evans, who had thought it could have been dealt with more amicably:

> For whatever reason, we don't know but Arnold obviously does, they followed up with a hostile move and actually overbid us eventually. He had to pay a huge amount of money to get it, certainly more than the business was worth even to us, and we had a massive tax advantage with it. They obviously judged it strategically. The value of the business for them was worth the money they paid for it. But certainly it is true that on the naval shipbuilding side Arnold always wanted to have a joint business with British Aerospace.[17]

The VSEL battle brought into the open much of the suppressed hostility between Britain's two most significant defence contractors. The boldness of Weinstock's move led to a belief in the business community that with VSEL and Britain's naval shipyards now owned by GEC he would launch a bid for British Aerospace. This would be a fitting grand finale for Weinstock, who intended to retire in September 1996, by which time he would be seventy-two.

But in many ways the moment had passed. GEC's best chance of taking over BAe would have been when it was in difficulties, and the deal could have been more easily sold to the MoD and others on financial grounds. Once BAe's fortunes had been somewhat restored, the logic of the deal faded. As well as the suspicion with which the two companies viewed each other, there were political obstacles. The MoD clearly found it useful to have two defence contractors whom it could play off against each other – as was the case when it came to selecting a consortium to build a replacement for the RAF's Nimrod maritime patrol aircraft. The choice for the £2 billion contract was originally seen as being between a BAe–Boeing alliance and Lockheed-Marconi, although a deal was brokered which gave both GEC-Marconi and BAe a share. Such compromises highlight the wisdom of Weinstock's decade-long war for more vertical integration in the UK's airborne platforms, particularly if trans-national European deals remain problematic. Over the longer haul the sheer force of the US mega-mergers is likely to prove Weinstock's thesis that seeking to maintain defence contract competition on the small canvas which is Britain will in the end prove counter-productive to the national interest.

Although time was clearly running out for Weinstock as managing director of GEC, his dogged determination to build durable defence ties for GEC-Marconi was maintained. Long, delicate and subtle negotiations with the leading French defence and consumer electronics concern Groupe Thomson, involving both the British and French governments, would lead in April 1996 to the formation of a £350 million Europe-wide alliance of sonar equipment makers for airborne and underwater use. The new company, Thomson Marconi Sonar NV, to be based in the Netherlands, was 50.1 per cent controlled by Thomson and 49.9 per cent by GEC-Marconi, employed 3500 people and would be a world leader in the field of sound-monitoring systems for warships, submarines, aircraft and minesweepers.

Weinstock saw this deal as a trailer for greater European alliances ahead. Its significance was twofold: it demonstrated Weinstock's willingness to make trans-European alliances in defence as he had in power systems and telecoms, despite his keen interest in vertical integration; and it provided a model for Europe-wide defence cooperation.[18]

It was not just the defence sector which was affected by the seismic geo-political movements of the early 1990s. As the market for military equipment shrank, reflecting the changing shape of international conflict, the nature of trade and finance also changed. The new geo-economics of liberalised financial markets and a more open trading scene became a dominant theme. The days when the three largest economic blocs – the European Union, the North American Free Trade Area, and the Japan and Asia region – could look to each other for their political, financial and trading relationships were past. To survive commercially meant forging relationships with the emerging market economies of the Pacific, Latin

America, Southern Africa and Eastern and Central Europe. Growth rates in the markets of developing countries were twice or more those in the industrial nations. The improved status of the developing world sucked in capital, investment and expertise from the industrial world. With this sea-change, reflected in new institutions such as the World Trade Organisation and the Asia-Pacific Economic Cooperation Group, commerce had to think in global terms.

It was to the credit of GEC, under Weinstock's leadership, that it saw the changes coming, and recognised that if it was to survive as a manufacturing powerhouse it could not do so alone in the global power and transport sector. It would require joint ventures like GDA (General Domestic Appliances, the 50/50 partnership with GE of America) in the consumer-white-goods business, GPT (GEC Plessey Telecommunications) and the partnership with Siemens in the telecoms sector. The company would draw its strength from this series of global alliances.

By far the most important of these was GEC–Alsthom, a combination in which Weinstock played a strong personal role. At the time when the merger was finalised by Weinstock and his French opposite number Pierre Souard in December 1988 Alsthom contributed twice GEC's volume of turnover, reflecting its sharper marketing skills, but only half its profit. An early objective was to implement the Weinstock system of management controls across both the French and British companies. This meant the introduction of monthly financial reports, reviews of projects underway and a much more vigorous procedure for tender approval. The tighter management system was seen by insiders as critical in bringing the two companies together and encouraging executives to explain their actions more clearly. Moreover, there was political advantage to an Anglo–French operation. Disputes between Britain and China over the governance of Hong Kong made it more politic for GEC–Alsthom to emphasise its French base when selling into the People's Republic of China. Furthermore, the French authorities have been more aggressive than their UK counterparts in providing export credit deals to secure contracts in overseas markets.

GEC–Alsthom managing director Jim Cronin, who started as an apprentice engineer at English Electric and now sits on the main

GEC board, believes that much of the credit for the good relations between the two companies rests with Weinstock's handling of the link-up: 'We started off originally with quite a structured company, and Lord Weinstock played a big part in the relationship with our French colleagues. He, of course, spent a lot of time in France with his horses and his music, and he developed a good relationship with the French management team.'[19]

In the power-generating arena GEC–Alsthom soon found itself competing in the global marketplace with the other major European players, Siemens of Germany and the Swiss–Swedish group Asea Brown Boveri (ABB). Much of the early battle was focused on the market for combined-gas cycle turbine power stations, the fastest-growing sector of the thermal power-generating market. The popularity of these systems was based on the widespread availability of low-cost natural gas, its perceived environmental advantages, efficiency and short lead-times in bringing them into operation. Employing technology based on aerospace gas turbines, the combined-cycle generator uses the waste gases from heavy-duty turbines to power a secondary steam generator which can increase thermal efficiency by up to 50 per cent. In the global fight with Siemens and ABB, GEC–Alsthom scored heavily: it was able to demonstrate scientifically that its combined cycle turbines had a higher efficiency rating than those of its competitors.

Equally importantly, GEC–Alsthom was able to ride on the coat-tails of General Electric of America by showing that its combined cycle machine worked best with the world's biggest turbine, the GE 212–226 megawatt machine, in which there was a degree of joint development. In the early 1990s GEC–Alsthom became the market leader in combined cycle orders, landing a huge contract at Eems in the Netherlands as well as several in the UK, in effect negating some of Weinstock's earlier concerns that electricity privatisation might destroy Britain's domestic power industry.

At the end of the 1995 financial year GEC–Alsthom had brought all its power generation companies together under one roof, the Power Generation Division. The company was able to boast an order book of £6.4 billion and a stream of contracts in the Pacific Basin including the Ling Ao and Luochang power stations in China and Sual in the Philippines, as well as combined cycle plants in

Greece and Thailand. Coal-fired units were being inaugurated in Inner Mongolia and Guandong province, and gas turbines had been sold to Japan, Italy, Spain and Turkey, as well as the UK.

Rationalisation and improved management controls also enabled GEC–Alsthom to improve its operating margins. Overall margins had been raised to 7 per cent, within reach of its main European rival ABB, and well ahead of Siemens, which was barely profitable in this area. The most successful US contractor, GE, has the best margins in the business, but it is essentially an equipment supplier rather than a contractor, as are the European power groups. GEC–Alsthom has established itself as one of the biggest and most successful global players. While GE is undoubtedly the world leader, GEC–Alsthom ranks second in the building of conventional power stations. Moreover, in transmission distribution, the movement of electricity from the power station to the ultimate user, GEC – having absorbed the German company AEG – is now the second player in the world behind ABB. In effect the GEC–Alsthom tie-up has given Britain a share of a competitive marketplace from which it would otherwise have been excluded. The belief that the UK's place in the global power industry would have been lost without the alliance is forcefully expressed by Jim Cronin:

> I personally believe that if we'd not had a merger we were on the beach. We would've been dead. There was a theory that Britain was back in the power business. They [the government] had ordered from us two nuclear power stations and three big 2700-megawatt coal-fired stations, and they all got cancelled. We were able to bring work into the UK units as part of a bigger programme which involved some of the nuclear units of the Korean systems and equipment we were selling abroad.
>
> It is a fact that we had four factories [at the time of the merger] and we now have two. Equally, we had more factories in France and we've been able to rationalise. As far as Britain is concerned, it's been very good in that the relationship between the government agencies, export credit agencies, in the UK and France, have learnt to work together in pursuit of these very big projects such as the

nuclear stations in China. Government support and joint financing was to become very important. In simple terms, if we sell a turbine generator, we make only stators in France and we make rotors in Britain. We were able therefore to invest in Rugby, in Stafford, very large sums of money because the throughput, the volume of components that we make in those locations, was several times that which we would have had as a purely British company. I believe it saved the power-generation turbine generators for the UK.[20]

The early 1990s were disastrous for British train manufacturing. After the privatisation of British Rail, investment in locomotives and rolling stock ground to a halt. London Underground, the other major buyer of rolling stock, also cut back its investment programmes. With the market so depressed the UK's domestic train-making industry, centred on British Rail Engineering Services (BREL), which had been bought out by GEC's rival ABB, was forced to cut back production and staff.

By contrast, the 1990s were a period of real growth and progress for GEC-Alsthom's train systems. Again, many of the orders gained were international. They include the Eurostar, whose high-speed TGVs are built half in Birmingham and half in France. This experience with high-speed systems has allowed GEC-Alsthom to win contracts further afield. Among those it gained in the 1990s were for the Seoul-Pusan high-speed link in Korea; a joint contract with Bombardier of Canada to supply twelve high-speed trainsets, fifteen electric locomotives and maintenance units for AMTRAK's high-speed Eastern Seaboard corridor linking Boston, New York and Washington; rolling stock for the Santiago metro in Chile; and a high-speed rail link in Sweden connecting Stockholm to Arlanda Airport. This series of projects, together with orders from France for a double-decker TGV, have put GEC-Alsthom well ahead of other power groups in the area of high-speed locomotives. 'In the railway sector we clearly are the leader, ahead of Siemens and ABB,' Jim Cronin observes. The GEC-Alsthom record in new and modernised railway systems contrasts favourably with the run-down of the rest of the British railway market. As with power generation, the combination of engineering skills with marketing and political clout has enabled GEC to become a genuine presence in global markets from Korea to Chile, benefiting from the new geo-economics. Following the completion of rail privatisation in Britain in 1996 GEC–Alsthom would quickly become a commerical beneficiary with orders from new franchises including South-West trains and Gatwick Express, making the case for floating it off from GEC stronger.[21]

If GEC–Alsthom has been the most successful of the international alliances forged by Weinstock, among the least satisfying has been GPT, the joint telecoms venture with Siemens forged in 1989, which has proved to be unduly restrictive for GEC and for Britain as a manufacturer in the global telecoms market. Weinstock has recognised that GPT is less stable than the GEC–Alsthom partnership, and has been disadvantageous to GEC as it has sought to become a more global company. Weinstock's successor George Simpson sought to extricate GEC from the joint ventures. In June 1998 GEC-Alsthom was renamed Alstom and floated on the Paris Bourse as an independent company putting a value of £4.3 billion on the enterprise.

On a purely financial basis, GPT is an impressive performer. Its operating margins of 13.6 per cent are among the highest in the industry, matched only by the mobile-phone maker Nokia,[22] and vastly superior to Siemens, whose returns are in the order of 3.6 per cent. GPT has achieved these high returns by avoiding low-margin commodity areas of the telecoms equipment market, concentrating on software and promoting costs savings. Unlike the GEC–Alsthom deal, which was a genuine cross-border merger of power interests into a new company, GPT was a marriage of convenience: right for its time, but without a clear rationale.

Essentially the company was formed as a result of the joint bid by Siemens and GEC for Plessey. But it was not a true joint venture: GEC retained a 60 per cent stake. The price of bringing Siemens in as a minority partner was to effectively exclude GPT from certain areas of activity: in the UK market it has been a major player, but in the rest of the world Weinstock concedes that GPT, which is excluded from selling superior Siemens technology, has nothing. Indeed, in critical overseas markets GPT has found itself in the bizarre position of competing against Siemens for sales. This is an unstable structure which has thus far proved difficult to disentangle. Weinstock would personally have preferred a full joint venture with Siemens in which research and development, production, management and sales and marketing were fully integrated.

Nevertheless, under the uncompromising leadership of Peter Gershon, GPT's energetic managing director, the joint telecoms operation has been a consistently strong performer within GEC. In fact Gershon was so effective in holding together a difficult structure and wringing good margins out of the operation that he was widely recognised as the best internal candidate to succeed Weinstock as managing director of GEC. When Gershon joined GPT from ICL in 1990 he found that the Plessey culture at the core of the enterprise was very different from that of GEC: more outward-looking, less tightly managed, and with a higher rate of capital investment, which in the main had proved sensible. Gershon immediately set about changing the company's structure. He rebuilt the board of directors, cut the workforce by 20 per cent to sixteen thousand, and introduced the tight financial controls for which GEC is renowned.

Weinstock was principally involved with dealing with the Siemens bosses directly. Relations were generally amicable, with problems between the two partners peaceably resolved. Siemens did, however, object when, as part of the process of putting GPT on a sound footing, engineers were fired – which was virtually unknown in the German skills- and investment-led approach. 'Siemens finds some of the things that GEC does frustrating, unexpected – and vice-versa,' says Peter Gershon.[23]

The benefit of the GPT partnership to GEC is that it has been able to combine its management controls with Siemens' world-class research and development capabilities. Among the problems which GPT had to cope with was the shrinking UK domestic market for its core product, the System X digital telephone exchange. To make up for this it has had to sell System X into overseas markets, where on occasions it has found itself head-to-head with Siemens. GPT has also sought to broaden its range of products, concentrating on high-tech equipment such as sophisticated payphone systems and video conferencing, a growth area. It has sought to build upon its software know-how by providing systems such as integrating switches, exchanges and headsets which can be used alongside the Siemens hardware. Among the new products which have been developed are devices, to be integrated into payphones, which will be able to read and process data downloaded from Mondex, the smart money card developed by UK banks.

However, behind the GPT structure there are uncomfortable strains. Siemens would like to increase its involvement, and Weinstock would have liked the ability to have piggy-backed more frequently on Siemens to gain access to new markets. At its current size, with non-UK sales of £400 million, GPT cannot be considered a world-class player. It thus needs to broaden its relationship with Siemens. The two parent companies announced in June 1996 that they would work more closely together in a 50/50 venture in private networks and extend their cooperation in public networks. But at its present scale and with a shrinking domestic market, GPT is not seen as providing great opportunities for payback on its research and development. As a result it has been increasingly dipping into Siemens' R&D pool, suggesting that the best way forward would be a broader merging of the telecoms interests of GEC and Siemens: something which Weinstock was unable to complete. It is his belief, however, that even if the Siemens partnership has been unbalanced, it is worthwhile. Without it, GEC would effectively have been out of the telecoms business altogether. His successor George Simpson disagreed, and in 1998 he bought out the Siemens stake for £700 million, renaming the wholly-owned venture Marconi Communications.

The ownership situation in the third of the defensive partnerships entered into by GEC in 1989–90 is more straightforward. In 1989 Weinstock sold 50 per cent of the company's white-goods (washing machines, clothes dryers, refrigators and dishwashers) business – which includes two leading brands, Hotpoint and Creda – to its larger and more powerful American counterpart General Electric for £238 million. GDA, the new company formed from the partnership, has an American managing director, Bruce Enders, and makes strategic sense to both partners. For Jack Welch's GE aims to dominate the global white-goods industry, and a strong British/European partner of GEC's calibre is part of that ambition. Joint ownership offers a spread risk, but GE has also bought into GEC's understanding of the British and wider European marketplace. At present the range of products is still dominated by the Hotpoint and Creda franchises, but production has been rationalised, the list of suppliers pruned and the products redesigned. As a white-goods producer GDA has become increasingly innovative: among its recent additions is Credanet, a central control pad which sends signals via the mains to control heating appliances throughout the home.

Logically, GEC's determination to hang onto its white-goods operation has seemed incongruous, given that it is the company's only business which sells directly to the consumer. It was unfortunate for GE that it acquired its stake in GDA just as the UK economy, and the housing market in particular, was entering one of its most prolonged downturns, making sales extremely difficult. Pressure on the division was also increased by competition among retailers in a highly competitive market. Nevertheless, with sales of £250 million and the Hotpoint brand the leaders in the UK and increasingly recognised abroad, GDA remains a significant asset for GEC.

Moreover, for Weinstock, whose industrial career started in consumer electronics, GDA has some sentimental value. He has never given up his dream of returning to television manufacture in Britain, reversing the Pacific tide: 'If you have a business like GDA,' he remarks, 'then as long as it is profitable the choice is there to keep it, or to sell it. There is no reason to sell it unless someone offers you a good price.'[24]

A long-standing criticism of Weinstock's management style has been his unwillingness to discard companies and brands which do not fit in with GEC's principal activities. In some respects this has proved an admirable quality: companies bought and sold regularly, rather than nurtured over the long run, are often neglected in terms of investment and management systems. Weinstock has always ensured that all the companies within GEC are subjected to the same rigorous management procedures, and that investments which can be justified by the manager responsible, will be approved.

However, as a result of Weinstock's unwillingness to be parted from what is GEC's – a trait perhaps born out of his unsettled youth – in the 1990s the group included a random series of activities loosely called the industrial division. Several of the companies comprising this division, such as Gilbarco, which manufactures petrol pumps, are leaders in their field. Others, including Picker, one of the US subsidiaries, which makes diagnostic imaging equipment for the medical market, are leading-edge companies. Picker has also won widespread plaudits for the aggressive management it has brought to the medical equipment business. As the *Financial Times* observed in 1992:

> The US businesses have taken great strides to streamline manufacturing through total quality programmes. Picker's de-unionised computer tomography factory on the outskirts of Cleveland, Ohio has cut its management layers from nine to three, reduced job classifications from 188 to six and pared average product costs 58 per cent of what they were four years ago. It is making 280 scanners a year with a staff of eighty-two, working on self-directed teams, compared with the 120 scanners it used to make with 180 staff. This has been the main force behind Picker's strong performance.[25]

Other parts of the industrial division, packaged up for instance with Marconi, might have been worth retaining for their technological capacity and ability to develop promising new products. But not all the parts of the division have performed and contributed with the gusto of Picker, and despite generating profits of around £200 million a year, the division has been viewed as underperforming because of a lack of focus which has drawn attention away from the better and most promising producers.

Picker is by far the largest single operation in the division, making profits of £20.7 million in 1988, on sales of £367 million. By 1994 this had grown to £54 million, on sales of £674 million. However, since then its performance has suffered as a result of continuing uncertainty over health-care reform in the US, a development which has made the marketplace far more competitive. Moreover, even though Picker has been remarkably successful in its field, it is a minnow in a huge market, trailing behind European players such as Siemens, which has sales of £3 billion. Picker is in an uncomfortable position, and needs better attention than it received in the Weinstock era, either through an alliance with a powerful partner or more direct management input from Stanhope Gate, giving strategic direction to the future.

Overall the operating profits of the industrial division plummeted after 1989, when much of the GEC management effort was focused on building up and developing the new alliances GEC–Alsthom, GPT and GDA, and augmenting the defence contracting business. At the end of 1989 the industrial division was producing operating profits of £225.7 million, but by the end of 1996 – the year of Weinstock's retirement – these were down to £184 million.

Of all the companies in the division, the ones which seemed to sit most awkwardly within GEC were the electronic meteorology concern Avery Berkel, the office equipment company A.B. Dick, and Wire & Cables. When Weinstock stepped down in 1996 the process of restructuring the division by disposing of non-core businesses had already begun, with the sale of Express Lifts to Otis in 1995–96. George Simpson, Weinstock's successor as managing director of GEC, would make no secret of his belief that reorganisation of the industrial division was one opportunity which his predecessor had fluffed. In July 1996, within months of taking over from Weinstock, Simpson unveiled the first stage of a group restructuring, resulting in the loss of a thousand jobs – many of them in the weighing machine business at Avery Berkel – and a restructuring charge of £160 million. Simpson identified four priority areas for change in the post-Weinstock era: development of strategy, making better use of the cash mountain, culture and developing organic growth. All had been perceived as shortcomings in Weinstock's GEC.

More than almost any industrialist in Britain, Arnold Weinstock, through the strategic relationships he forged with European and American manufacturing corporations in 1989–90, recognised the new economic order of the coming decade. It was a period when Weinstock's philosophy appeared to be all-conquering. The cash mountain built in the eighties provided GEC with the cushion it needed in the deep recession provoked by Britain's membership of the exchange rate mechanism; it also provided a shock absorber in case any of the huge contracts being secured by GEC–Alsthom in China and the Pacific Basin went wrong. The alliances Weinstock made in defence, power, telecommunications and consumer white goods ensured that GEC remained a serious operator in all these industries despite severe competitive pressures.

Nevertheless, however well GEC performed financially and industrially, and however shrewd its strategies appeared, Weinstock only intermittently received the credit. Increasingly, the picture of the industrialist to be gleaned from the financial press and analysts was of an ageing executive, past his sell-by date and clinging to the reins of power long after it was sensible for GEC or its major shareholders. The management practices installed by Weinstock, the informal gatherings of an old guard in the managing director's office, were now derided. The fashion in British industry was for more activist boards, with strong non-executive directors and organisation charts which made the succession or potential succession immediately apparent. Corporate individualism of the kind represented by Weinstock was distrusted, and corporate governance – with its stress on more transparency and clear lines of control and succession – all the rage. Instead of being praised for his intelligence, Weinstock was deprecated for his failure to prepare the way for the kind of clear succession which the City craved.

In his heart of hearts there was only one successor Weinstock really wanted: his son Simon. Having lost his own parents at an early age, his family was extraordinarily precious to him. When Weinstock, after many years of seeking to preserve his independence, had finally gone to work with his father-in-law Michael Sobell at Radio & Allied, he found the going difficult, as is often the case in family businesses. But the two men came to an understanding. Weinstock brought his financial and managerial skills to the enterprise, Sobell the entrepreneurship and marketing which came from being an old-fashioned trader. Some forty years on, Weinstock still credits Sobell with the stroke of genius which led the company to develop a larger television screen, which proved popular with the public. In the early 1950s most receivers were equipped with twelve- or at best fourteen-inch screens: 'But my father-in-law Michael Sobell correctly suggested that it would be better to offer a bigger one, provided we could still sell it at an attractive price.'[26]

Although Weinstock did not harbour dynastic ambitions for their own sake, he preferred to work with people he trusted and liked; perhaps this provided him with the security that was missing from his childhood. No one was closer to him than Simon, who was the embodiment of everything he wanted in a son. Simon's education at Winchester and Magdalen College, Oxford in Classics gave him the background which his father had missed out on. Weinstock had never hesitated to put important family business into Simon's hands. When Simon showed an interest in bloodstock breeding and racing, his father gave him free rein to manage the Ballymacoll stud farm at County Meath in Ireland. For more than two decades all the major decisions at Ballymacoll were taken by Simon, who had an encyclopaedic knowledge of bloodlines.

Weinstock encouraged his son to gain his apprenticeship at GEC's merchant bankers S.G. Warburg, then brought him across to GEC in 1983. There he quickly established himself as part of the inner cabinet who would gather in the managing director's office to hammer out policy, and he was elevated to the main board as commercial director in 1987, with responsibility for GEC's most profitable division. In much the same way as Simon had taken over the family horse-racing interests, Weinstock wanted to see Simon in charge of GEC. What he failed to grasp was that in the era of corporate governance, the succession was not necessarily in his gift. Although there were examples of the leadership of British public companies being allowed to cascade down the generations, like the Wolfson family at Great Universal Stores, such arrangements were increasingly frowned upon.

Moreover, Weinstock failed to appreciate what some of his closest associates had recognised some time earlier: despite Simon's fine qualities, he did not have the driving ambition necessary to take on the mantle of GEC. Simon was far happier managing his horses, searching out a gourmet meal or attending La Scala with his father than wrestling with strategies for industry. Moreover, the breadth of his experience was also suspect: 'He was never allowed to leave Stanhope Gate. His father wanted him around,' a GEC non-executive director observed.[27]

Weinstock's hope that Simon would succeed him was one of the reasons he delayed finalising the details of his retirement for so long. The question of his own future coloured much of the press coverage of GEC, but Weinstock refused to be hurried, despite increasingly adverse comment and open discussion about GEC being a company at war with itself over its future. In a 1991 assessment of Weinstock's era, the City Editor of the *Independent* did not mince her words:

> Lord Weinstock once said he would know when to leave GEC. Nobody would have to tell him. But after twenty-eight years as managing director of Britain's biggest electronics company that time has come. Once regarded as the country's most brilliant industrialist, his reputation has become tarnished. Arnie has outstayed his welcome. The company he created through an unusual combination of spark and attention to detail is in decline, with falling profits and a lagging share price.[28]

There was a recognition inside GEC too that change would have to come. Essentially those seeking it fell into three groups. There was Weinstock and his small inner cabinet, who wanted an evolution in management within the group which had run the company from Weinstock's personal office. They favoured some sort of carve-up of responsibilities between Simon and the finance director David Newlands. Weinstock would remain close to the centre of power, providing guidance on strategic issues and wielding his legendary influence at home and overseas.

A second group felt that there must be a radical break with the past. This meant pushing the company into new areas and removing not just Weinstock, but Lord Prior from the chairmanship, and disbanding the cabinet around the managing director's office including such close advisers as veteran deputy managing director Malcolm Bates and community affairs director Sara Morrison. Richard Reynolds, a main board director and chairman of GEC's telecoms offshoot GPT, would eventually go public with these views, losing his post on the board as a consequence.

Then there were the compromisers. These were essentially the non-executive directors, representing the interests of shareholders, who demanded an orderly timetable for Weinstock's departure, a wide search for a new chief executive, and an independent chairman less in thrall to Weinstock and his methods.

241

In the event the plan for an internal succession involving Simon was to be sidelined by his fatal illness, which tragically coincided with the final stages of the saga. The dissidents were to be vanquished and a conventional corporate solution, bringing in a well-qualified outsider, was to resolve the issue.

At the heart of the process was Ron Artus, the former investment director of the mighty Prudential insurance group, which was GEC's largest shareholder with 7 per cent of the equity. Artus believed it was unlikely that Simon would succeed his father. Like others in the City, he felt that although Simon had many qualities, he lacked the forceful leadership required to steer a large public company, and had never operated sufficiently far from under his father's wing to prove his management skills. Artus had a mammoth task in persuading Weinstock, who was not even convinced that there was an issue, either about his own retirement or the succession of Simon. His first job was to convince Weinstock that he needed to set a date for the transfer of power, and to let him know that the City would not accept Simon taking over as managing director: 'I went and had sessions with Arnold about all this, because I knew perfectly well that it was not going to be acceptable in the City. He seemed to think I wanted him to go public, and he said he was not prepared to exclude Simon alone of the current executive directors from that possibility. But he also made it clear that it wouldn't be something that he was working to bring about.'[29]

Gaining this understanding was a singular achievement, but the Prudential's role was not yet over. Weinstock was still not convinced about the City's determination to remove him, and never felt any particular urgency about the matter: 'It was all rather nebulous. Only the chairman, at some time or the other, mentioned that there was a feeling around that I should be replaced by someone else. No one put me under any pressure,' he says.[30]

Artus initiated discussions with the chairman Lord Prior and another non-executive director, Lord Rees-Mogg, a former editor of *The Times* and an old friend of Weinstock, in an effort to persuade Weinstock that he should at least set a retirement date, even if he did not resolve the succession. In the summer of 1994, shortly before the release of GEC's annual results, Weinstock baldly told the board, without any warning or open discussion, that he would be retiring in two years' time. As had often been the case in the past, Weinstock regarded the board as the last place he would discuss sensitive issues like the succession.

The public announcement was typically low-key. Lord Prior dropped it into the chairman's statement on the results between some comments on group strategy and financial details, as if the end of a managing director's thirty-one-year reign was a matter of routine. 'As to the future management of the group,' Prior stated, 'Lord Weinstock reaches the age of seventy in the current year. He has agreed to the board's request that he should continue as managing director for a further two years.'

With a formal date for retirement now pencilled in, it was hoped that the issue of what would follow the Weinstock era would, temporarily at least, be put to rest. But among the non-executive directors at least there was a recognition that the starting gun had been sounded in the search for a new managing director, and that although speculation about Simon continued, his father had started to realise that his son would not immediately step into his shoes. The process had not been an easy one for Arnold. Having run his own show for so long, and having delivered with such regularity for GEC's shareholders, he was not pleased that his hand had been forced. But even he recognised that he could not go on for ever.

Among the internal candidates, the strongest was perceived to be Peter Gershon, then in charge of the telecoms division and since moved on to become managing director of GEC-Marconi. Most of the other possibilities at Stanhope Gate were considered either too old, or to lack the necessary breadth of experience of global business.

Weinstock began to suspect that he might have made a mistake in failing to groom candidates of the right age within GEC. An informal search committee was established, involving Weinstock, Prior and Sebastian de Ferranti, the former chairman and managing director of Ferranti, and a non-executive director of GEC since 1982. Ron Artus, representing the City through his time with Prudential, the biggest shareholding interest on the GEC board, was kept in touch with developments by Prior. While some public speculation continued to focus on Simon, those involved in the search had already privately agreed on his exclusion.

Among the possibilities was a merger with Carlton Communications, a high-profile television, film and media group much admired in the financial community, whose chairman was the ebullient Michael Green. A link with Carlton was by no means illogical: US General Electric had moved into the multimedia world with an audacious takeover of the NBC television network. Michael Green attracted Weinstock because they spoke the same language. Green was a product of the West End Jewish culture with which Weinstock could identify, and his parents had been Weinstock's travel agents. The two men agreed a price for the merger, and Green was brought to Stanhope Gate to meet GEC's directors, but the deal fell through when he failed to negotiate a satisfactory future role for Weinstock, who remained unwilling to leave the scene before the appointed time.

Weinstock was also drawn towards Alan Sugar, the rough-edged founder of Amstrad and chairman of Tottenham Hotspur Football Club, whose expertise in branding and marketing electronic consumer products – an area in which GEC had had only limited success – would have made him an interesting choice. As with Green, Weinstock was attracted by the prospect of leaving an enterprise forged by Jewish industrialists in the post-Second World War era in the hands of a new generation of management with which he felt culturally attuned, and which understood the new multimedia and electronic technologies and the significance of marketing.

From a personal viewpoint, Weinstock's self-imposed July 1996 deadline for the succession was proving spectacularly unfortunate. Unbeknown to the journalists and City analysts urging a solution to the question of the succession, and the fund managers making less than sensitive comments about the process, Simon Weinstock had become seriously ill. What had first been noticed as a mole changing colour on his arm had developed into a virulent melanoma. Weinstock could delay no longer. His son was dangerously ill, although the full gravity of his illness was unknown to the public. Simon's death on 18 May 1996 left Weinstock physically and emotionally devastated. But he buried himself in work, refusing to take any time off until his August vacation.

The clamour in the financial community, partly generated by dissident GEC director Richard Reynolds, was intensifying, and

Weinstock and his fellow directors, notably chairman Lord Prior, were under pressure to reach a decision about the succession.

It was during GEC's extensive talks with British Aerospace about merging the defence interests of the two companies in 1993 that Weinstock had his first close look at BAe's deputy chief executive George Simpson. Simpson was widely credited with having turned BAe's Rover subsidiary back into a viable company before eventually selling it to BMW. After Simpson moved from Rover to become chief executive of the leading car components and electronics group Lucas in 1994, Weinstock began to court him, pointing out that the position at the head of GEC, with its leadership in defence, power and manufacturing, was the most important in UK industry.

Jim Prior took an instant liking to Simpson, and Weinstock, more difficult to please, felt comfortable with him, largely because he did not come across as over-sophisticated and was 'not too much of a big-head'.[31] In an era when chief executives have been endowed with qualities of glamour by the media, Weinstock was attracted by Simpson's plainness. At a series of interviews with the non-executives Simpson impressed the board with his maturity, his experience and his knowledge of the industries in which GEC was involved. The only drawback was that he was already in his mid-fifties, which would mean he would always be viewed as a stopgap. Nevertheless, the non-executives took the view that he was the best choice, as there was no outstanding candidate inside the group.

For Weinstock personally, the position of Simon had always been a confusing element in the succession. He had never fully come to terms with the fact that his son was not capable of following him. However, as Simon's illness became more serious, he accepted the choice of Simpson, who seemed to him a 'good guy'.

Uncharacteristically, Weinstock, who normally thrived on detail, was largely disengaged from the decisions on his successor's remuneration. He was, however, determined that his stewardship of GEC would not end with the annual general meeting in September 1996. GEC was far more to him than simply a corporation: it was the enterprise which he and Kenneth Bond had welded together from the remains of Britain's electrical engineering industry. Stanhope Gate was more than just an office: it was the place where he felt most secure and spent most of his waking hours, and it would not be relinquished easily. Eventually a compromise was reached, and a terse, formal press release was issued on 18 March 1996:

> The Board of GEC announces that it intends to appoint Mr George Simpson as managing director as soon as he is free to take up the appointment. Lord Weinstock will retire from the board on Mr Simpson's appointment. The board and Mr Simpson have asked Lord Weinstock to accept the honorary position of Chairman Emeritus so as to have available the benefit of his long experience and profound knowledge of the company.[32]

The curious title 'chairman emeritus' was in fact an appropriate one, reflecting the precision which Weinstock had always valued. His was not to be the honorific title of 'president' enjoyed by such people as Lord King of British Airways, who had been formally sidelined. As chairman emeritus he would have a continuing advisory role, and the new managing director would make full use of his expertise in dealing with complex Continental partnerships.

In his final days as managing director there would be one further incident which illustrated that in the new world of the Cadbury code, setting out the rules for corporate governance, and the Greenbury code, establishing the framework for the pay and share options of the directors of public companies, Weinstock, known throughout his years at GEC for protecting shareholders' funds, was oddly out of touch. In August 1996 George Simpson's contract was made available for inspection by the GEC company secretary. It revealed that the new managing director would receive an annual remuneration of up to £1.5 million, including pension contributions, plus a complicated grant of share options based on £4.8 million worth of shares or eight times his salary. The big institutional shareholders were outraged. Weinstock was on holiday at Cap d'Antibes with his grandchildren. With the row filling the columns of the newspapers and the new managing director branded a 'fat cat' before he had even had a chance to take possession of his desk at Stanhope Gate, Lord Prior was forced to act. At a meeting with the Association of British Insurers, representing the interests of big shareholders, it was agreed that the original package which could have delivered

Simpson up to £10 million in pay, pensions and bonuses should be toned down, and the bonus terms made more exacting.

Nevertheless, it left a sour taste. The same corporate governance dogma which had dogged Weinstock's final years at GEC had brought his company grief yet again – this was ironic, given Weinstock's notorious meanness about payments to his executives. The episode irked Weinstock, whose only instruction had been that Simpson's package at GEC should match what he was receiving at Lucas. He was to vent his anger at his farewell annual general meeting and in a valedictory interview with the *Financial Times*: 'I didn't happen to see the final arrangement we made with George Simpson, and I agree the threshold figure was silly, but there was nothing outrageous about it. His remuneration was not at all unreasonable for the job, and mostly he only got what Lucas was already giving him. If that is an example of the way Greenbury is meant to work, I am afraid it doesn't work.'[33]

Weinstock's final annual general meeting as managing director of GEC was held at noon on 6 September 1996, at the London Hilton. Two hundred and fifty shareholders assembled beneath the twinkling chandeliers for the last appearance of the old master. When almost everyone else had taken their places Weinstock made a quiet but nevertheless dramatic entrance, joining the rest of the board lined up on the stage behind a long table, beneath a simple GEC logo in yellow on a plain blue background. He was greeted by applause. Lord Prior, as chairman, made the customary tribute to Weinstock's brilliance, which was received with a half-hearted standing ovation.

Then came the moment the shareholders had been waiting for, the final speech. But it was to be a disappointment, which gave no sense of the importance of the occasion. GEC's record, Weinstock stated matter-of-factly, was the result of a team effort: 'No one does these things on his own. It is a team, each of whom puts their ego behind them.' When it came to corporate governance, the tone of his remarks changed sharply. While it was true that there had been some examples in Britain of 'greed and unrestricted exploitation of privileges', much of the pressure put on directors bordered on 'persecution'. The principles of Greenbury and Cadbury, the two corporate governance codes, were not, in Weinstock's view, 'tablets of stone handed down from Mount Sinai', and should be treated as principles, not unbendable rules. Weinstock clearly distrusted the corporate governance revolution, of which he saw himself as a victim.

The long-drawn-out debate over who would follow Weinstock, and the subsequent dispute over George Simpson's salary, detracted from the achievements of Weinstock's final years at the helm of GEC. Rather than pandering to the short-term interests of the stock market and the demands of the analysts and the financial press for a higher share price, Weinstock spent those years with higher strategic goals in mind. Through the consolidation of the defence industry and the alliances he made on the Continent he demonstrated the determination of GEC to remain a military contractor in the post-Cold War era. Moreover, the alliances in the power sector and telecoms showed a mastery of the new global economics, sadly not equalled by most of British industry, which ensured that GEC would remain a world-class player.

The succession struggle, though, proved to be Weinstock's Achilles heel. By his failure to prepare an orderly internal succession, he ensured that his last years as managing director of GEC were marked by factional disputes, leaks and criticism which did much to damage the reputation for clear-headed management he had built up over three decades. There was also personal tragedy, first with the realisation that the City would not tolerate a family succession with Simon talking the helm, then with Simon's illness and death. However, the final tribute to Weinstock's industrial prowess was the realisation by his successor George Simpson that once the industrial division had been tidied up, his role would be to build on the value and strategic directions of other businesses that had been personally sculpted by Weinstock.

But it was also a signal that the old era of Weinstock domination at the most senior levels of GEC was at an end. Within a month of Simpson's taking over in September 1996, his allies were appointed as heads of personnel and strategic planning. By early 1997 a purge of Weinstock loyalists was under way.[34]

# CHAPTER EIGHT

## *The Man and his Passions*

THE BALLYMACOLL STUD, occupying some three hundred acres of rolling limestone pastures in Ireland's County Meath, is something of an anachronism. In an age when bloodstock breeding and racing in the British Isles are increasingly dominated by an elite of super-rich Gulf potentates like the Al Maktoum family from Dubai, Bally-macoll, with its slightly faded turquoise-and-yellow paintwork and crumbling stable yard, is owned and controlled – down to the last detail – by a shrewd businessman of Polish-Jewish descent: Arnold Weinstock. In an age when the individual racehorse breeder has given way to slick, globally promoted stud farms like Coolmore, controlled by the racing magnate John Magnier, the Ballymacoll operation is testimony to different values. It is a gentle place surrounded by neatly clipped hedgerows and well maintained stud fences, but has the same old-fashioned, slightly musty feel as the headquarters of the General Electric Company at Stanhope Gate. Unlike the nearby studs owned by Middle Eastern bloodstock bree-ders there are no high electronically controlled gates, security cameras or new, architect-designed stable blocks and foaling areas. Behind the pretty main building in the Ballymacoll yard are stables which are in such a state of disrepair that they can no longer be used; the floodlighting for the tennis courts at the stable yard has never been installed, even though the poles went up a long time ago, because the cash ran out. Many of the same strict accounting disciplines which have been applied by Weinstock to his business life have been applied to the bloodstock operation – an irony, in that even the most frugally run stud must be viewed as an extravagance.

When it comes to breeding racehorses, the stallions are generally regarded as the stars of the show. It is the winners of the Group

One races (the twenty-five classic flat races of international importance), like Dancing Brave, syndicated for stud purposes to a group of investors for £14 million after a brilliant racing career, who are the glamour boys of the racing fraternity, the belief being that the talent of the stallion will be bred into the progeny. At Ballymacoll, they take a different view. The stud manager Peter Reynolds, who has been working with bloodstock since he was a teenager, stoutly maintains that the brood mares, which provide 50 per cent of the carefully nurtured gene pool for any racehorse, are just as important as the stallions. Reynolds currently has twenty-five mares on the go for the Weinstock family, having cut the number from forty-five over the last seven or eight years in an effort to focus on the most promising bloodlines and keep costs under control. In a racing year Ballymacoll will produce twenty-two or twenty-three birthings.

Among the most important decisions to be taken at any stud is the choice of stallion to send to the mare. Although Arnold Weinstock, as proprietor of Ballymacoll, had taken these decisions for as long as can be remembered, at the stud it was his late son Simon who was the ultimate arbiter, recalls Reynolds: 'Simon used to pick the stallions, which stallions to put with which mares and how much to pay. He had a photographic memory for horses and pedigree. He could look at any horse, remember its name and its breeding. He was quite young, still at school and very shy when he took an interest in the stud. I remember the old man [Weinstock] telling me to get him out and about in the horse business, it could do him some good.'[1]

Since Simon's death, which was perhaps more deeply mourned in the close world of racing than anywhere else, Weinstock has picked up the pieces. Even during his long reign as managing director of GEC he could always find time in his schedule for racing and breeding decisions. In his otherwise stark and dimly illuminated offices at Stanhope Gate the only brightness is provided by the gleam of the picture lights on oil paintings of his winning thoroughbreds. Like many of Weinstock's colleagues in the business sphere, Peter Reynolds, a distinguished figure in tweeds with a gentle Irish lilt to his voice, has become used over the years to the late-night phone call from the old man, who has spotted something to question in the stud books, or decided to send one of his injured horses back to the stud for a season of recuperation. Alternatively Reynolds will confer with Weinstock before he leaves for Stanhope Gate in the morning, on for instance the stud plans for a particular mare or the yearlings to be put up for sale at Newmarket.

Over recent decades horse-racing has had to struggle to keep its reputation clean in the face of drugging, horsenapping and other scandals. The sport has been used by some owners, including some who have set up in Ireland, as a form of tax avoidance. Weinstock has studiously avoided the seedier side of the game. The same scruples – some would say meanness – which he has applied to his business dealings are characteristic of his handling of the stud. First-cut hay, the crop from a newly cultivated field, is deemed as essential for brood mares and yearlings on a stud farm, to ensure that they receive the best protein and nutrition. Since most stud farms are not large enough to produce their own supplies, it has to be bought in from outside. Most stud managers find a reliable supplier and negotiate a regular supply. Not at Ballymacoll. Weinstock checks each hay invoice personally, and has in the past demanded that the contract goes out to tender each year, in case the supplier tries to cheat the stud.

His integrity can at times seem inflexible and obsessive. On one occasion Reynolds, on behalf of the stud, sold an unpromising yearling at the local horse fair for £600 to a trader who handed him a shoebox full of cash. When Reynolds suggested the cash be used to pay the stable lads their Christmas bonus, Weinstock's reply was emphatic: 'I pay tax on what I earn; you, Peter, pay tax on what you earn; so why should anyone else be paid in cash? Put it in the bank.'[2]

On other occasions Weinstock has offered members of his stud staff or his trainers the use of a GEC jet to attend a race meeting on the Continent or a distant auction. Whereas in some public companies this would be regarded as one of the perks available to the managing director's colleagues, that was never the case for Weinstock. Each flight would be carefully logged, and the individual or the stud billed for it.

Weinstock's love affair with horse-racing, to which he was drawn by his father-in-law Michael Sobell, is an enigma. Despite his prudence and caution in business, which has led to criticism, there has always been a more raffish side to his character, a liking for the good life to which bloodstock racing provides ready access. The same man who would scrutinise the cost of a bale of hay, or resent the idea of a tax-free bonus for his stable lads, would think nothing of taking a private jet to Deauville for a day's racing, flying to La Scala for the first night of an opera or taking his whole family to Barbados on Concorde for Christmas. Weinstock has mused that somewhere way back in his Polish-Jewish ancestry, about which he has shown surprisingly little curiosity, there was an inveterate gambler. Certainly, horse-racing has always attracted prominent members of the Jewish community. James Joll was a legendary Jewish racehorse owner, and the betting enclosures of racecourses are still populated by Jewish bookies and their runners. Britain's largest and most successful betting chain, Ladbrokes, was largely the creation of Cyril Stein, a confidant of Weinstock and a traditional Jew. Moreover, at the racecourse – notwithstanding the snobbery of the Royal Enclosure at Ascot – anyone who can afford to be there is an equal, whether Arab or Jew. Amid the discussion of breeding and betting, form and odds, handicapping and bloodstock, there is a great levelling process, a sense that behind the veneer of professionalism everyone is being foolhardy together. Weinstock recognises this. Talking of his horses, he says: 'I less enjoy spending money on them than seeing them win races. The spending bit is not all that fun, the spending bit goes with hope. Owning racehorses is a game for people who are optimistic, and I am naturally not all that optimistic, so it goes a bit against the grain.'[3]

As investments go, horse-racing might not be the first choice of a hard-headed businessman. Behind the façade of glamour and the headline figures in their millions of pounds, it is all but impossible to beat the odds. The average return on expenditure for a racehorse in the British Isles is 21 per cent: in other words, a horse can be expected to win just a fifth of what it costs to keep. The bigger the operation and the more control there is over the breeding, the better the chances of beating the statistics. Weinstock has done better than most. Between 1990 and 1995 his horses accumulated £1.4 million in prize money, and far higher figures would have been earned from putting his winners out to stud.[4] Despite this success, however, the Weinstock family are relative minnows in the racing world: Sheikh Mohammed and the Al Maktoum family are estimated to have poured up to £1.5 billion into the sport since 1980.

Weinstock and his father-in-law Michael Sobell's formal entry into the world of horse-racing came in 1957, at the time they were preparing to launch Radio & Allied onto the stock market. Acting on the advice of the revered jockey and trainer Sir Gordon Richards, the two racing novices bought a little-known four-year-old stallion, with apparently little to commend it, called London Cry for 3,500 guineas. Richards felt that the horse might improve with a change of stable, and he was quickly proven right. London Cry went on to win six of its first nine races, among them the Cambridgeshire Handicap at Newmarket, where it came in at 20 to 1, carrying a record weight. When London Cry retired from racing, it took a great deal of persuasion to stop Sobell from putting it out to pasture at his house at Englefield Green near Windsor.

The unexpected success of London Cry instilled the bloodstock bug in its novice owners. Their boldest move came in 1960 with the death of one of the great characters of British racing, Dorothy Paget, who had set new standards of lavishness and eccentricity as an owner-breeder between the wars, financing her habit with the fortune she inherited at the age of twenty-one. She intensely disliked the company of men, and surrounded herself with women minders and horses. As an owner she was exasperating to deal with, which led to constant tensions: she would dine at 7 a.m., sleep during the day, get up for a vast breakfast in the evening, and then begin phoning her trainers. Her odd and high-handed ways attracted a great deal of publicity, but her investment in racing brought her some notable successes, such as Golden Miller, which won the Cheltenham Gold Cup five times in a row between 1932 and 1936, and is the only horse ever to win the Gold Cup and the Grand National in the same year. When she planted a kiss on Golden Miller's nose after one of his victories, one racegoer suggested it was probably the first time she had kissed a member of the opposite sex. 'And he's a gelding,' pointed out another.[5] She was also a successful owner and breeder on the flat, winning the Derby in 1943 with Straight Deal.

Dorothy Paget was a huge gambler, once betting £160,000 on

an 8 to 1 outsider, which duly obliged by winning. When she died in 1960 her then favoured trainer Sir Gordon Richards looked around among his other owners for a buyer of her racing interests. His first port of call was the Greek shipping magnate Stavros Niarchos, but when that fell through Richards turned to Michael Sobell. In June 1960 Sobell and his son-in-law Arnold Weinstock brought the Paget bloodstock and facilities for a quarter of a million pounds. For this relatively modest outlay they received a substantial package:

> The deal comprised the Ballymacoll Stud Farm, three hundred acres of prime stud-farming land in County Meath, near Dunboyne, a favourite meet of the Ward Union hounds, together with more than 120 head of stock of all denominations, horses in training, mares, yearlings and foals ... Amongst the twenty-two mares were Cychnet, destined to become the dam of champion sire Wolver Hollow (Eclipse Stakes) and Straight Bod, who features as the grandam of Peleid (St Leger).[6]

Pinned on the wall of Peter Reynolds' office at Ballymacoll are the bloodlines of the current crop of mares dating back to 1931. The oldest line is descended from Jamaica Inn, which was bought as a yearling at Doncaster.

It was one of Dorothy Paget's eccentricities which was to bring the Sobell–Weinstock collaboration its first successes after they bought up her stud and stock. Among her unusual breeding tactics was the practice of buying mother and daughter whenever the opportunity arose. In 1942 Miss Paget purchased Third Act and her daughter Second Act as in-foal mares at Newmarket. They were part of a job-lot of horses from Lord Portman's bloodstock and seemed to have little to commend them, coming from less than distinguished bloodlines. Despite this, Second Act's first filly, Internaval, bred from Jamaica Inn, proved remarkable, winning a series of races in Ireland and going on to produce Matal and Bandrilla, the first winners for Sobell and Weinstock.

The source of the partnership's greatest success was to be La Milo, who was not generally seen as a class horse, but who had remarkable stamina and courage. As racing mare she won four consecutive handicaps and as a dam, breeding at Ballymacoll, she produced seven winners. In the 1970s many of the breeding decisions at the stud passed to Weinstock's son Simon, still in his twenties, whose interest in racing began while he was still at school. Flying in the face of his father's advice, Simon proposed that La Milo be covered by the stallion Petingo. At 8.30 p.m. on 25 March 1976, having gone three weeks over the normal gestation period, La Milo produced Troy. The foal seemed to be rather backward, but this did not worry Peter Reynolds, who believes that it is often the phlegmatic foals which know how to avoid trouble when they are young which turn out to be the best prospects. More advanced and lively foals can injure themselves, and can prove to be unreliable when raced. In Troy, Reynolds' judgement was proved correct.

Before Troy was a yearling he had been orphaned. The eleven-year-old Petingo suffered a fatal heart attack, and his dam La Milo, who had been so productive, was put down after Troy had been weaned, when her hind pasterns gave out. As a colt Troy was trained by Major Dick Hern at the West Isley stables in Berkshire, which the increasingly successful Sobell–Weinstock partnership had acquired from Sir John Astor in 1965. The two-year-old Troy began his first racing season promisingly enough. On his debut at Salisbury in June 1978 he finished second over six furlongs, and he went on in the same season to win at Newmarket and Goodwood over seven furlongs, starting as favourite in both races. The following year, as a three-year-old, Troy embarked on an astonishing winning sequence. He began the season by winning the Sandown Classic Trial Stakes on 28 April, took the Predominate Stakes in May, and went on to Epsom for the two hundredth running of the Derby on 6 June. Even before the race Sir Michael Sobell, eighty-six years old but still as spry as ever, was supremely confident of the horse which had been bred as a result of his grandson Simon's intuition. 'Troy may be the best horse I have ever owned,' he publicly declared.[7]

At the halfway stage of the race Troy was badly placed, and appeared to be struggling. As he entered the straight there were still at least a dozen horses in front of him when his jockey Willie Carson, wearing the distinctive light-blue and yellow Ballymacoll silks, switched him away from the rails. Troy's quality began to show as he picked up speed and left the opposition standing, storming away to win by seven lengths, the biggest winning margin in the Derby since 1925. After the race the two owners, along with Carson and trainer Dick Hern, were invited to the royal box by the Queen, whose entrant Milford had been rejected by Carson in favour of Troy.

Despite his cultivated reputation for meanness, Weinstock shared Troy's glory with his colleagues. William Waldegrave, later to become a Conservative cabinet minister, was Weinstock's personal assistant at the time, and was struck by Weinstock's thoughtfulness and generosity:

> It was the two hundredth anniversary Derby and he won with Troy. And that was terrific in every kind of way. Caroline [Waldegrave's wife] and I were quite impoverished at the time; he wasn't paying me very much. Why should he? Anyway, I got a cheque for a quite useful but rather odd sum, like £132.47, and a note saying, 'You remember that when Troy entered the Derby the odds were such and such on the first day, and you remember that I put on a pound for you' – of course, I hadn't. 'Here are your winnings.' I thought it was an elegant way of giving all your friends some recognition.[8]

Even after this triumph, Troy's season was still far from over. He went on to win the Irish Sweepstakes Derby on 30 June, the King George VI and Queen Elizabeth Diamond Stakes on 28 July and the Benson and Hedges Cup on 21 August. At this stage Sobell and Weinstock were still undecided as to whether to race Troy for another season as a four-year-old, or to put him straight out to stud. Weinstock told an interviewer at the time: 'As long as he enjoys his racing we will not be thinking too much about him going out to stud. But each time he races he is taking on the best. I suppose the horse will tell us, but at this stage I can't say whether he will race as a four-year-old or where he will stand at stud.'[9]

The only classic mountain left for Troy to climb was the Prix de l'Arc de Triomphe on 7 October, where he finished third in a field of twenty-two runners. Despite this setback, it had been a remarkable

Henry Kissinger, briefly a GEC adviser, with Weinstock and Lord Rothschild.

*Right* Two future GEC chairmen, Lords Carrington and Prior, leaving 10 Downing Street after a Cabinet meeting.

*Below* Chairman Lord Prior celebrates GEC's centenary, April 1986.

Simon Weinstock in 1993, three years before his untimely death at the age of forty-four.

*Left* Weinstock at his country mansion at Bowden, Wiltshire, 1987.

*Above* In the study at Bowden.

*Above left* The Hon. Sara Morrison, Weinstock's confidante and GEC director.

*Above* Weinstock and Lady Netta.

*Left* Weinstock in his office at Stanhope Gate, surrounded by pictures of racehorses.

*Overleaf* Weinstock in 1995.

season, with eight wins and three places, earning £450,494 in prize money. Troy was the first horse ever to make a clean sweep of all the Group One events for which he qualified in one season, eclipsing the records of such greats as Nijinsky, Grundy and The Minstrel, none of which was Anglo–Irish bred. But Troy was more than just a winner: he was seen as underlining the quality of breeding in the British Isles.

Once the value which Troy could yield at stud became clear, there was little doubt that he would not run as a four-year-old. He was put out to syndicate by the Queen's racing manager Lord Porchester, acting on Sobell and Weinstock's behalf. Forty shares in the stallion were sold for £180,000 each, placing his value at £7.2 million. Among the buyers was the Queen. Troy's syndication, as much as his winnings, changed the whole economics of Ballymacoll's breeding operation. There was now money to invest in upgrading facilities, and any doubts Weinstock may have been harbouring that the stud was rather too expensive a hobby were eased. Although Troy was not notably successful at stud he did sire for the Weinstock colours Helen Street, which triumphed in the Irish Oaks in 1985.

After Simon's success in producing Troy, many of the main breeding and training decisions at Ballymacoll were passed on to him. The circle of trainers patronised by the Weinstocks broadened beyond Dick Hern to include the French trainer David Smaga, who prepared Lancastrian to win the 1983 Prix Ganay at Longchamp. Others with strong Weinstock connections were John Hammond, Lord Huntingdon, Peter Chapple-Hyam and Michael Stoute.

Simon cleverly purchased Ela-Mana-Mou in 1979, and it went on to win the Eclipse Stakes at Sandown and the King George VI and Queen Elizabeth Diamond Stakes in 1980. The Weinstocks' best filly was Sun Princess, which won the Oaks by twelve lengths as a maiden in 1983 and went on to further classic success in the St Leger. In recent years the Weinstock colours have triumphed at the 1995 Irish Two Thousand Guineas with Spectrum, who also went on to win the Champion Stakes at Newmarket.

The ultimate goal for the Weinstock partnership has always been the Prix de l'Arc de Triomphe, the race which eluded Troy, Homeric, Ela-Mana-Mou and Sun Princess. But there was some consolation in October 1996 when the jockey Walter Swinburn, just recovered from serious injuries suffered in a fall in Hong Kong, rode the Weinstock colours to victory on Pilsudski in the Breeders' Cup Turf at Woodbine Park in Toronto. This race, which comes at the end of the European season, is the richest and among the most highly regarded bloodstock events in the world.

As he watched the replay of his victory, an emotional Swinburn recalled his own recent brush with death, and the loss of the breeder-owner Simon Weinstock who had brought Pilsudski on to triumph: 'I remember lying there [in Hong Kong] thinking that this could be the end of my days as a jockey, but my family and the doctors pulled me through, and I dedicate this victory to them. There have been many sad things and I can't tell you what this victory means to me.'[10]

Coming as it did within a month of the memorial celebration of Simon's life at the Royal Opera House, Pilsudski's win brought into sharp relief Weinstock's memories of his son's involvement with racing. In Simon's encyclopaedic knowledge of breeding and form, the Weinstock racing partnership had lost one of its greatest assets.

However, after his retirement as managing director of GEC, Weinstock, theoretically at least, has more time to indulge his passion for racehorses, which always had to take second place to the responsibilities of the boardroom. The personal touches in his new post-retirement offices at GEC are the horse paintings on the walls and a television monitor which provides a comprehensive closed-circuit feed from racecourses around the country. His involvement in decisions affecting the stud and training is as close as ever, and he never ceases to amaze those who work in his racing operations at how outrageous he can be when it comes to questioning judgements, decisions and spending. It is exactly the same technique he uses in all his dealings: he enjoys the cut and thrust of debate, often delivering his cuts sardonically, with a twinkle in his eye. For the uninitiated, unfamiliar with the subtleties of his moods, his interventions can be misinterpreted as rude and hostile. An obsession with detail, whether it be in the form book, the score of a Mozart opera or a balance sheet is deeply rooted in Weinstock's personality and is partly, as he has conceded, based upon fear of failure.

*     *     *

If Weinstock had chosen any career path other than business, the strong likelihood is that it would have been music. His devotion to bloodstock came relatively late, but music, particularly choral music, was part of his life from childhood. As a boy at the Stoke Newington Central School he appeared in the chorus of *The Yeomen of the Guard* and would spend nights high in the gallery at Sadler's Wells; later, after the death of his parents, he sang in the choir at the Poet's Road Synagogue; and while at the LSE at Cambridge he would work to the accompaniment of classical music.

Although Weinstock is far too reserved to display his musical prowess in public, his great friend the Italian conductor Riccardo Muti is convinced that Weinstock could as successfully conduct a major orchestra as he can organise the syndication of a stallion or dominate a takeover bid: 'If Lord Weinstock had chosen to be so, he would have been a great musical talent. If he stood in front of an orchestra, he would be capable of conducting it. He moves his arms well and has the range. He has a great ear, understands the cadences of the music and would make a great conductor. He would be fine in front of an orchestra. He is not uncritical and has told me if he has a problem with an opera I am conducting.'[11]

Though Weinstock's Jewishness has never played a large part in his public life, to this day he traces his love of the choral sound back to those schoolboy days in the Poet's Road Synagogue, and he believes that cantorial music, one of the great traditions in Jewish worship, shares many characteristics with grand opera.

Music is an integral part of Weinstock's daily routine. Every morning, after he has had breakfast at his Grosvenor Square flat – usually with Netta, although she also spends time at the family's country home at Bowden in Wiltshire – the emeritus chairman of GEC retreats to his dressing room, puts on an operatic compact disc, and turns the volume up as high as if he were at a live performance. He sporadically waves his toothbrush in the air as he listens, conducting the music. If he has chosen an emotional piece he will be quickly moved to tears. His choice of opera will vary with his mood: in the course of a takeover bid he might listen to Rossini's *William Tell*, in which the beautiful music symbolising the fight for Swiss independence is filled with the call of the hunting horn.[12]

Weinstock's tendency to linger in his dressing room listening to opera to psyche himself up for the day ahead partly explains some of his unusual habits as a business figure. In an age when it is *de rigueur* in most companies for the chief executive to be in the gym, or planted at his desk at dawn, Weinstock conducts himself in a much more leisurely way. Quite often he does not arrive in the office until mid-morning, although he may have taken some phone calls at home. But a day which starts at an unconventionally late hour also tends to stretch on until mid-evening, with Weinstock still clearing his backlog of phone calls until at least 8.30 in the evening, unless he has to leave for a dinner, a concert or the opera.

Weinstock's musical hero is his friend Riccardo Muti. Indeed, he could almost be described as a Muti groupie, and cannot bear to miss the Italian conductor's opening nights at the Teatro Alla Scala in Milan, arguably the most revered temple of opera. In some respects the dark, athletic, virtuoso conductor and the captain of industry make an odd couple. Muti first registered on the British musical scene in December 1972 when at the relatively young age of thirty-one he made his debut with the Philharmonia Orchestra at the Royal Festival Hall. He brought with him a formidable reputation. His career as a conductor had begun in Milan in the mid-1960s when he won the Cantelli competition for conductors. In 1969, after making his professional debut, he conducted a concert at the Maggio Musicale festival in Florence. This was such a success that he became the festival's chief conductor. As Muti's reputation grew rapidly he was invited to appear at the Lucerne, Montreux and Salzburg festivals, and made his debut at the Vienna State Opera conducting a new production of *Aida*, and at Paris with *Il Trovatore*. In 1974 he began a twelve-year association with London's Philharmonia, in the course of which he transformed the struggling orchestra into a great ensemble by virtue of his hugely energetic talent. He went on to do the same for the Philadelphia Orchestra before landing the prized position of musical director at La Scala in 1986. Muti has been recognised as much for his campaigning and intellectual approach to musicality as for his energy. It is the intelligent quality of his conducting, characterised by his efforts to remove what he regards as corrupt performing practices from nineteenth-century Italian opera, which is so appealing to admirers like Weinstock.

When he appeared on *Desert Island Discs* in May 1993, Weinstock set a precedent by becoming the first guest to choose the same conductor for all of his eight recordings. He acknowledged that he was Muti's greatest fan: 'Given the necessity to choose eight records from the great mass of music I love, I found that quite impossible unless one reduces the number of variables. So I took a couple of constant things. One was that since I have a special relationship with Muti, who I have been friends with for many years, I chose to have records performed by him; and secondly, all the performances which I chose are things which I actually saw happen.'[13]

Describing his first choice, Gustav Mahler's Symphony No. 1, Weinstock explained to the presenter Sue Lawley that his love of music originated in the synagogue choir and that he was attracted to Mahler as he was born a Jew, although the composer was later baptised. Weinstock chose a moment in the symphony at which, he said, the conventional Viennese music suddenly becomes 'very Jewish', with the music of a Jewish wedding creeping in. His other choices included passages from Mozart's *Così fan tutte*, conducted by Muti at the Salzburg Festival; Vivaldi's *Gloria*, which demonstrates Muti's special talent with choral music; Handel's *Water Music*, played by the Berlin Philharmonic; the Verdi *Requiem* from La Scala; part of the first act of Bellini's *I Capuleti e i Montecchi* as performed at the Royal Opera House; and the Vienna Philharmonic's rendering of Johann Strauss's *Egyptian March* from one of Muti's now traditional New Year's Day concerts. His choice of book was the twenty-volume *New Grove Dictionary of Music and Musicians*.

The relationship between Muti and Weinstock is not like that between musician and patron, in the traditional sense. It is far more personal and deeply rooted. In Weinstock's greatest hour of need, after the death of his son Simon, Muti immediately volunteered his time to conduct a memorial concert at Covent Garden. Sitting in his dressing room at the Royal Festival Hall, with the sounds of the orchestra warming up filling the corridors, Muti says: 'I am very fond of Lord Weinstock and Lady Netta. I love him as a brother. He is the most rewarding person that I know.'[14] The softly-spoken Weinstock still retains the good singing voice of his youth, and it is not unknown for him and Muti's wife to burst into duets while the two families dine together in Rome.

261

The mutual admiration between Weinstock and Muti dates back to the early 1970s when the two men were guests in Tuscany of Sir Ronald Grierson, one of Weinstock's oldest business associates. The up-and-coming young conductor was working in Florence before taking up his appointment at the Philharmonia, and the meeting was memorable because of the heat of the discussion, with Weinstock challenging Muti's interpretation of *Così fan tutte* (he was eventually to concede that Muti was right). At that time Weinstock's taste in music was largely centred on Bach, Mozart and Haydn, and Muti claims that it was he who educated the industrialist about nineteenth-century Italian opera and more modern composers, and also takes credit for converting Weinstock to the *Ring* cycle, although he instinctively – like many Jews – distrusts Wagner. Muti demonstrated that *Parsifal* was in fact based upon Gregorian chant, eventually converting Weinstock.

Weinstock may intensely dislike travelling on business, preferring the security of his own office, but when it comes to Muti's performances he willingly catches a plane. Whenever possible he attends Muti's first nights at La Scala and Salzburg. On one occasion he flew to New York for the opening night of *Tosca* at the Metropolitan Opera, only to find the performance had been cancelled, so the two men retired to a restaurant for dinner. Weinstock always steers clear of Muti before performances, and has never asked him for tickets – an occupational hazard of conductors. On occasions when Weinstock has met up with him after a performance, Muti has been conscious of the 'moistness in his eyes'.

Weinstock sometimes takes guests to Muti's performances, and when Margaret Thatcher was prime minister he invited her to *Così fan tutte* at the Salzburg Festival. Mrs Thatcher was less than pleased with the opera, which she believed reflected badly on women, but Muti soothed her somewhat by explaining that it was neither pro-man nor pro-woman, and that in fact the feminine '*tutte*' in the title reflected female dominance.

Weinstock's musical friendship with Muti has not been one-way. He has recruited Muti to his own causes, including the staging of a production of Bellini's *I Capuleti e i Montecchi* at Covent Garden (Muti believes that without Weinstock's support some of the lesser-known Bellini operas might never have been produced, and a recording of this production was one of his desert island choices) and appearances at the Ravinia Festival, the annual summer gathering in a park in Chicago at which the events include concerts by the Chicago Symphony Orchestra and visiting orchestras as well as jazz performances.

Unlike other prominent Anglo-Jewish businessmen, such as Sir Stanley Kalms of the electrical retailers Dixons and Cyril Stein of Ladbrokes, Weinstock has never sought to play a public role in Jewish community life. His heavy involvement in his grand passions of horse-racing and music, and his work as a very active Trustee of the British Museum, together with his punishing work schedule, left little time for such activity. Moreover, until his death at the age of one hundred in 1993, Weinstock's father-in-law Sir Michael Sobell was one of Anglo-Jewry's greatest benefactors, providing leadership in an area which his son-in-law preferred to give a wide berth. Sobell's public philanthropy, which still lives on through his charitable foundation, was a model for the rest of the community. He was a great supporter of Britain's main rabbinical seminary Jews' College, the home for the elderly Nightingale House, and he funded the Michael Sobell Sinai School and the Michael Sobell Day Centre in Golders Green. In Israel, Sobell was a benefactor of the Haifa Technion (a technological/research-based university), the Bar-Ilan University, to which he donated a sports centre, and Magen David Admon, the Israeli ambulance service. His philanthropy was not confined to Jewish causes, and he sought to give something back to the country which had adopted him: he supported cancer charities and endowed two sports centres in his name in South Wales and Islington, North London. On his death he left the bulk of his £47 million estate to the Sobell Foundation, which continues to establish sports centres and support day centres.

From Weinstock's point of view it was far better for his father-in-law, rather than him, to be seen as the great benefactor of the Jewish community. GEC was dependent on overseas markets for its commercial success, particularly in its defence production. Until the Middle East peace process began to advance in the mid-1990s it was better for Weinstock and the shareholders of GEC that he and the company were not too closely identified with Jewish causes and with Israel in particular, because of the threat of Arab black-listing.

This does not mean that Weinstock turned his back on his Jewish heritage – far from it. Unlike his father-in-law he preferred his contributions to Jewish and Israeli causes to be anonymous, and to let others take on the community leadership role. Nevertheless, even though he would practise his Judaism lightly, Weinstock's commitment to his background has been profound, and friends and colleagues recount many acts of personal kindness. Moreover, in his business dealings and his extensive relations with politicians, Weinstock would use his treasure chest of Jewish humour to good effect, and he has never been shy of peppering his conversation with the Yiddish words of his Stoke Newington childhood. 'He is conscious and proud of being Jewish,' says the former Chairman of the Conservative Party Lord Tebbit, who came to know Weinstock when he was minister at the Department of Trade and Industry in the 1980s. He remembers a dinner conversation in 1995 when he told Weinstock that he infinitely preferred the Old Testament to the New. Weinstock retorted: 'There is a holy bible and a New Testament!'[15]

In many respects Weinstock's attachment to Judaism has been more cultural and emotional than activist, as he has led a very assimilated life. But as a prominent figure in British business he was sometimes the target of racial stereotyping. One of those involved in the mishandled attempted to take over GEC in the 1980s, the leader of the Metsun consortium Lord Cuckney, says of Weinstock: 'It sounds racist, but he has an extremely Shylock approach. Very difficult to describe, but it's a slightly aggressive bullying manner, which I find very, very unattractive.'[16]

At the time of the epoch-making GEC bid for AEI in 1967 Weinstock's son Simon, then at Winchester, was the butt of anti-Semitic abuse, which may have contributed to his detachment from his Jewish background. During the same bid there were also mutterings about the concentration of so much power over Britain's electrical industries in the hands of the son of Polish-Jewish immigrants.

Similarly, during one bitterly-fought takeover battle Weinstock came to suspect his opposite number of what one participant has called 'blatant anti-Semitism'. Weinstock was deeply scarred by the experience, as he had encountered little prejudice of this type during his long period at the top of British industry, where people are mainly judged by performance rather than by having been to the right school or having the right ethnic background.

Weinstock's main spiritual attachment is as a member of the New London Synagogue in St John's Wood, where the religious leader is Rabbi Louis Jacobs, one of Anglo-Jewry's most prominent intellectuals, who split from mainstream United Synagogue orthodoxy in 1964 to establish his own 'Masorti' ('traditional' in Hebrew) movement. Rabbi Jacobs, who in his previous incarnation as a traditional United Synagogue rabbi officiated at the wedding of Weinstock and Netta in 1949, believes there is a middle way in Judaism which strikes a balance between the extremes of the religion. In a recent book he argues that Masorti seeks a balance between Orthodox and Reform Judaism, 'taking issue with Orthodoxy in its theory and with Reform in its practice'.[17] In Jacobs' view his form of Judaism, of which Weinstock is an adherent, affirms the validity of traditional observances but is more open to change. Weinstock's observance of his faith has been irregular, although he usually attends the synagogue on Kol Nidre, the solemn eve of the Day of Atonement (Yom Kippur) service, when Jews around the world gather to ask God to annul all religious vows as part of the process of forgiveness and redemption.

However, at times of family crisis it is to Louis Jacobs that Weinstock turns. When his son Simon died in May 1996, there were serious questions as to whether he was entitled to a Jewish funeral, given his church marriage to a non-Jew. But at Arnold's request Rabbi Jacobs was among the officiants at Simon's Jewish burial in Willesden, even though his sense of his Jewish identity had been slight.

If there is a major regret in Arnold Weinstock's life, it is that the rich Jewish heritage of his childhood was not passed on to Simon. In recent years, as Weinstock's own Jewish feelings have strengthened, he has been comforted by the fact that his daughter Susan, although she too married a gentile, has decided to bring her children up in the Jewish faith. In traditional Judaism the faith passes down through the female line, which means that Susan's children Clare, Karis Anne and Jerome are considered Jewish, despite having a

non-Jewish father. In recent years Susan has affirmed that background by sending her children to Hebrew classes and becoming
closely involved with the local Liberal Jewish community. This
reaching out to a Jewish past has given Weinstock a great deal of
pleasure and satisfaction. Watching his grandchildren grow up with
a Jewish identity partly makes up for his own failure to instil a
stronger sense of his Jewishness in Simon.

Weinstock's growing closeness to his Jewish roots has been
reflected in his charitable giving. When the Anglo-Jewish com-
munity sought to erect a memorial to Raoul Wallenberg, the
Swedish hero of the Holocaust, a nine-foot bronze statue by the
Sussex sculptor Philip Jackson in front of the Western Marble Arch
Synagogue, Weinstock was among the first to make a donation to
Sir Sigmund Sternberg, the Jewish entrepreneur and philanthropist
organising the venture. Similarly, he has been a willing giver to
Anglo-Jewish educational causes, including Britain's only Jewish
public school, Carmel College at Wallingford in Oxfordshire – often
known as the Jewish Eton – which before its closure in 1997 sought
to combine the best of public school academic and sporting instruction with traditional Jewish values. One friend with a more traditional background says of Weinstock: 'There is a Jewish spark, a
soul there.'[18]

As a result of GEC-Marconi's role as a major defence contractor,
with important customers in the Middle East, Weinstock's support
for the State of Israel has been circumspect. His sympathy with
Zionism was clear from an early age, and was reflected in his visit
to the embryonic Jewish state shortly before his marriage in 1949.
But by the 1960s GEC had become a big exporter of arms to the
Arab world, and although Israel let it be known that it was interested in buying GEC equipment, Weinstock dared not risk supplying it directly. However, apparently with the secret help of the
Israeli embassy in London, arrangements were made for some
limited supplies to be sent via third countries.

On the Monday morning after the outbreak of the Six-Day War
between Israel and its Arab neighbours in June 1967 a leading
figure from the Joint Israel Appeal, a British organisation which
offered Israel financial and moral support, was rung by Weinstock,
who bluntly asked: 'What can I do?' The immediate reply was to

send a cheque, and one duly arrived from the Weinstock Trust, which had been set up to make charitable donations. More importantly, however, Weinstock was also put in touch with officials at the Israeli embassy at a moment in the war when Israel was desperately short of supplies and spare parts.

Weinstock quietly arranged for a planeload of supplies for the Israeli armed forces to be sent by the Israeli carrier El Al, demonstrating a level of commitment to the Jewish state far beyond that which has been generally recognised. The risk Weinstock took in doing this was enormous. If details of his actions, which demonstrated an extraordinary degree of commitment to Israel, had slipped out it could have had dangerous consequences for him personally, for GEC, and for Britain diplomatically. Indeed, it is questionable whether he would have been able to remain at the helm of the group he had done so much to create. At the time when Israel was most threatened and all but friendless internationally, Weinstock was willing to take the most startling risks on its behalf. He was arguably a greater hero of the Israeli people than the many wealthy diaspora Jewish benefactors whose names are scattered on monuments, buildings, parks and colleges all over the country.

Despite Weinstock's commitment to the Jewish state, seen most vividly in 1967 and underlined over the years by regular cheques to the Joint Israel Appeal (although perhaps not of sums commensurate with his reputed personal fortune of £160 million[19]), he has not, like other successful diaspora Jews, sought to set up a second home there, or even been a frequent visitor. When he last visited Israel with his children in the 1980s he was disappointed. He found Jerusalem's luxury King David Hotel, with its rich history and views over the Old City, unimpressive – the paint in his room was peeling. He moved his party north to the coastal resort of Haifa, but there they encountered torrential rain, of an intensity known only to those who live in the Middle East, and he felt a cold coming on. This was enough of the Holy Land for Weinstock, who takes an obsessive interest in health matters, and he cut his visit short and flew back to London, with little desire to return.

The decision to abandon his holiday and to blame Israel, rather than the hoteliers and the weather, for his unsatisfactory experience is very characteristic of Weinstock. Places, people and associations are very important to him and forever become connected in his mind with events, however unfair that may be. He also tends to be shy of the unknown, and does not enjoy leaving the security of his Stanhope Gate offices, his Grosvenor Square apartment and his country home in Wiltshire, where he famously enjoys acting out the role of the country squire.

In much the same way as Weinstock has shied away from strong public commitments to Jewish causes and to Israel, he has generally kept his personal political views under wraps. He is among only a handful of individuals in British public life who can lay claim to having remained at the top of the ladder through nine changes of government and six prime ministers, and to have successfully ridden out the dramatic swings in Britain's post-war business cycles and industrial policy. Weinstock was knighted by a Labour government and ennobled during Margaret Thatcher's first administration.

Over the decades GEC's success has been largely dependent on maintaining good relations with government, whatever its political stripe. Until privatisation took off in the 1980s GEC's markets were dominated by government contracts, and one of the most persistent criticisms of Weinstock's period at the head of the company is that he became so fond of big government contracts that GEC failed to make the necessary investment in marketing, sales and new products which were necessary in a world without the security of public-sector contracts. In recent years, post-privatisation, GEC has become much more global in its outlook, winning large orders from Malaysia, China and other countries. But even these big international deals have been largely dependent on working closely with government in areas such as export credits. The necessity of remaining on good terms with government has been a constant concern for Weinstock. His disagreements with Margaret Thatcher did not prevent him from maintaining good relations with other Tories, including Michael Heseltine, and he has worked with a range of trade, defence and prime ministers

Moreover, Weinstock has not been averse to taking former leading politicians into Stanhope Gate in both executive and non-executive capacities. Successive chairmen of GEC Lords Carrington and Prior were exiles from Margaret Thatcher's Conservative Party.

Sara Morrison, the director responsible for all GEC's external affairs and a close confidante of Weinstock, has worked at his side since 1980, after being ejected from the Heathite Conservative Central Office when it was purged by Mrs Thatcher. William Waldegrave, who served in the Thatcher and Major administrations, most recently as Chief Secretary to the Treasury, was once Weinstock's personal assistant. In 1995 the former Conservative Trade Minister Richard Needham controversially moved straight to the GEC board-room. Demonstrating Weinstock's non-partisan tastes in politicians, (Lord) Denis Healey was asked to join GEC as chairman soon after Labour's disastrous defeat in the May 1983 election, to replace the former Tory Foreign Secretary Lord Carrington, who was being tipped to become Secretary General of NATO. Healey declined the offer, as he wanted to stay in politics.[20]

Despite his record of deploying the skills of former politicians, with the possible exception of the Wilson governments of the 1960s Weinstock has never been particularly associated with one political party. He was not among the group of fashionable 1980s industrial-ists like Lords Hanson, King and Shepherd who became so closely linked with the Thatcherite cause that it was all but impossible for them to extricate themselves from the web that had been woven when Margaret Thatcher was removed from office in 1990 and replaced by the less ideological John Major.

Given the importance to GEC of government contracts, Wein-stock has sensibly straddled the political fence. However, like much of Britain he was strongly sympathetic to the Attlee governments of the post-Second World War period which established the Welfare State and did much to lay the foundations for economic prosperity. 'I thought the Attlee government was a good thing. It had right on its side, insofar as there is a difference between decent behaviour towards the masses of people and indifference. The government cared about the people. Later it got its policies distorted and a lot of things went wrong, but the original basic intention was sound, it a little on the unrealistic side.'[21]

The principles which drew Weinstock to the Attlee government have never really wavered over the decades. While he came to admire Margaret Thatcher, particularly in her early incarnation as a union-buster, he has always had a keen sense of social justice.

Sacking people, as has often been necessary, particularly when bedding down mergers, has never come easy to Weinstock. Over the decades he has taken an enlightened attitude towards employees suffering personal or family problems. He has generally avoided the more ostentatious trappings of power and wealth and the outright disregard for workforces and society at large which became so prevalent and divisive in the later Thatcher era. While he has never disclosed how he votes, close friends are convinced that he voted for the Wilson governments of the 1960s, believing that their ideas for concentrating industrial power and modernising the structure of British industry were intellectually soundly based, if poorly carried out. In 1996 one of the major industrialists prepared to entertain the policies of New Labour and appear on a platform with Tony Blair was George Simpson, Weinstock's hand-picked successor at GEC.

One of GEC's main conduits to government in the Wilson era was Ronald Grierson of the Industrial Reorganisation Corporation. It was Grierson, who later joined the GEC board, who introduced Weinstock to the late Richard Crossman, a combative luncheon guest at Stanhope Gate. Weinstock's conversations with Crossman were very much in keeping with his approach to politics, which is generally issue- rather than party-oriented. It was under Crossman's own mentor, Harold Wilson, that Weinstock had risen to prominence. Five years after Wilson had come to power Weinstock was the largest private sector employer in the country, with a workforce of 250,000 people. GEC controlled 54 per cent of the market for automation equipment, 51 per cent of aerospace, radar and defence, 90 per cent of traction, 70 per cent of the grid switchgear and 53 per cent of radio communications. Without the tacit support of Wilson's government Weinstock's emergence as Britain's merger genius might never have taken place.

Weinstock's interest in policy as opposed to party meant that while he admired much of what Mrs Thatcher did in smashing the power of the miners in 1984–85, he would also use his seat in the House of Lords to oppose telecom privatisation, which he instinctively regarded as unnecessary and harmful to GEC.

Those who have seen Weinstock at close quarters in the GEC boardroom regard him as something of a political gadfly, because of the speed with which he can change his opinion on issues. One associate who sat on the board of GEC from the mid-1950s recalls Weinstock writing a memorandum on why incomes policy was necessary, and then changing his mind. Colleagues used to tease him about what would happen if he were a minister: his constant chopping and changing would mean he soon ran out of political allies. In their view Weinstock liked to believe he could apply his method of running a business to running the country, but he would have had considerable difficulty in doing that in a democracy.

If there is a common theme of Weinstock's political relationships it is his ability to have a working relationship with politicians of all parties. The same industrialist who worked so closely with the Wilson government and politicians of the left in the 1960s, including Tony Benn (although they eventually fell out), enjoyed similarly fruitful relationships with politicians of the right including Norman Tebbit, Alan Clark and Mrs Thatcher in later decades. In much the same way as he admired the Attlee government for shaking up Britain after the Second World War, so Weinstock came to value Mrs Thatcher for her willingness to restructure the British economic system in the 1980s. Although Weinstock was not part of the prime minister's inner circle, she appreciated successful business people, and would listen to him. Cecil Parkinson, one of the politicians closest to Mrs Thatcher during her years in office, found this curious: 'I was quite surprised over the years how often she said, "I saw Arnold last night," or "I was at dinner with Arnold last night," and they certainly met socially. And she had a high regard. And he had the ability to cause a lot of trouble, because she would meet him and make remarks like, "You've got electricity wrong." You would spend the next couple of days clearing it up.'[22]

Among Weinstock's skills has been his ability to remain an insider, whichever government is in power. This has on occasions allowed him to influence government policy, for instance on the best way of doing business overseas. It was always Weinstock's view that it was mad for two British contractors to be bidding for the same power station contract: far better for the government to decide who was best qualified, or to put a consortium together. Weinstock was regarded within government as one of the great lobbyists, using both the telephone and personal meetings to sway ministers on issues in which he was interested; a former industry minister referred to him as 'chairman of the industrial claimants' union'.

One means of burnishing his contacts with government has been through the 'Other Club,' an organisation originally intended to be anti-Establishment, which has itself become profoundly Establishment. The Other Club was founded by Winston Churchill after he was blackballed from the Tory citadel the Carlton Club for criticising the Conservative Party, and meets around ten times a year for dinner in the Pinafore Room at the Savoy Hotel. Its membership is limited to fifty, of whom no more than twenty-four are MPs, who are paired across party lines. Most former and present prime ministers have been members, but not Mrs Thatcher, although leading Labour figures like Harold Wilson and John Smith have been. Weinstock relishes the cut and thrust of these events, at which the quality of conversation is very high and there is a great deal of informal betting about the outcome of political events. His membership of this group has given him a bond with many of the nation's leading politicians as well as other businessmen and people from the arts such as the playwright Tom Stoppard.

Like many of the Thatcherite exiles who found refuge at Stanhope Gate, Weinstock's politics are on the Butskellite wing of the Tory party. If there is one political contemporary who has been on the same wavelength as him it is Michael Heseltine, a towering figure in defence and industrial policy in the long period of Conservative government from 1979 to 1997. Weinstock saw Heseltine as 'the right sort of minister for a government and country like ours . . . Michael is intelligent, with energy and charisma to match, he wants to get things done and he will. Heseltine is a really big man.'[23] He and Heseltine dine together at their respective country houses, and more often than not have found themselves on the same side on public issues. Most dramatically, Weinstock expressed his willingness to join the European consortium to take over Westland Helicopters in 1983 when Heseltine asked him to do so, even though it was not necessarily in his own best interests. (As a result, however, Weinstock was later rewarded by Ministry of Defence support for GEC's role in the AWACS surveillance aircraft.)

As well as admiring Weinstock as an operator and businessman,

272

Heseltine is fond of his impish sense of humour. He could imagine him laughing to himself when he told Sue Lawley on *Desert Island Discs* that he was just a speck of sand in the deserts of time. Heseltine believes that there is no industrialist in Britain who has done more for the country over the last four decades, having survived while others fell by the wayside.

In many ways Weinstock's politics are the politics of convenience. He learnt by experience that industry has to co-habit with government, and that principle has always guided him through the political thickets. That does not prevent him from taking a strong stand on issues such as Europe, where his closest associates believe he has moved towards the Eurosceptic camp. Nor has he been afraid of using his seat in the House of Lords to voice his objections to the way in which telecoms and electricity privatisation was handled. The luncheon table at GEC has always been a place of lively political discussion, whether the issue be pensions or nuclear weapons, although the debate is often inspired as much by Weinstock's thirst for the dialectic as by strongly-held beliefs.

Arnold Weinstock is a man of contrasts. There is little room in his character for shading. He is a man of grand passions, of obsessions, as is manifested by his approach to horse-racing and music. Despite his reputation for financial carefulness, having decided that blood-stock racing was part of his life he has been prepared to spend an estimated million pounds a year in the pursuit of excellence.

Similarly, in his pursuit of musical excellence Weinstock has essentially placed his trust in one person, Riccardo Muti, believing that in this conductor he has discovered the sublime. There is no second best: excellence has to be pursued, even if that means flying halfway around the world to attend a performance by Muti. It is not enough for Weinstock to simply state that a love of music was implanted in him as a young boy in North London by a synagogue cantor. That does not explain a love which can make him weep before he sets foot in his office in the morning, or send him into waves of ecstasy.

Weinstock is a creature of habit, as his closest associates frequently testify. But outside the world of business he can indulge in wild flights of fantasy. As a young man he would blow his wages on a gourmet meal or in luxurious lodgings, and later in life he would underwrite a major opera recording at Covent Garden to ensure that a performance by his friend and brother in music Muti was captured for posterity.

The apparent contradiction between such grand gestures and Weinstock's meanness of style in his management of GEC is one of the hardest aspects of his character to grasp. What is sometimes forgotten is that Weinstock's reign at GEC has been so long, and that the really grand gestures, the huge mergers which turned GEC into a £10 billion enterprise which spans the globe and can command the attention of prime ministers, are now far in the past. The takeovers of GEC, AEI and EE were in their time epoch-making events which gave Weinstock leverage over vital aspects of Britain's industrial base and a considerable proportion of the private sector workforce. The image his critics present, of a management-accounting freak controlling his empire from a single telephone on his desk, is inaccurate. Certainly his management techniques are relatively old fashioned, and his vision may seem less dynamic than that of younger chief executives like Jack Welch of US General Electric. But Weinstock was doing major deals before Welch's generation was out of the starting gates.

If there is anything fuddy-duddy about the way Weinstock works, it is mainly because his business techniques were formulated in an earlier era. He has found the security he never had in childhood in his business environment. Office and home have become one and the same, work overlapping with his personal time at night and with his home life early in the morning, when he takes phone calls.

The familiar is what Weinstock likes. After his old lieutenants David Lewis and Kenneth Bond retired he had to create around him the security of a new group of trusted decision-makers – his son Simon, David Newlands, Sara Morrison, Michael Lester and Malcolm Bates – who would gather in his office to thrash out issues confronting GEC. This collegiate form of management was exclusive rather than inclusive, turning the company's hundreds of managers of subsidiaries into outsiders, rarely allowed into the inner court. This acted as a form of protection for Weinstock, safeguarding him from those who were unfamiliar; but also for the managers themselves, who were thus shielded from a cruel irony and wit which was as likely to destabilise them as to encourage them. On occasion managers have been so deeply wounded by Weinstock's sharp tongue that Sara Morrison has had to bring them back for a second meeting, to correct an impression which Weinstock had no intention of leaving.

No one is more important to Weinstock in his business environment than Sara Morrison, who has been at Stanhope Gate since 1980, when she was removed from Conservative Central Office by Margaret Thatcher's forces. At sixty-one she is a vibrant, intelligent woman whose eccentricities include bringing her faithful dog to the office each day. She is the gatekeeper to Weinstock's office and the fielder of his telephone calls, and has an uncanny understanding of the swings in his mood and the workings of his mind. She instinctively knows what Weinstock is thinking, and recognises the deeply rooted insecurities which have made his office a place of refuge he finds hard to leave. When Weinstock assembles with his inner cabinet at around 6.30 p.m. with a glass of orange juice, it is Sara Morrison who is at his elbow as he makes the phone calls he has postponed during the day. She guides him through the unsorted papers on his desk, demanding he deal with the issues he has put off because he finds them psychologically difficult. All interviews and photographic requests are channelled through her, and it is she who must interpret Weinstock to business colleagues and visitors foxed by his fluctuations in mood.

During the dark period of Simon's illness and eventual death, which ran in parallel to the succession crisis at GEC, it was Sara who provided the comfort and protection which Weinstock needed in his public life. In her company he finds the solace and sound advice which some powerful figures are prone to eschew. Like all strong women close to the font of power in an organisation, Sara Morrison has been the subject of much fevered personal speculation, at all levels of GEC and in the business community at large. 'I've heard some scurrilous rumours on the subject of Sara,' says the chairman of one of Britain's top companies, who has had extensive dealings with Weinstock and Morrison, 'and they may be true, they may not be true. She's the Honourable Sara Morrison, isn't she? Deputy chairman of the party, Paris Sorbonne-educated, an expensive piece of decoration.' 'She's the ultimate executive perk,' said one envious comtemporary of Weinstock's.

However, although in the work environment Sara Morrison behaves much as a spouse might, in her willingness to serve and to speak bluntly to her boss, there is no evidence to suggest that between them there is anything more than a remarkably strong business bond, of the kind Weinstock excels in developing with those he likes. Others he can treat with contempt. When Lord Nelson was GEC chairman Weinstock was habitually rude to him, reading the newspaper while Nelson attempted to discuss business matters.

On occasions Weinstock's dislike can turn to vindictiveness. Larry Brook, an MSF (Manufacturing, Science and Finance) union official who generally admires Weinstock, describing him as the most impressive industrialist he has ever come across, saw the other side of the GEC chief when the MSF mounted a legal challenge over Weinstock's decision to reduce redundancy terms to employees who came into the firm with the Avery and Plessey takeovers. In 1992 Weinstock sent Brook an infamous Christmas card on which the words 'Best wishes' had been crossed out and replaced by 'See you in court.' Later, when Brook wrote asking for clarification of GEC's interest in the joint telecoms venture with Siemens, GPT, he received what he describes as a 'raging, vindictive letter' which accused him of 'fraudulent behaviour', and added that his support for GEC was 'unwelcome'.[24]

Brook himself acknowledges that the Christmas card may simply have been an unsuccessful attempt by Weinstock at a joke. Nevertheless, there was no mistaking the underlying bitterness and anger, and perhaps a sense of betrayal, contained in the subsequent letter. Many GEC managers who have felt the managing director's wrath over a poor set of budgetary figures came to regard Weinstock as a bully, whose voice booming down the telephone was enough to give them sleepless nights.

Similarly, the memoranda churned out from Weinstock's office over a period of thirty years reflect the different sides of his character. On first reading, a Weinstock memo can give the impression of coming from an incredibly narrow figure, more interested in structures than businesses, cost ratios than the people who produce them. But running through them is an enormous sense of context, of responding to a political or economic imperative. Moreover, the severity and harshness of Weinstock's language – much of it intended for his senior executives in the field – is counterbalanced by teasing touches. It is as if the reader can see Weinstock in his office, eyes twinkling, quietly enjoying a smile at the thought of the discomfort which a formal missive from Stanhope Gate could bring. The tone is schoolmasterish, and the demand for quick responses reflects Weinstock's determination to be in control of events. He hates surprises, and demands order in his management. In December 1993 Weinstock, in his end-of-year note to managing directors, was at his most high-handed: 'I should like the narrative part of monthly reports to be more meaningful and less rhetorical. There is too much repetition, besides iteration of numbers which appear clearly in the schedules. Will managing directors please not deal with ratios, salient figures and capital employed statements as if they were in themselves subjects.'[25]

In such notes, with which his files are littered for over thirty years, there is much of the real Arnold Weinstock. First and fore-most there is the stickler for form and language, a legacy of his Admiralty days which he has never lost. Then there is the evidence that as managing director, he must be heard and listened to. He is the master of the enterprise, the person in control, who tolerates few deviations from the norm in what he expects his senior execu-tives to produce. But within the language there always remains a wryness: for those who know Arnold Weinstock, even the most pompous pronouncements contain an element of exaggeration for the sake of it. There is that extra bit of toughness which can be turned on its head and interpreted with a degree of good humour.

For almost every example of Weinstock's mean-spiritedness there is an act of kindness, especially when the health of someone at GEC or their immediate family is concerned. Jim Cronin, managing director of GEC–Alsthom, tells of the speed with which Weinstock intervened when his nineteen-year-old son Michael was taken ill. Within hours of Weinstock accidentally learning of the young man's illness he had called two London specialists and made arrangements for him to go into hospital for extensive tests. 'Arnold was concerned that I could afford it, and the insurance was right and so forth, and would regularly ask after the boy. A few months later I put Michael back in the same hospital, only to be told by Arnold, in no uncertain terms, that I was being stupid. It wasn't an emergency any more, and there were cheaper ways of doing it.'[26]

Throughout GEC there are such tales, offering a strong counterpoint to those who have felt slighted or disturbed by Weinstock's sharp, half-joking point-scoring. They underline the mystery in Arnold Weinstock's character, the wild swings from resentment and the desire for revenge to kindness itself.

Those who work with him are all too aware that Weinstock is subject to quite extraordinary mood swings. On the downswing difficult issues, like seeing City analysts, whom he cannot abide, are best left alone, and it is best to steer clear of the managing director. But when his mood is up, Weinstock, speedy in his decision-making, brilliant in his analysis and fearsomely wise in his advice, is simply electrifying company.

Weinstock has to be coaxed into a good mood, almost like a child, and the great expert at this over the years has been Sara Morrison. Perhaps this is another legacy of a childhood cut short by his parents' death and rural exile in Warwickshire, which would be weighty psychological baggage for anyone to carry around, let alone one of the leading industrialists of his era.

There are hidden demons in Weinstock. He does not take criticism lightly, and likes to control his public image: when television reporter and business journalist Graham Turner produced a book which offended him in the 1970s Weinstock moved to suppress it, threatening author and publisher with libel suits and eventually buying the manuscript for several thousand pounds so that it would never see the light of day.

In his desire to control what is said and written about him, and his assumption that the media and the City are enemies, Weinstock can display almost Nixonian paranoia. In the 1970s he was as likely to issue writs against stories he did not like as two more notorious users of the courts, James Goldsmith and Robert Maxwell. In a flurry of writs in the middle of the decade he sued the satirical magazine *Private Eye*, the *New Statesman*, the *Guardian* and a former Labour Mayor of Greenwich over articles and comments on his business affairs which he found offensive or inaccurate. A stickler for detail, Weinstock regarded sloppiness in the media as a fault which had to be aggressively challenged rather than lived with. Yet his readiness to use the full power of GEC's legal machine to protect his reputation, at a time when all that really counted was the company's generally stellar performance against all the economic odds, suggested deep insecurities.

In his management techniques Weinstock is the master of the rational. Decisions are based on logic assisted by the power of numbers and management reports, rather than on instinct. His approach is that of the professional rather than the entrepreneur, which suggests that he might have been less successful than he thinks had he chosen a career in the world of property rather than industry. Like so much of his character, the cool rationality, the ability to bottle up his emotions and lose himself in work, dates back to his childhood. For much of the time his emotions are deeply suppressed, and at times of trouble he finds it easiest to put up the barriers and immerse himself in his business affairs.

When he does let himself go, in the privacy of his dressing room, at a Muti concert or with his family, Weinstock is transformed. He can be a highly emotional figure, easily moved to tears by music or by family news. His home has always been his retreat. When his late brothers were in London the reunions, sometimes at GEC headquarters, were lively, raucous affairs full of the Jewish humour which is so much part of the Weinstock persona. His wife Netta is always present, in the background, and friends like Muti are as fond of her as they are of Arnold.

Since the death of his son Simon, Weinstock has found comfort in his daughter-in-law Laura, who has worked at his side on his musical and other charitable activities. His grandchildren have become greatly important to him as he seeks to fill the chasm opened by his son's departure. This is not the rational businessman, but the Jewish father and grandfather, letting his emotions drive him. Although he has odd working patterns, often remaining in his office until late at night, his family has always been at the centre of his being.

Weinstock's home life is incredibly ordered. Visitors to his country seat in Wiltshire are astonished by its decorousness. This is not a country house in the normal English mode, with mud on the carpets, bikes in the hallway and sleeping dogs shedding their hairs on the rugs. Instead there is a striking perfection in the decor, the silk hangings and the highly polished furniture which is said to reflect Netta's taste. Despite Weinstock's passionate involvement with horses the stables are empty except for a huge electric train set dating since Simon and Susan were young. Family occasions are renowned for their punctuality, although it is always likely that Susan, who is regarded as a rebel, with a less than impressive French husband, will arrive late as part of the revolt against her parents' obsessiveness.

Despite his running battles in the libel courts, Weinstock has generally been respectfully treated by the media, with most profiles littered with references to his penetrating mind and analytical skills. His ability to understand the most complex technologies, read a balance sheet and see industries strategically is an unusual combination, particularly for a man who never received a scientific or formal business education. It is this mastery of everything that he is involved in, be it a Mozart score, the bloodstock lines of a Group One race-winner, or the intricacies of a new advanced semiconductor, which has made Weinstock such a prodigious intellectual force on the British industrial scene. Others may have higher degrees from better universities than Weinstock, but his exceptional brand of practically applied intelligence, together with a touch of *chutzpah*, has made him a unique and towering figure in post-Second World War British business history.

# CHAPTER NINE

## *The Record*

ARNOLD WEINSTOCK'S CLAIM to be Britain's premier post-war industrialist rests mainly on the fact that he was at the top of one of the country's most prominent manufacturing companies for more than thirty years. During a period when British manufacturing was in steady decline, GEC not only survived but prospered for most of that period. He certainly left the company in a much stronger state than when he took over.

But Weinstock's stature has declined rather than grown with the years, and important questions remain about his legacy, both at GEC and in the wider business arena. His influence on managers outside the company he ran has been limited because of his disdain for both personal publicity and the forums of top management such as the Confederation of British Industry. It could have been much more significant, because he anticipated by almost thirty years many of the management trends which have swept the business world in the 1990s, notably the innovation of the lean, flat organisation which chops away excess overhead costs.

On the other hand, Weinstock has ignored much of the management wisdom of his era, from the growth of marketing in the 1970s, through the importance of corporate strategy in the 1980s to the human relations insights of the 1990s. While many of the fashionable ideas have merely been fads, the cultural transformation which has revitalised companies such as British Aerospace and ICI in the 1990s could also have been important to GEC.

A fundamental of Weinstock's reign appears to be his conduct of affairs at the top of the company – the management of the boardroom and of his own succession; what has come to be called governance, and which has become a major corporate issue in the 1990s. The Cadbury Committee was established by the City following scandals such as the Robert Maxwell pensions affair and the collapse of Polly Peck. Reporting in 1993, it laid down guidelines for good boardroom practice. The most important of these concerned the role of non-executive directors in supporting and scrutinising executives and acting to prevent the kind of abuses which emerged in the late 1980s. The Cadbury guidelines suggested that the roles of chairman and chief executive should not be held by one person, so as to avoid an excessive concentration of power, and that there should be a minimum of three non-executive directors, who should be the sole members of audit and remuneration committees and the main members of a nomination committee which controlled board membership.

GEC was not significantly out of line with most leading British companies on most of these issues. Its board always contained a significant group of non-executives, and Weinstock was always responsible to a chairman. Only when GEC gave his successor, George Simpson, the same contract he had enjoyed at Lucas was there any suggestion that GEC was playing fast and loose with its shareholders' money. Indeed, Weinstock was more commonly accused of excessive tight-fistedness: his strictness on directors' expenses included their having to pay for their own newspapers and health insurance. But while GEC complied in form with most of the Cadbury rules, in substance Weinstock exhibited precisely the excessive dominance of the figure at the top of the organisation which had prompted those rules.

When he accepted the job of managing director in the summer of 1962, one of his conditions was that there would be no interference from the chairman. In GEC's condition of near collapse, this was an understandable demand, and it was acceded to. But, as was to happen with so many other aspects of Weinstock's years, he and the company failed to change with the circumstances. Splitting the top roles was irrelevant because Weinstock's chairmen had little influence on matters of substance, and virtually no control over him. Lord Nelson was well-liked, and admired for his passionate interest in technology and his desire for the success of GEC and the electrical industry in general. Yet Weinstock treated him with scant respect, and was always furious if Nelson knew something

282

that he didn't. Lord Carrington's brief period at GEC was so insignificant even to him that it barely merited a mention in his autobiography. He did not think it sufficiently interesting to say how he came to be appointed, why he accepted the job, what he found while he was there, or what he thought of the company and its managing director. Lord Prior eventually managed to build a meaningful relationship with Weinstock, and a role for himself, beyond what many had expected when he took over from Carrington. But he had no more control over the board or business matters than his predecessors, and struggled with what was his most important task – the succession to Weinstock. He was known to complain that Weinstock regarded him merely as a super-salesman, sending him off to China or other faraway markets to butter up important customers – a role at which he turned out to be excellent.

The most telling failure of all these chairmen was to build a balanced and effective board. Many of those appointed to the board were Weinstock's friends, notably Lord Rees-Mogg and Sara Morrison – or in the case of his son Simon, even a member of his family. It is astonishing that there were only two years during Weinstock's thirty-three as managing director when there were no board changes. In many years three or four directors came and went. Frequently they stayed for only a brief period. Heinz boss Tony O'Reilly joined the board in 1990–91, for example, only to depart two years later. Sir David Scholey of Warburgs also lasted only two years. Both Arthur Walsh and Roy Gardner left the group the year after being made directors.

In a sense, though, the membership of GEC's board was irrelevant, because it has never functioned in the style expected of modern company boards. Weinstock gave a famous explanation of his management style early in his tenure, telling an enquirer during the AEI bid battle: 'The board is in constant session.' But in practice the board met only four times a year, each meeting preceded by a fine lunch at which Weinstock and one or two other directors would display their wit and wisdom. Two of these meetings were dominated by formal approval of the half-year and annual accounts, and otherwise directors' time in board meetings was taken up mainly with hearing a formal presentation on the state of each unit's finances. Discussion of key issues was not considered appropriate for this forum, as was illustrated by the fact that the decision in 1994 to set a two-year limit on Weinstock's tenure was simply announced to the board, with no previous discussion or consideration.

The conduct of the board was clearly unsatisfactory, just as Weinstock clearly remained at the helm for too long. But it is unreasonable to blame Weinstock for these failures. He always insisted that there should be a chairman to whom he was responsible, telling his first chairman, Lord Aldington: 'You are the only person who can save the GEC from me if I go mad. The board is there to sack me.' The process of finally persuading a reluctant Weinstock that it was time to step down was undoubtedly a difficult one, especially given a natural desire to manage the process through agreement and to avoid conflict or compulsion. Yet the failure to manage that process properly was a failure of the board, and especially of the chairman and the non-executive directors, not primarily of Weinstock. Similarly, he cannot be blamed entirely for the unsatisfactory nature of GEC's board proceedings and membership. The responsibility for that must lie first with the chairmen who allowed him to dictate matters, and with major shareholders who failed to insist that matters be handled differently.

When Weinstock ended his thirty-three-year reign as managing director in September 1996, GEC's sales were almost £11 billion, its profits virtually £1 billion, and there was £1.4 billion in the bank. In 1963, when he began the long adventure as an unknown entrepreneur, the company was heading for bankruptcy. Sales were a mere £147 million, yielding profit of just £6 million. By any standards, and even making full allowance for inflation over the intervening years, that represents a remarkable advance. But the figures tell only a small part of the story. An assessment of Weinstock's impact on both the company and the wider British economy must take into account many other factors, considering what was not achieved as well as what was, and comparing his successes with those of his peers. The key question is whether he could have done much more, had his character, style of management, and the circumstances in which he operated been different. Or whether, had he been less skilled, the company he led would have gone the way of so many other British manufacturers – either out of business or into the hands of foreign owners.

The question has to be asked in the context of the economic and industrial environment in which Weinstock operated. The years from the early 1960s to the mid-1990s were a period of radical change in the world economy which saw dramatic developments in all industrialised countries, and particularly sharp political, industrial, social and economic shifts in the UK. In the 1960s, government-driven consolidation of key industries helped Weinstock to acquire AEI and English Electric, but Harold Wilson's technological revolution did little to prepare British industry for the rigours of two oil-price shocks in the 1970s. The failure of the Labour government to push through industrial relations reforms left a bitter legacy. Ted Heath's Conservative administration fared worse in its battle with the trade unions, and ultimately fell in the contest, but the union question eventually opened the door for Margaret Thatcher's brand of free-wheeling, union-reforming Conservatism.

Industrial relations was only one of the causes of the unprecedented turbulence that British industry had to face in the 1970s. The oil-price hike in 1973 caused economic troubles in Britain's major markets overseas, as well as record levels of inflation at home and a financial crisis so serious that it threatened the entire banking system. The sense that Britain's economy was out of control was confirmed in 1976 when the government had to turn to the International Monetary Fund for emergency financial support – a move which had hitherto been the resort of shambolic developing nations, not one of the world's leading economic powers. The combination of chaotic macro-economic management with uncontrollable labour relations left large sections of British management demoralised and demotivated by the end of the 1970s.

The Thatcher government quickly began to change that mood of dark pessimism, with tax reductions to put more cash in managers' pockets, and a steady erosion of trade union rights capped by victory over the coalminers in the long-running national dispute of 1984–85. The privatisation programme which was to be one of its most lasting legacies hit directly at GEC's customer base, however, and together with a deliberate policy of opening UK markets to overseas competitors, made life substantially more difficult for the company.

More broadly, economic policy mistakes in the early years of the Thatcher government made life impossible for many of Britain's manufacturers, while the hubris and then dissent of its later years created first an untenable consumer boom, followed by a second recession which was made worse by Britain's membership of the European Exchange Rate Mechanism.

The early target of the Conservative government's economic activity was inflation, and it set out to stifle price rises and change the country's inflationary mentality through control of the money supply, set out in the Medium Term Financial Strategy. But this strategy was accompanied, almost accidentally, by an astonishing increase in the value of sterling in foreign currency markets, the pound rising by more than a third between 1978 and 1981. This appreciation of sterling, allied with Britain's new-found status as an oil-producing nation, left the pound 50 per cent higher than it had been in 1976, effectively cutting exporters' prices by a third over that period. The pound hit 4.8 deutschmarks and 2.4 dollars in January 1981, while manufacturing output fell by 14 per cent between the start of 1980 and the end of 1981.

It was the government's apparent lack of concern for the lethal impact the pound's rise had on many manufacturers which in 1985 prompted the House of Lords Industry Committee, with the aid of Lord Weinstock, to highlight the accelerating decline of the manufacturing sector. Their Lordships' fulminations, though, did not slow the decline. In 1996 less than one in five of the British workforce was employed in manufacturing, compared to one in four in 1983, while one in three of the top hundred manufacturers and a quarter of the manufacturing capacity that was left were owned by foreigners.[1] A prime example is the motor industry, where the remnant of British Leyland, Rover, is now owned by BMW and the rest of the supposedly British car industry is owned by American, French and Japanese companies. The same applies to newer technologies. ICL, which was created as Britain's premier computer company, originally part-owned by English Electric, is now owned by the Japanese company Fujitsu, contributing to the fact that 70 per cent of computers made in the UK are manufactured by foreign-owned companies.

While this decline is shared to some extent by most of its major competitors, Britain's record on manufacturing output and investment was substantially worse than theirs. In the recession of the early 1990s, as Weinstock was nearing the end of his reign, British manufacturing output was barely ahead of its level in the early 1970s when he began the task of building the unified electrical company he created. Among major competitor nations, France was closest to this British performance, but even it managed a rise of almost a fifth in manufacturing output over the twenty-year period. Italy and Japan showed increases of almost 70 per cent.

Manufacturing in general may have fared badly in recent decades, but one key sector for GEC – electronics – has seen success of sorts. A review of the industry in 1988 showed that the UK electronics market had grown faster than any of its major competitors other than Japan in the years 1976 to 1986.[2] As a result it was larger than that of France and Italy, and not far behind Germany. Some of that growth had been met by imports, but production in Britain was in line with the average for major countries, with a growth rate well ahead of European competitors and marginally ahead of the United States.

The analysis also showed, however, that British companies had largely missed out on this growth. Employment by UK electronics companies had actually fallen, and their sales growth was well behind that of competitors in other countries. Most of the British growth had gone to foreign companies operating in Britain, partly because UK companies were over-represented in the low-growth defence industry, and partly because they appeared unwilling to invest sufficiently in more promising areas, especially those requiring global scale.

Britain's capital markets, and the dominance of the financial markets over industrial affairs, are regarded by many as being responsible for the country's poor industrial performance. The debate over alleged short-termism has raged for years, with critics arguing that British public companies are prevented from investing adequately for long-term development because of the demands of shareholders for steady dividend and earnings growth, and the readiness of institutional investors to sell their shares to predators who pounce on companies which are prepared to sacrifice short-term profits for long-term market position.[3]

Weinstock has been largely immune from such pressures, however. His tight management of GEC has ensured that he has never needed to go to investors for cash, even to finance major acquisitions. He has never pandered to City opinion, to the extent of ignoring criticism of his strategies and his running of the group, and has refused to put significant effort into investor relations in the style of most modern public companies. Only in the late 1980s was GEC ever a serious takeover target, and rather than having a negative impact, the threat helped Weinstock push through the key joint ventures which helped strengthen two of his main businesses.

He has nevertheless often been accused of short-termism, because of his heavy concentration on immediate financial results at the expense of building long-term market positions. It is certainly true that Weinstock has always been suspicious of allowing losses now in the hope of profits at some stage in the future. But there are examples of such investment strategies being pursued in parts of the group, and Weinstock has been remarkably lenient in allowing poor results, both in Marconi during the 1980s and in some of the smaller businesses, notably A.B. Dick. While he has also been chary of fashionable notions such as 'vision' and 'strategy', that has not prevented his thinking deeply about long-term issues in the development of the industries GEC has operated in. (Nor has it prevented GEC from joining the fashion to adopt a 'mission statement'; the first was published in the annual report for 1988–89.) One leading fund manager recalled Weinstock's impressive grasp of strategic issues (even though, with his aversion to the term 'strategy', Weinstock himself might not have been happy to hear his thinking described thus): 'He was always terribly convincing about giving a picture – a firm grasp of the strategic position of the various industries.'[4]

But GEC has been inextricably bound up with the process of Britain's manufacturing decline. Its own employment record exemplifies the dismal story. By the early 1980s the group's UK employment had halved from the 228,000 workers Weinstock inherited following the English Electric takeover. In the subsequent ten years the rate of decline accelerated. By the mid-1990s only fifty-seven thousand people were employed in GEC's UK factories. The group has been both a victim of the hostile macro-economic environment and a contributor to the negative culture on the ground which has played down innovation and risk-taking, glorifying instead cost-cutting and tight management, squeezing the most out of the least assets. One writer has cited the company as the arch example of successful defensive management in the face of adversity:

> The history of GEC provides a big clue to the extraordinary combination of dynamic productivity and dismal growth in manufacturing output that has characterised the British economy over the past two decades. Bad macro-economic management has fostered an extremely defensive managerial culture in industry. Weinstock was the prime exponent of that culture, and his temperament was very suitable for managing a capital-intensive manufacturing business in a period of poor policy, difficult labour relations and exceptionally high inflation.[5]

The story of Trafford Park fuses the legacy of general manufacturing decline with the history of GEC. Its heritage lies in the tension between traditional landed wealth and commerce, while its history encapsulates both the triumphs and the failures of British manufacturing. The 1200-acre estate on the edge of Manchester was owned by one of the North-West's leading families, the de Traffords, who had lived there since Elizabethan times. Disillusioned by the encroachment of commerce, and especially the sight of ocean-going ships passing along the newly-constructed Manchester Ship Canal, the family sold the land in 1896, and it was developed into what Manchester has always claimed to be the first and largest industrial estate in the world. On 10 July 1889 the developer won its first tenant, when George Westinghouse wrote on behalf of his newly-formed British Westinghouse Electric and Manufacturing company to secure a large plot at the southern tip of the park, known as Meeting Waters Farm. It was to be the site of the company's glorious but over-ambitious factory, eventually becoming Metrovicks and subsequently one of AEI's leading plants.

The factory finally built in 1901 was a monument to the optimism of the new century. It became a symbol of engineering excellence, and Metrovicks the region's leading employer. Its distinctive hooter, which signalled the start of work each morning, the beginning and end of the lunch break and the end of work in the evening, could be heard for miles around. As far away as Rusholme the hooter was known simply as 'The Westinghouse'.

Westinghouse was quickly followed to Trafford Park by hundreds of other companies, including food giants Kellogg's and Procter & Gamble, although some, such as Henry Royce of Rolls-Royce, and the Ford Motor company, did not stay for long. The park became a magnet for technology-based new ventures, including Manchester's first airport.

The Westinghouse factory was not only a major turbine plant and training ground for generations of Manchester's engineers. It was also the location of Britain's first radio broadcast in 1922, as Westinghouse was part of the private consortium (including GEC and Marconi) which established the privately-owned BBC. At its peak during the Second World War the factory employed twenty-three thousand people, making Manchester and Lancaster bombers and many other instruments of war. Trafford Park as a whole employed seventy-five thousand people during the peak war effort.

The era of thousands of men flooding out of the factory gates as the hooter sounded the end of the working day was over by the 1970s. The Westinghouse factory, under Weinstock's direction following GEC's takeover of AEI in 1967, remained an important site for some time, eventually becoming part of the GEC–Alsthom joint venture when that was established in 1989. But it declined along with the rest of the Trafford Park estate, which by the mid-1980s could boast only six hundred companies employing just twenty-four thousand people – a total close to the number employed by Westinghouse alone in the 1920s. In 1995, with turbine production transferred to Rugby, and office staff to the suburb of Knutsford, demolition of the factory began. By its centenary, all that will be left standing will be the original six-storey, gabled red-brick office block which was modelled on the Westinghouse headquarters in the United States, and that only because it is a listed building.

The rest of the estate has fared better, under the direction and with the funding of a development corporation established in 1987. The corporation has invested in modern infrastructure, although in 1997 Trafford Park was still an odd mixture of new roads and rapid transit railways, clashing with the rusty and disused remains of the original rail tracks against a background of old warehouses and factories.

Distribution is a key factor, and the park's original asset of proximity to the ship canal has been replaced by the modern equivalent, motorway access, while Manchester Airport is just a short drive away. Sandwiched between the GEC site and Manchester United's Old Trafford football ground is the grandly titled World Freight Centre, a huge container terminal. Much of the park now consists of modern single-storey 'business units' housing the new breed of company for Britain's post-industrial economy: distribution and service businesses. One services the kind of electric motors which used to be made at the Westinghouse plant. It is Korean. The biggest irony of all is that the man who has chaired the development corporation which has overseen this transformation is Bill Morgan, the former GEC commercial director who pleaded in vain during the 1970s for the company to be more ambitious.

Despite the hostile environment which has seen manufacturing give way to distribution and service throughout Britain, Weinstock left a substantial edifice when he stepped down as managing director of GEC in September 1996. The group was still Britain's twenty-fifth-largest company by stock market value, and the largest truly industrial company. To a casual observer, GEC might seem a collection of disparate businesses operating with varying degrees of success in various parts of the world, and Weinstock's lack of interest in public relations did nothing to dispel this rather haphazard, fragmented image. But behind the superficial fragmentation lay a concentration on key businesses and key markets. There remained a long tail of miscellaneous businesses spanning activities as diverse as Express Lifts, Gilbarco petrol pumps and medical electronics, and it slowly emerged in the 1990s that many of these were unofficially up for sale.

To those who subscribe to the fashionable 1990s theory that the future lies with leading global businesses, these peripheral operations are an indictment of Weinstock's leadership. His argument is that in a group with excess cash, there is no need to sell operations which produce an adequate return on capital unless somebody offers a sum which would yield an even better return. This was his response to the management of Hotpoint, which, before the joint venture with GE, put together a proposal for a management buy-out of the business. 'What would I do with the money?' Weinstock asked chief executive Jeff Sansom. Yet he also refused Sansom's pleas to forge a European merger at a time when European competitors such as Electrolux were pursuing such a strategy to gain economies of manufacturing, development and marketing scale.

Some of the peripheral businesses have failed the basic Weinstock test of delivering an adequate financial return. The office equipment company A.B. Dick is the most conspicuous example. This 1978 US acquisition was a disaster almost from the start, making recurrent losses despite a succession of new management teams, and was eventually sold early in 1997. The only saving grace was the emergence from the company of the Videojet non-impact printing operation, which was a resounding success.

The acquisition of Picker medical equipment was much more satisfactory, but here Weinstock stands accused of failing to build beyond the United States, leaving Picker vulnerable to the power of global market leaders. This is a particularly telling criticism, because Weinstock highlighted the attraction of expanding Picker's reach in merger talks with Philips' medical business which were aborted at the last moment in 1987. A combination of Philips and Picker would have been a powerful global player, but Picker remains essentially an American business.

Between the extremes of A.B. Dick and Picker lies a collection of largely nondescript businesses which do not have the scale to make a significant contribution to GEC's performance, and which probably gain little from being part of a large group.

Weinstock never saw GEC as a coherent organisation, to be managed as a separate entity from its constituent parts, which is one reason why he and his critics have often failed to connect. He has always regarded GEC as a holding company for a collection of what he liked to describe as autonomous units. He would pore over each unit's set of monthly returns with the same degree of interest, regardless of its size or the field in which it operated. As one colleague commented: 'He views every tree in the woods, not the woods.'[6] But, as a senior non-executive director has said, this is an unusual way to run a huge multinational empire: 'As a method of running a group of that size, it is inappropriate. A lot of that function should be left to the finance director. A chief executive should properly be spending his time in more creative ways.'[7]

Creativity was largely left to the managers of the 'autonomous' units, who in Weinstock's view were responsible for strategy, and should not be dictated to by Stanhope Gate. The notion of 'a strategy for GEC' was therefore meaningless to Weinstock, just as he was uninterested in 1990s ideas about 'core competences' of large groups. But after the joint ventures of 1989, GEC came to concentrate on three activities – or, in the terminology of the time, it focused on three core businesses. These were telecommunications, through the GPT joint venture with Siemens; power engineering, through GEC–Alsthom; and defence electronics, through Marconi, the only wholly-owned core business. These three activities contributed a growing proportion of sales in the 1990s.

Telecoms and electronics had always been GEC's most substantial businesses, and drove sales growth through the 1970s and 1980s. Power, on the other hand, had begun to shrink in the second half of the 1980s as public sector orders dried up. Nevertheless these three businesses contributed around 60 per cent of sales in the 1980s. Following the joint ventures, however, this proportion grew to almost three-quarters, and the dominance of these activities was finally acknowledged. In his brief report accompanying the half-year results in December 1992, chairman Lord Prior described them for the first time as GEC's 'three principal activities', and explained: 'These are sectors in which we have concentrated considerable investment in capital and effort in recent years to advance our competitive position internationally.'

As the only wholly-owned business, Marconi is the core of the core. It is a broadly-based defence electronics contractor, with its main strength in airborne systems but with a strong presence in the naval and underwater sectors, including the Yarrow and VSEL shipyards. The division also includes civil electronics activities, notably for the aerospace industry, but has found it difficult to translate defence expertise to civil products. Marconi's technological skills are widely admired, despite some well-publicised disasters, such as Nimrod in the 1980s. But the business was slow to react to the changes in defence procurement introduced by the Thatcher government. Only when Peter Gershon took over at Marconi in 1995 did the company seriously begin to come to terms with the new environment. He forced the business to address the issue of increased risk, to focus on key in-house technologies and manage the associated risks, while laying off risks on less critical activities to sub-contractors or partners.

Having come to terms with the new way of doing business, however, Marconi faced a more substantial problem. The world's defence industry was rapidly consolidating during the mid-1990s, as contractors reacted to the slowdown in military spending following the collapse of communism, and the rising costs of developing new equipment. In 1994 Marconi ranked fifth in the world, behind Thomson-CSF of France and three US giants, GM-Hughes, Martin Marietta and Raytheon. By 1997, however, a series of American mergers had dramatically changed the ownership of the top of the industry, leaving Marconi adrift.

In response to these developments, GEC was keen to enlarge Marconi. It missed its best chance, however, when it failed to make a takeover bid for British Aerospace in 1992, when the aircraft company was plunged into a financial crisis. Many at GEC subsequently accepted that the acquisition of BAe at the low price which would have been possible because of its troubles would have been beneficial. One City critic of Weinstock described GEC's failure to bid as 'a loss of nerve'.[8]

As a result, Marconi remains an equipment supplier in a world where the power is increasingly moving to the prime contractors such as BAe, whose recovery since 1992, plus its pole position in the shake-up of the European defence industry, illustrates the opportunity that was lost. GEC has subsequently seen an opportunity to enhance Marconi's position by means of some form of deal involving Thomson, which was being privatised by the French government during 1997.

GEC's power engineering business, covering electricity generation and distribution and rail transport systems, already has a French partner, through the joint venture with Alsthom set up in 1989. This is generally regarded as the most successful of the joint ventures, as well as the best-positioned of GEC's businesses. It has combined predominantly French management with GEC's financial and management systems, and French orders to compensate for the lack of business in the UK, while the combination of French and British heritage has left GEC–Alsthom well positioned in the growth markets of Asia. The company is some way behind the Swiss–Swedish market leader ABB in scale, but nevertheless has strong positions in fossil-fuel, nuclear and hydro-electric generation. In rail transport it is one of the world market leaders, with products including the TGV high-speed train in France. For all GEC–Alsthom's success, it has been alleged that Weinstock has effectively handed the company over to the French. When this accusation was put to him by one trade union official, Weinstock's response was to dial the French chief executive and harangue him for a quarter of an hour about anything and everything that was happening at Alsthom. When he eventually put the phone down, he said: 'That shows you who's in charge.'[9]

The other major joint venture, GPT, is in a less promising position. First, GEC's relationship with its partner, Siemens, is more difficult because it was not a full merger, unlike Alsthom. GPT is merely one of the German giant's many interests, and essentially its route into the UK market. GPT remains predominantly a UK supplier, small by world standards, in a business which is becoming increasingly global. In addition, GPT depends substantially on Siemens for technology, being unable to afford to develop new-generation equipment on its own. It is clearly the weakest of the three main businesses, and there seems little prospect of it improving its global market, leaving the likelihood of its eventually being absorbed completely into Siemens.

Telecommunications has undoubtedly been Weinstock's least successful major business, although typically it has remained highly profitable. The original GEC was a relatively small player in telecoms, but the addition of AEI's substantial business and the electronics skills of English Electric should have provided a good base in what has been one of the greatest growth businesses of recent decades. Weinstock can reasonably argue that he was hampered by British government policy and by the behaviour of the nationalised telecom operator. The embarrassing failure of the first electronic exchange, installed in 1961 in North London, led the GPO to delay introducing a new generation of exchanges, thus hampering the ability of its suppliers to compete internationally. Thus GEC's telecoms exports, which were a third of its output in 1961, steadily shrank, while companies such as Ericsson of Sweden gained market share. The GPO also operated a cosy cartel of suppliers, which provided little incentive for innovation.

Although managers with a long-term vision should have foreseen the necessity to build a global business, British manufacturers were also hampered by the GPO's insistence on an exchange system different to that of other developed countries, making it difficult to export. GEC was also prevented in the 1980s from increasing its scale in the UK by the Thatcher government's refusal to allow the acquisition of Plessey on monopoly grounds. Weinstock has also argued strenuously that he was disadvantaged in that decade when British Telecom's purchasing policy opened the UK market to overseas competition, while British operators were not similarly allowed to bid for business in many countries whose attractive markets were preserved for domestic suppliers.

GEC's greatest failure, however, has been in mobile telecoms, where the company accepts that it completely failed to perceive the market opportunity. Marconi opted not to bid for the first licence to operate a mobile phone network, allowing Racal to build its Vodafone business into a huge success. Subsequently GEC failed to launch a takeover bid for Racal which would have allowed it belatedly to buy into the cellular market. The success of companies such as Nokia also highlights GEC's failure to capitalise on the market for mobile phone equipment, as well as missing out on the communications network.

While GEC's telecoms operations failed to perform on the world stage, the group cannot generally be accused of the common British failure of neglecting overseas markets. GEC's exports to China represent two-fifths of all British business there, for example. The group was always highly international, although in common with most British companies its overseas efforts were concentrated in the Commonwealth countries. In the 1970s, however, the UK still accounted for around half total sales, and while this proportion dipped at the beginning of the 1980s it rose again in the second half of that decade, reaching a peak of 60 per cent in 1989. The joint ventures changed that dramatically. UK sales actually fell in absolute terms during the recession of the early 1990s, and shrank to less than 30 per cent of the group's total by 1996. The addition of Alsthom's French business boosted sales on the Continent, which overtook British sales in 1996, while successes in China and elsewhere in the Far East saw Asian sales rising to 15 per cent of the total. Only the United States remained disappointing, with sales stagnating at around the £2 billion mark, representing just under a fifth of the group's total, no higher a proportion than in the early 1980s.

GEC's high level of exports has attracted some criticism, however, from those who believe globalisation requires much more of a local presence than the group has generally been interested in creating. This theory is more relevant to consumer industries than GEC's power and other businesses. But it does raise the question of how sustainable its position in China and other Far Eastern countries will prove to be if it remains as an importer into those countries rather than an indigenous manufacturer.

GEC's performance under Weinstock can only properly be judged in the context of its peers. There are none in the UK, its original competitors either having been devoured, as in the case of AEI, EE and Plessey, or disappeared, as with Ferranti. This is the strongest case for Weinstock's defence against charges of failure: virtually alone among substantial British electrical engineering companies, GEC is still here, and in a strong financial state. It has also avoided the crises which have hit other large industrial companies such as British Aerospace and Rolls-Royce.

Comparisons must then be sought abroad, with the likes of the US General Electric, Philips of the Netherlands and Siemens of Germany. One way of making them is by examining share price performance. The share price is a very broad indicator; it has no subtlety, but in GEC's case it does at least reflect the financial community's judgement on Weinstock's thirty-three years at the top. Taken overall, GEC's share price has performed better than the stock market average, and better than its international competitors (see Appendix 5, pp.321–4).

But breaking the period down tells a more pertinent story. The message then is that Weinstock did a wonderful job of putting together the three big companies and transforming their profitability, but that he lost his way once that process had been completed. For example, over the whole thirty-three-year period GEC easily outperformed the US General Electric. But that outperformance took place entirely during the 1970s; since the early 1980s GE's shares have done much better than GEC's. Weinstock fared slightly better against his European competitors in the 1980s than against GE, but GEC's shares were still a worse buy than Siemens or ABB, while even Philips' dismal performance was not much different to GEC's.

This broad comparison says nothing about the varying economic and other conditions pertaining in each country during the period, but it does suggest that Weinstock failed to maintain his early momentum. The same picture emerges from an examination of the league table of electrical companies. When he brought together GEC, AEI and EE in 1968, the new group ranked third in the world on the basis of sales, behind GE and Westinghouse, and slightly ahead of Philips and Siemens. Trailing in sixth place was the Japanese company Hitachi. By 1997, however, GEC was well behind the pack, while Hitachi (which acquired, *inter alia*, GEC's television business in the UK) had grown so much that it was neck and neck with GE at the top, although under Jack Welch GE became the most profitable company in the United States in 1997. The sales of each of these two giants were the equivalent of nearly £50 billion, four and a half times those of GEC (in 1968 GE had sales only two and a half times GEC's).

GEC's European competitors also easily outpaced its growth. By the mid-1990s Siemens had grown to three times GEC's size, while Philips was twice as large. But the outstanding success story of the 1980s was ABB, the Swiss–Swedish merger whose component parts were not major players in 1968, but whose sales in 1996 matched those of Philips. Even the Swedish company Electrolux has equalled GEC's sales of £11 billion, despite the fact that it concentrates on appliances such as washing machines, a field in which GEC failed to transform its operations into a global or even a European business, and which had sales of just £250 million in 1996.

Weinstock's record cannot be judged merely on the basis of sales growth, however. First, his sales would have been much higher had GEC not seen its aircraft and computer interests taken away through nationalisation. Second, GEC has been prevented by government from making some important acquisitions, such as Cable & Wireless in the UK before it was privatised, and defence businesses in the United States.

Third, the stories of GEC's peers contain mixed messages for an assessment of Weinstock's achievements. The other US member of the original grouping, Westinghouse, which spawned the mighty Trafford Park plant, has effectively disappeared, having turned itself into a media company through the disposal of most of its manufacturing businesses and the acquisition of the American media group CBS. While ABB, Hitachi and GE have been outstandingly successful, the growth of other groups hides many problems. AEG, the German company Weinstock came close to buying, has ceased to exist as a separate entity, after a tale of mismanagement which illustrates that Weinstock's caution was not entirely unjustified. Philips has grown to twice the size of GEC, but it has also experienced years of financial troubles, including huge losses and a failure to pay a dividend during the early 1990s. Philips did what many critics argued GEC should have done: it competed head to head with the Japanese in electronic consumer goods, ploughed enormous sums into the development of new consumer products such as compact discs and digital tape players, and as a result it continued to employ 250,000 people. But the consequence was a non-existent or low dividend for shareholders, insecurity for tens of thousands of those employees, and profits which were no more than GEC's despite sales being twice as high. In France, Thomson Multimedia provides similarly eloquent testimony to GEC's wisdom in steering clear of consumer electronics. The huge losses run up by this consumer electronics division of the Thomson electronics company were instrumental in delaying the privatisation of the group in 1996. In Italy, Olivetti's financial crisis in the mid-1990s showed the difficulty of operating in the personal computer market. Even Siemens, the most successful of GEC's direct European equivalents, has found it difficult to justify financially its determination to remain in mainstream semi-conductor manufacture.

On straightforward financial comparisons with its rivals, GEC's performance is clearly better than average. A comprehensive City assessment in 1994 concluded that GEC was a middleweight by international standards, but that it punched above its weight according to most financial criteria. Compared to a group which included GE and ABB, GEC turned out to have the highest return on capital employed, the most commonly used measure of profitability. Other conclusions were:

> At an operational level, GEC's day-to-day management of its businesses is world class.
>
> It does not appear to be underspending on self-funded research and development.
>
> GEC has the lowest cost base in Europe, while in some areas (telecommunications, for example) its apparent productivity is comparable with the best in Europe.[10]

GEC's spending on research and development has been a bone of contention ever since Weinstock took over as head of the company. Along with his investment record it has been cited as an illustration of meanness which would eventually cripple the group. There are no clear ways of testing the accusation, nor even satisfactory definitions of R&D which ensure that cross-company comparisons are valid. Yet the record seems to show that GEC's spending in this area has been on a par with that of its main rivals. The picture is confused by the extent to which the group's basic research in its main areas of defence electronics and telecommunications was traditionally funded by government or by nationalised industries. Comparison is also clouded by the different mix of businesses within each group, those with a greater high-tech content being expected to spend a higher proportion of revenues on research.

With these caveats, GEC's spending seems to have been at least comparable to its rivals'. Following the Plessey takeover and the late-1980s joint ventures, the group was spending more than £1 billion a year on R&D, more than 11 per cent of sales. About 60 per cent of this was funded by customers, but that still left over £400 million of GEC's own money pouring into the research labs and development operations. That company-funded element was a smaller percentage than most of the peer group's, but the total was higher than all of them except the totally electronic, nationalised Thomson of France. Yet the grounds for criticism are clear. While GEC's sales rose from just £9 billion in 1991 to nearly £11 billion at the end of Weinstock's reign, total R&D spending edged up only from £1040 million to £1130 million, and company-funded spending failed even more dramatically to keep pace, actually falling marginally from a peak of £435 million in 1991.

Investment also seems to have tailed off in the 1990s. Again there are no clear measures, and it is difficult to compare companies operating under different accounting regimes, but throughout the 1980s GEC invested substantially more than the level of its annual depreciation charge, which might be regarded as the minimum level necessary to maintain the asset base. Between 1980 and 1989 GEC's annual investments represented an average of 1.25 times its depreciation. But the level fell from 1.5 times in 1980 to 1.2 times or below in the second half of the decade. And in 1990 investment was slightly less than depreciation for the first time, slipping to barely 0.75 times depreciation in 1993. Only in 1995 did investment creep ahead of the depreciation charge again.

These narrow financial criteria give some insight into Weinstock's record at GEC. The numbers show that his custody of the group has been adequate to protect it and preserve it, but they do not answer the larger criticism that he has not been able to grow it into a world-class operator fit for the twenty-first century. The broader records of a small number of GEC's competitors hint at what might have been had Weinstock's brilliance at analysis and control been matched by greater daring and vision during the 1980s and 1990s.

ABB is the European competitor which stands out as an example of what could have been achieved at GEC with greater boldness as well as tight management. The company has been voted Europe's most respected business twice in recent years, while its Swedish chairman and chief executive Percy Barnevik has become one of the world's most respected managers. He is seen as the European equivalent of Jack Welch, the head of GE. Like Welch, and like Weinstock before him in the late 1960s, Barnevik slashed and burned his way through the corporate bureaucracy after the merger of Swedish Asea with the Swiss Brown Boveri in 1988. But unlike

Weinstock, Barnevik has been bold positively as well as negatively. He has invested heavily in Eastern Europe, describing it as 'the Asia-Pacific on our doorstep' and spending $300 million there on acquisitions. Nor has he neglected Asia-Pacific, pumping money and management into India and China. While sharing Weinstock's distrust of management theory, he has also spent heavily on management training and development, and operates a matrix system of management, combining country and product responsibilities, which has had business school professors purring.

Yet there are similarities between Barnevik and Weinstock, and between ABB and GEC. Like GEC, ABB operates as a confederation of small businesses, with each profit centre reporting its results to Barnevik every month. Like GEC, ABB is ferocious in attacking stock levels and productivity. Like GEC, ABB has a remarkably 'flat' management hierarchy, with only two levels between country manager and Barnevik, enabling rapid decision-making. But there are two important respects in which ABB is different. First, Barnevik is an inspirational figure. Weinstock has inspired deep devotion among the small coterie of managers with whom he has been in frequent contact; but for the wider community of quite senior executives within operating companies, who rarely see or hear from him except for the occasional complaint, he has been a distant, anonymous figure. Secondly, GEC operates only one part of the matrix. Weinstock has deliberately avoided, and in some cases actively prevented, cross-fertilisation between business units, a factor which ABB believes has been crucial to its success.

Different lessons emerge from an examination of the remarkable rise of the US General Electric under Jack Welch, who has become one of the world's most respected managers. Welch has also exhibited the fondness for lean organisation, which Weinstock led the world in bringing to GEC in the 1960s. And he has pushed GE relentlessly to higher productivity, shorter 'cycle times' for developing and producing products, and more effective use of capital. Weinstock could claim to have been first in the field with all these aspects of business efficiency. Welch has added to this, however, a boldness which has usually been lacking in GEC since the late 1960s. Weinstock tinkered with financial services in the 1980s, buying a stake in the Summit group, whose main activity was lease

302

finance, and hiring a merchant banker to make some tentative investments. Similarly he has toyed with media, backing London Weekend Television when it was bidding for one of the capital's ITV franchises in the late 1960s, and with the detailed talks for the takeover of Carlton Communications shortly before Weinstock's retirement as managing director. Welch, on the other hand, has built the financial arm of his group, GE Capital, into a major global operation, representing a third of group profits, and has a strong stake in the media industry through the acquisition of the US television network NBC as part of the RCA conglomerate (whose main attraction was its defence activities).

In his 1995 report to shareholders, Welch described the transformation of GE in ways which identified some of the strengths and weaknesses of GEC under Weinstock. He explained the decision in the 1980s to concentrate on leading global businesses, resulting in the sale of $10 billion-worth of assets which would never fit that category, and $19 billion of acquisitions to build the remaining operations into world number-one or number-two positions. Weinstock managed the joint ventures in power and telecommunications, which pushed those businesses some way up the global ladder, but he did not clear out the industrial tail of marginal operations, nor did he have the ambition to build on the scale of GEC's counterpart. Of the company's three core businesses, Marconi was looking increasingly vulnerable as the consolidation of the defence electronics industry accelerated in the late 1990s, while GPT remained predominantly a domestic player, dependent on Siemens, in a telecoms market dominated by global giants. Only GEC–Alsthom could truly be said to be on a par with the world leaders in its industry.

Welch's 1995 report also mentioned the 'delayering', simplification and culture change at GE which was aimed at giving businesses the freedom and self-confidence of entrepreneurs. In the mechanics of these changes, GE was following where Weinstock had led twenty years earlier: 'We cleared out stifling bureaucracy, along with the strategic planning apparatus, corporate staff empires, rituals, endless studies and briefings, and all the classic machinery that makes big-company operations smooth and predictable – but often glacially slow.'[11]

Welch could teach nothing about such matters to Weinstock, who had cleared out the bureaucracies of GEC, AEI and EE in 1967 and 1968, and maintained a paranoia about overheads which kept GEC's head office and operations so lean that there was no scope for delayering. But he did have useful lessons for Weinstock in the area of culture. The bulk of his report was not about what he described as 'changing the hardware' of systems and structures, but 'changing the software' of attitudes and processes. Welch reported that GE had sought to build self-confidence by involving all its 222,000 employees in decision-making as far as possible and by developing managers who could make such an approach work, as well as by the relatively straightforward business of freeing people from oppressive bureaucracy. One of the biggest stumbling blocks to this process of liberation was the attitude of some managers; and, as Welch said, the crucial point in overcoming it was the decision to get rid of those – known in GE as 'Type IV' managers – who did not believe in or implement the new values, even if they delivered results:

> One is always tempted to avoid taking action, because Type IVs deliver short-term results. But Type IVs do so without regard to values, and in fact often diminish them by grinding people down, squeezing them, stifling them. Some of these learned to change, most couldn't. The decision to begin removing Type IVs was a watershed – the ultimate test of our ability to 'walk our talk', but it had to be done if we wanted GE people to be open, to speak up, to share, and to act boldly outside 'traditional lines of authority' and 'functional boxes' in this new 'learning, sharing environment'.[12]

Weinstock might dismiss such attention to values as mere management theory, but he cannot dismiss the remarkable success of GE since the early 1980s – the period when GEC has largely stagnated. And GEC exhibits the culture described by Welch as 'grinding people down, squeezing them, stifling them'. Weinstock developed and led a culture in which managers were often tested to destruction, where there were always complaints and criticisms, virtually never compliments, praise or thanks. One former GEC director recalls:

> I had to do an urgent report for a meeting one evening, which I sent over by car because it was the only way to get it to Weinstock on time. At about eleven o'clock that night I got a phone call. No mention about the report, he merely said: 'Why did you put it in a fresh envelope?' That was his way of not being able to say thank you and to try and score a point.
>
> He did once say thank you. I could have almost fallen off my seat. He had asked me to do an appraisal of something somewhere else in GEC, and he actually rang up and said: 'That's one of the most constructive reports I have ever read.' I thought to myself: what the hell have I done wrong?[13]

Another explained why he had decided to leave GEC after only five years:

> I could see I was going to get crushed. I was going to get battered every day until in the end you become some sort of Pavlov's dog. Five years was a tremendous learning experience; twenty years and you become a loyal servant – you've had all the initiative bashed out of you. You're doing a solid job of work and you're probably underpaid for it, but you've developed a sort of dependency.[14]

As another disillusioned former employee described it, 'It is a bullies' culture. You survive either by creeping to the bullies or by being a bully yourself. Most creep.' Weinstock habitually acted the part of the bully, despite his deep sentimentality and humanity. He was aided and abetted in many cases, especially after the departure of David Lewis and Kenneth Bond, by colleagues and staff who were unable or unwilling to stand up to him. One former main board director observed that GEC was like a medieval court, with most of the courtiers playing safe in order to keep their heads: 'Weinstock needed other great men around him, the greatest of which was clearly Sir Kenneth Bond. The fact that they have gone shows, because quite frankly he is surrounded by courtiers who do not give him wise counsel and do not counter the negatives within his personality. Like courtiers they tend to work for place or position.'[15]

Weinstock has never been able to accept these criticisms. In his eyes he operates a simple, straightforward system within which any efficient manager should be able to perform. His bullying style, haranguing and chasing managers, has not been vindictive. It has been intended to test their mettle and their ideas, to ensure that responsibility is not ducked, that ideas have been properly thought through and that risks have been properly recognised and assessed. The trouble is that the Weinstock style works only with Weinstocks – managers with the same level of ability and arrogance to stand their ground and fight for what they believe is the right solution. GEC head office, and Weinstock himself, never told managers what they should or should not do. The responsibility was theirs. Arguments would be presented by Stanhope Gate as to why something should not be done, and it would be opposed fiercely, for months, in many cases. But so long as it did not require cash from central resources, a manager was entitled to pursue his chosen option – always knowing, however, that failure would be fatal. Hence, among lesser managers, the culture of caution which gave GEC and Weinstock such a bad name in the 1990s. It was described by one former director: 'If you don't try, and fail, you can't be criticised for the failure. So new ideas can get stifled by hesitant management lacking the courage to want to do it, and to take on a system which will regard them as being out of their depth if they want to do something which is out of kilter with the balance sheet. And the paradox is that the man at the top – Weinstock – would actually be in favour of it, but he doesn't properly understand that he runs a system that frustrates it.'

Some strong managers have been able to pursue projects which involved substantial investment with no immediate returns because they were able to argue that they would help the long-term future of the company. One example was the GPT transmission business in the early 1990s, where 20 per cent of revenues were ploughed into developing new products to build what is now a successful international company.

A current main board director stressed that the failing of the

Weinstock culture was a failure of managers to understand their freedom and back their judgements.

> He doesn't say: 'You can't do this'; equally, he doesn't say you should do something else. This has been interpreted by a large number of managers as: 'We have to run the company according to the financial rules.' But if you want to do something which you believe is in the interest of the business, Arnold won't stop you. But you have to have the courage of your convictions.
>
> I think too many managers in GEC have seen their job in too narrow a term. They haven't had the courage of their convictions to recognise they have to manage their businesses and that businesses have to change. They have got to be able to stand up to Arnold and justify what they want to do. The easy route is not to change, so you don't have to stand up to Arnold, just hope the numbers will keep going right and you'll survive that way.[16]

But Weinstock must bear the key responsibility for this failure. It is the job of a leader to create an environment which brings out the best in his staff. That is something which Weinstock was unable to do after the early years in which survival and sound finances were the overriding priorities. His combative style suited a few, but bred excessive caution and defensiveness in many. His shallow judgements of managers, and especially his fickleness, were identified as key weaknesses even by some of his greatest admirers within the company. One colleague said:

> He assumes that if a business is going well, that is because of the manager, and similarly a bad business is the fault of a manager. in fact you can have good people struggling because of the businesses they are in, and poor people who look good. It has led to businesses declining, losing momentum. There have been some very good businesses in parts of Marconi, for example, which have gone sick because of that.[17]

GEC has been served by excellent managers, but they have emerged by a process of elimination, and in some cases survived by luck rather than good management. Another former director also remarked on Weinstock's shallow assessments and swiftness in demanding a manager be sacked even if he had previously been well regarded: 'He just looks at the red ink and draws completely false conclusions about the abilities of management and management teams.'[18]

The most consistent example of this confusion between bad management and bad business was A.B. Dick. The company was a mistaken acquisition. Its technology was outdated and it was struggling in an office equipment market increasingly dominated by leading global companies. Yet rather than admit the error of the acquisition, GEC persisted with the company for years, through losses and inadequate profits, making frequent changes of management.

Because Weinstock presided over a culture with only vertical links, so that managers did not talk to each other across the group, even within operations such as Marconi, there has been little potential for cross-fertilisation of the kind which Jack Welch has encouraged at GE and Percy Barnevik at ABB. Weinstock kept his managers in their own little boxes, communicating with the centre but not with each other. MSF union official Larry Brook recalled a meeting of national officers attended by several senior GEC managers. One of the trade unionists observed to the head of the power division that it must be boring hearing Weinstock running through the group's operations time after time. On the contrary, the manager replied. This was the first time he had ever heard so much information about GEC's other operations.

The practice of treating each operation as a separate entity even allowed Weinstock to tolerate a situation in the 1980s where Arthur Walsh, head of the Marconi defence business, was not on speaking terms with Jack Pateman, who was running Marconi Avionics. As a result, the avionics operation remained separate rather than being integrated with the communications, instruments and defence business. One former director said: 'There's a lack of trust of people. There seems to be a need to divide and conquer, which is very strange, and unlike any other successful business I know.'[19]

The creation of the Board of Management in 1985 was an attempt to deal with the compartmentalisation which was Weinstock's

308

natural inclination. It quickly fell into disuse, however, because it did not fit into Weinstock's style of operation. Although happy to talk through ideas interminably with individual managers or small groups, he was utterly impatient with larger discussions, and could not abide presentations. His paranoia about unnecessary overhead also predisposed him against any kind of liaison group or other structure which might be interpreted as merely an expensive talking shop.

Such an excessively uncoordinated approach has been identified as a key weakness in building global businesses. A 1988 report on the UK electronics industry by leading management consultants McKinsey observed that British companies tended to have organisational structures suited to the management issues of the 1960s and 1970s, not the 1980s and 1990s:

> Many UK electronics companies have structures and management processes which were state of the art for the management of diversified portfolios in the late 1960s and early 1970s, but which have worked against the development of successful international businesses . . . These organisational structures and processes are an obstacle to growth in global markets. Decentralisation to small units has limited the scale of ambition to that of the units rather than the company as a whole. Numbers-driven rather than issue-driven planning has reinforced a focus on shorter-term results rather than long-term investment to create major new businesses. The limited role of the centre in many UK companies has meant that the potential synergies and scale benefits of a large company – in creating a customer franchise, in product development and in attracting and developing highly talented management – have not been achieved. And the failure to develop a truly international or global organisational structure makes it difficult for the UK companies to pursue global scale.[20]

In mitigation, however, the report also noted that the needs of the defence and telecoms industries, which have dominated GEC's electronics activities, made it difficult to develop alternative styles which would have been suited to other businesses, and that this problem was evident in other companies, including American examples, which were major defence suppliers.

Summing up Weinstock's remarkable career, it is difficult to avoid making conditional judgements rather than arriving at neat, absolute conclusions. There have been many creditable achievements, and few of the criticisms that have been levelled at him can be supported without caveats. In particular, accusations of short-termism, of a refusal to invest in research and to invest in new initiatives, are far too simplistic.

Nevertheless, it is undeniably remarkable that a shy, evacuated North London orphan should have reached the dizzy heights of running one of Britain's most significant industrial companies. Weinstock's rise is at least partly explained by his sharp intellect, which fuelled an arrogance that gave him more self-belief than would be expected of most young men from his background. That intellect was evident throughout his entire business career.

Weinstock's thirty-three years at the helm of GEC need to be divided into three sections if a proper assessment is to be made of his contribution.

In the early years he exhibited a steely will, combined with a clear view of how a business ought to be run, which swiftly turned what had been an ailing company into the best-run business in the industry. The parts played by Kenneth Bond and David Lewis in developing contract bidding and management processes and financial controls should not be underestimated, but Weinstock was the leader of the small team which positioned GEC so that it was able to undergo the essential rationalisation which followed. The team's success continued with the integration of AEI and English Electric. The combined entity which these three companies produced was, as intended by the Wilson government and the Industrial Reorganisation Corporation which acted as midwife, substantial enough to become a major UK representative on the world stage. Looking back from the vantage point of the late 1990s, however, GEC did not capitalise on that position to the extent which it could have done. The brilliant success of the first stage of Weinstock's rule, roughly from 1963 to 1973, was not sustained.

There were considerable achievements in the middle period, and several mitigating factors which explain why GEC's success was not greater. The company's main achievement was not only to survive the turmoil of the 1970s but to end that decade, which was riven by industrial unrest and economic chaos, in a stronger financial and market position. That position would have been even stronger if government purchasing policies had been more supportive. But GEC would have entered the 1980s in better shape if Weinstock had been bolder in international expansion and more responsive to the ambitions of many of his senior managers to build their businesses rather than merely building the group's bank account. The company needed to evolve from the culture of tight control and a fierce focus on managerial responsibility which had been essential in saving the British electrical industry. But Weinstock's inability, for reasons of character, background or temperament, to move to a more open, supportive culture and to shift the emphasis from survival to growth, left GEC a less formidable competitor than it might have been in the 1980s.

Those failures were repeated and exaggerated in the third phase of the Weinstock era, roughly from the early 1980s to his departure as managing director in 1996, which must be regarded as his least successful period. Again, a number of factors, including government economic and industrial policies, did not help. But managers must make the best of the circumstances in which they find themselves, and Weinstock's continued failure to adapt meant that that could not be said of him during this period. First, he failed to react swiftly and substantially enough to the fundamental changes which occurred in the group's main markets of defence and telecoms. Second, he failed to accept the impact of globalisation, which should have caused GEC to concentrate on its key businesses and to build powerful positions in those areas. And third, he failed to recognise the potential of modern ideas of 'people management' which, in competitors such as ABB and GE, have yielded dramatic business results. A recognition of these failures was implicit in the first moves of Weinstock's successor George Simpson, who quickly appointed directors of strategy and human resources, and stated key objectives to use GEC's financial resources more creatively in building a more focused, global group.

Ultimately GEC's shortcomings were the result of a failure of leadership – a failure to project the values the company needed in the 1990s and to create the conditions in which managers and the group could grow. At the beginning of Weinstock's reign, his clarity of purpose provided the necessary leadership. For some managers he could be personally inspirational, especially in his earlier years. 'He had the tremendous ability to lift people up and make them feel they could go and do something superhuman when they left the room – those who hadn't been murdered, I mean,' one close colleague observed.[21] But the same man, who regards Weinstock as 'one of the most phenomenal people you could ever have worked with in your life', admitted that people were Weinstock's key weakness. Preferring to treat his managers merely as instruments – even though he himself has often acted impulsively and emotionally – he has behaved as if people don't matter, only the goals they have been set. This narrow approach has demeaned many of his managers and diminished Weinstock himself, who must be judged to have achieved great things in his early career, but to have allowed those achievements to wither.

# APPENDIX 1

## *Chronology*

| | |
|---|---|
| 1800–1850 | forerunners created of companies such as Elliott Automation, Napier Engineering, Stevenson engines |
| 1870s | foundation of electrical industry |
| 1883 | forerunner of GEC opened as a shop in London |
| 1889 | GEC established |
| 1896 | British Thomson-Houston set up as subsidiary of GE of America |
| 1897 | British Marconi formed |
| 1899 | British Westinghouse set up |
| 1903 | Michael Sobell arrives in Britain |
| 1917 | first attempt at merger between GEC and Westinghouse |
| 1919 | Metrovick formed from merger of Westinghouse and British Thomson-Houston; formation of English Electric |
| 1922 | merger talks between GEC and BT-H |
| 1924 | birth of Arnold Weinstock (AW) |
| 1926 | talks about merging GEC, EE, Metrovick and BT-H |
| 1928 | creation of AEI from merger of BT-H and Metrovick |
| 1930s | Sobell radio business set up |
| 1944 | AW starts work at Admiralty in Bath |
| 1946 | EE acquires Marconi |
| 1947 | AW starts working for Louis Scott in property |
| 1951 | AW marries Netta |
| | Sobell begins making radios and TVs for EMI |
| 1953 | Sobell Industries sold to EMI |
| | GE of America finally sold out of AEI |
| 1954 | Sobell bought back and AW joins Radio & Allied |
| 1958 | Radio & Allied floated on stock exchange |

| 1960 | Radio & Allied bought by GEC for £8 million; merger talks with EE |
|------|---|
| 1962 | semi-conductor business into joint venture with Mullard (finally sold in 1969); Jack Scamp joins board |
| 1963 | AW appointed managing director of GEC; Kenneth Bond joins board |
| 1964 | GEC buys Cannon cookers; David Lewis joins board |
| 1960s | AEI puts various peripheral businesses into joint ventures with Thorn and EMI |
| 1965 | GEC sells turbo generators to Parsons |
| 1966 | GEC fails to buy Pye and Telephone Rentals |
| 1967 | EE buys Elliott Automation; GEC acquires AEI |
| 1968 | GEC merged with EE |
| 1970 | AW knighted; stake in LWT |
| 1971 | AW appointed director of Rolls-Royce |
| 1973 | AW blackballed at Brooks's |
| 1974 | AW argues for strong 'third force' Liberal presence against socialist extremism; GEC donates £25,000 to Liberal Party |
| 1976 | BAC nationalised |
| 1977 | capital repayment to give back some cash; GEC involved in attempt to save Meriden motorcycle business |
| 1978 | first losses in TV and radio; AW elected to Jockey Club |
| 1979 | Hitachi joint venture in TV; GEC acquires A. B. Dick |
| 1980 | AW peerage; GEC acquires Avery; demerger rejected |
| 1981 | GEC acquires Picker; Sara Morrison joins board |
| 1982 | capital repayment; |

|      | David Lewis retires; |
|------|----------------------|
|      | GEC sells Morphy Richards |
| 1983 | Lord Nelson retires, Lord Carrington chairman |
| 1984 | GEC finally sells out of TV; |
|      | AW highly critical of BT privatisation; |
|      | Lord Prior takes over as chairman; |
|      | GEC attempts to buy British Aerospace before privatisation |
| 1985 | acquisition of Yarrow; |
|      | AW's controversial participation in Lords Select Committee on industry; |
|      | GEC board of management formed |
| 1986 | GEC's first offer for Plessey blocked by Monopolies Commission; |
|      | development of private mobile phone network |
| 1987 | failure to merge Picker with Philips medical; |
|      | acquisition of Creda and Microscope |
| 1988 | creation of GPT as joint venture with Plessey; |
|      | acquisitions of Lear Astronics and Gilbarco; |
|      | 40 per cent stake in Summit (finance); |
|      | Simon Weinstock joins GEC board |
| 1989 | joint ventures with Alsthom, Siemens and General Electric |
| 1990 | sale of Osram lighting business; |
|      | various Ferranti purchases; |
|      | Kenneth Bond retires |
| 1991 | Matra space joint ventures |
| 1992 | out of mobile telephony |
| 1993 | Michael Sobell dies |
| 1994 | AW two-year time limit set |
| 1995 | acquisition of VSEL |
| 1996 | Simon Weinstock dies |
|      | AW becomes chairman emeritus of GEC |

# APPENDIX 2

## *The Genesis of GEC*

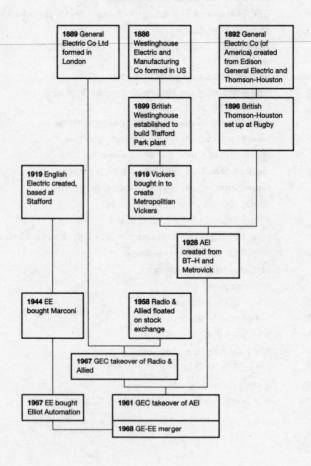

**1889** General Electric Co Ltd formed in London

**1886** Westinghouse Electric and Manufacturing Co formed in US

**1892** General Electric Co (of America) created from Edison General Electric and Thomson-Houston

**1899** British Westinghouse established to build Trafford Park plant

**1896** British Thomson-Houston set up at Rugby

**1919** English Electric created, based at Stafford

**1919** Vickers bought in to create Metropolitian Vickers

**1928** AEI created from BT–H and Metrovick

**1944** EE bought Marconi

**1958** Radio & Allied floated on stock exchange

**1967** GEC takeover of Radio & Allied

**1967** EE bought Elliot Automation

**1961** GEC takeover of AEI

**1968** GE-EE merger

# APPENDIX 3

## GEC in 1963

*The Board*

A. L. G. Lindley, chairman

T. B. O Kerr ⎫
Lord Aldington ⎭ deputy chairmen

O. W. Humphreys, vice chairman

A. Weinstock, managing director

R. N. Millar, managing director (technical)

K. R. Bond, finance director

Other directors: D. G. W. Acworth

W. J. Bird

Lord Catto

R. C. Giggins

C. F. Richards

A. J. Scamp

M. Sobell

| Company activities | sales (£m) |
|---|---|
| Engineering | 32 |
| Consumer products | 32 |
| Telecoms and electronics | 40 |
| Other | 27 |

317

# GEC in 1996

| Company activities | sales (£m) | profits (£m) | no. employees (thousands) |
|---|---|---|---|
| Electronic systems and defence (GEC-Marconi) | 3049 | 291 | 43 |
| Power systems (GEC-Alsthom) | 3752 | 177 | 38 |
| Telecommunications (GPT) | 1070 | 158 | 12 |
| Consumer goods (Hotpoint/Creda) | 250 | 11 | 4 |
| Metrology (Gilbarco, Avery Berkel) | 550 | 50 | 8 |
| Office equipment/ printing | 299 | 37 | 3 |
| Medical (Picker) | 675 | 32 | 4 |
| Electronic components | 387 | 34 | 6 |
| Industrial apparatus (wire, cables, fans, control systems) | 348 | 20 | 4 |
| Distribution and trading | 428 | 20 | 3 |

# APPENDIX 4

## *GEC and its Peers, 1968–1996*

### Electrical industry rankings (£billion sales)

| 1968 | £bn | | 1996 | £bn |
|------|-----|---|------|-----|
| General Electric (US) | 3.2 | | General Electric (US) | 49 |
| Westinghouse | 1.2 | | Hitachi | 48 |
| GEC | 0.9 | | Siemens | 33 |
| Philips | 0.9 | | Philips | 21 |
| Siemens | 0.8 | | GEC | 11 |
| Hitachi | 0.6 | | | |

# APPENDIX 5

## *Share Price Performance Charts*
### Share Price Performance 1963–1997

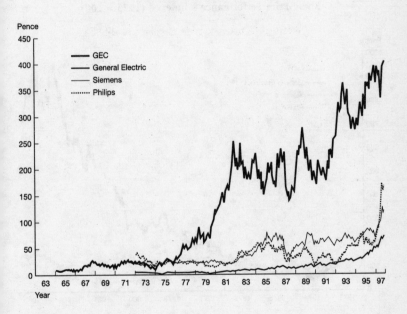

## Share Price Performance – Indexed (1973 = 100)

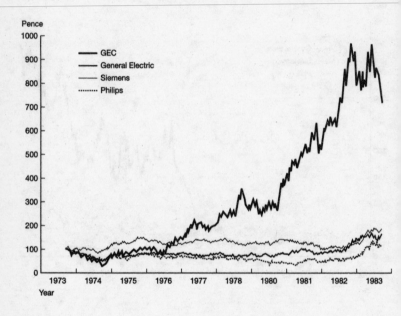

## Share Price Performance – Indexed (1983 = 100)

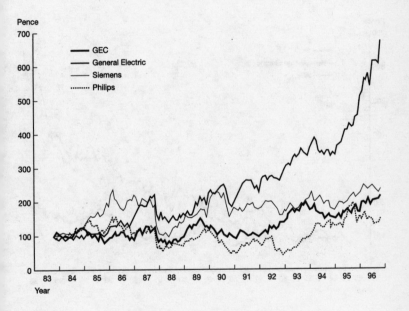

## Share Price Performance – Indexed (1983 = 100)

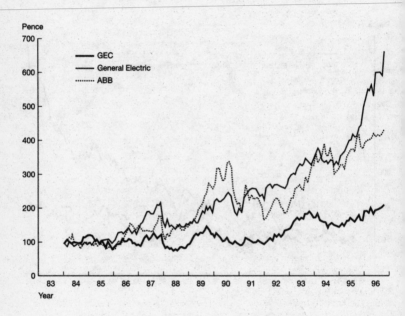

# NOTES

PRELUDE: *Final Days*

1 Lord Weinstock, letter to the authors, 20 August 1996
2 Lord Weinstock, *Desert Island Discs*, BBC Radio 4, 23 May 1993.
3 Riccardo Muti, interview with the authors, 9 May 1966
4 'Behind the Weinstock Enigma', *Financial Times*, 9 July 1992
5 Richard Reynolds, interview with the authors, 12 September 1996
6 Lord Prior, interview with the authors, 4 July 1996
7 Confidential interview with the authors, 1996

CHAPTER ONE: *New Beginnings*

1 Alan Adelson and Robert Lapides (eds), *Lodz Ghetto: Inside a Community Under Siege*, Penguin 1991, p.xiv
2 Old Ordnance Survey Maps: Stoke Newington 1914 (London Sheet 30), commentary by Jenny Golden, published by Alan Godfrey
3 Lord Weinstock, interview with the authors, October 1996
4 Lord Weinstock, *Desert Island Discs*, BBC Radio 4, 23 May 1993
5 Stephen Aris, *The Jews in Business*, Jonathan Cape 1970, p.220
6 Gordon Hill, interview with the authors, 20 August 1996
7 W.H.L. Jones, in *Stoke Newington Central School Magazine*, May 1936
8 Cary L. Cooper and Peter Hingley, *The Change Makers*, Harper & Row 1985, p.5
9 Jeanette Barnett, interview with the authors, 1995
10 Louis Golding, *The Jewish Problem*, Penguin 1938, pp.150–4
11 Lord Weinstock, interview with the authors, October 1996
12 *Stoke Newington Central School Magazine*, May 1936, pp.16–17
13 Kit Dew, interview with the authors, 1995
14 Harborough Magan School, Headmistress's War Diary, Warwickshire County Council archives
15 Albert Wood, interview with the authors, 1995
16 Lord Weinstock, *Desert Island Discs*, BBC Radio 4, 23 May 1993
17 Gordon Hill, interview with the authors, 20 August 1996
18 GEC fax to Willans Works, 4 August 1989
19 Ralf Dahrendorf, *A History of the London School of Economics and Political Science 1895–1995*, Oxford University Press 1995, pp.325–9
20 Talking points from LSE Reunion at Peterhouse, Cambridge, 30 September 1989
21 Betty Evans, *née* Bond, 'Reminiscences', 1993, LSE archives
22 Ken Gay, letter to the authors, 20 March 1996
23 Lord Weinstock, *Desert Island Discs*, BBC Radio 4, 23 May 1993
24 Dahrendorf, p.350
25 Stanley S. Bloom, letter to the authors, September 1995
26 Lord Weinstock, interview with the authors, October 1996

27 Ibid.

28 Cooper and Hingley, p.5


CHAPTER TWO: *Man of Property*

1 Lord Weinstock, *Desert Island Discs*, BBC Radio 4, 23 May 1993

2 Oliver Marriott, *The Property Boom*, Abingdon 1989, pp.45–6

3 Saul L. Magrill, FSVA, 'Notes on the Property Market circa the Late 1940s and 1950s: Louis Scott', 14 June 1995

4 'The Man Who's Always Right,' *Observer*, 12 November 1967

5 Marriott, p.1

6 Aris, p.221

7 Obituary of Sir Michael Sobell, *Jewish Chronicle*, 18 September 1993

8 'Mr Weinstock, This is Your Wife . . .', *Evening News*, 10 November 1967

9 Lord Weinstock, interview with the authors, December 1996

10 Peter Clarke, *Hope and Glory: Britain 1900–1990*, Allen Lane 1966, pp.249–54

11 Lord Weinstock, interview with the authors, December 1966


CHAPTER THREE: *Into the Hot Seat*

1 Heads of agreement between Sobell Industries and EMI, 5 March 1951

2 EMI board minute 2938, 24 September 1953

3 S.A. Pandit, *From Making to Music: The History of Thorn EMI*, Hodder & Stoughton 1996, p.75

4 Lord Weinstock, interview with the authors, December 1996

5 Sir Kenneth Bond, interview with the authors, March 1996

6 Sir Harry Moore, quoted in Robert Jones and Oliver Marriott, *Anatomy of a Merger*, Jonathan Cape 1970, p.212

7 'Big Demand for Radio and Television Shares', *The Times*, 5 June 1958

8 Jones and Marriott, p.77

9 Sir Kenneth Bond, interview with the authors, March 1996

10 e.g. *The Times*, 26 June 1958

11 'GEC's Uncertain Prospects', *The Times*, 27 July 1960

12 Confidential interview with the authors, June 1996

13 '2,300 Television Sets a Week', *The Times*, 20 July 1960

14 'Board Changes', *The Times*, 11 December 1962

15 Confidential interview with the authors, June 1996

16 Sir Kenneth Bond, interview with the authors, March 1996

17 Anthony Sampson, *Anatomy of Britain Today*, Hodder & Stoughton 1965


CHAPTER FOUR: *White Heat*

1 Ben Pimlott, *Harold Wilson*, HarperCollins 1992, p.130

2 Ibid., p.304

3 'The National Plan', Cmnd 2764, 1965

4 David Lewis, interview with the authors, May 1996

5 Confidential interview with the authors

6 Sir Joseph Latham, *Takeover: The Facts and the Myths of the GEC/AEI Battle*, Iliffe Books 1969, pp.67–75

7 *Cynon Valley Leader*, 25 October 1963

8 GEC annual report 1964–65

9 Former GEC manager, confidential interview with the authors, 1995

10 'Strong Nerves Needed but Little to Lose for TR Supporters', *The Times*, 27 February 1967

11 Quoted in Sampson, p.552

12 Ronald Grierson, *A Truant Disposition*, Weidenfeld & Nicolson 1992, p.34

13 Pandit, p.21

14 Jones and Marriott, p.247

15 Ibid., p.270
16 Latham, p.59
17 Jones and Marriott, p.269
18 Sir Kenneth Bond, interview with the authors, March 1996
19 'AEI Says "Take Offer" ', *The Times*, 10 November 1967
20 Jones and Marriott, p.298
21 'More Mergers, Urges Blackett', *The Times*, 21 February 1968
22 Richard Crossman, *Diaries of a Cabinet Minister*, vol. 3, Hamish Hamilton & Jonathan Cape 1977, p.187
23 'The Man Who's Always Right', *Observer*, 12 November 1967
24 *The Money Programme*, BBC Television, 9 May 1968
25 'Sense of Fulfilment Gained from Doing One's Best', *The Times*, 2 December 1968
26 Tony Benn, *Diaries 1968–72: Office Without Power*, Hutchinson 1988, p.25
27 Ibid., p.144
28 Ibid.
29 Crossman, p.887

CHAPTER FIVE: *Turmoil*

1 'The Woolwich Case', *The Times*, 6 February 1968
2 Confidential interview with the authors, March 1996
3 *The Money Programme*, BBC Television, 9 May 1968
4 'Sack!', *Daily Express*, 4 September 1968
5 Sir Kenneth Bond, interview with the authors, March 1996
6 Confidential interview with the authors, 1996
7 Confidential interview with the authors, 1995
8 Ibid.
9 Confidential interview with the authors, March 1996
10 Confidential interview with the authors, 1995
11 'Blackball Row as Banker Quits Club', *Daily Mail*, 11 May 1973

12 'GEC will Fulfil "Half-Baked Ideas" ', *Daily Telegraph*, 17 June 1974
13 *Talking Politics*, BBC Radio 4, 25 August 1975
14 'The Weinstock Way', *Observer*, 2 March 1975
15 *Talking Politics*, BBC Radio 4, 25 August 1975
16 Report of the Committee of Inquiry on Industrial Democracy, Cmnd 6706, 1977
17 'United, We Can Take the Road to Riches', *Daily Express*, 26 September 1975
18 Sir Michael Bett, interview with the authors, December 1995
19 'The Man in the Seat of Power', *The Times*, 19 June 1978
20 'Weinstock Picks Cross for California', *Guardian*, 7 December 1977
21 Confidential interview with the authors, 1996
22 'The Man in the Seat of Power', *The Times*, 19 June 1978
23 'GEC to Refuse Merger', *Guardian*, 16 May 1977
24 'Arnold's Slap-up Secret', *Daily Express*, 1980

CHAPTER SIX: *The Thatcher Years*

1 'Too Many Cash Riches for Comfort at GEC', *Daily Express*, 6 July 1979
2 Hugo Young, *One of Us*, Macmillan 1989, p.362
3 Lord Prior, interview with the authors, June 1996
4 Sir Kenneth Bond, interview with the authors, March 1996
5 *Hansard*, 27 November 1980, Col. 232
6 Ibid., Col. 236
7 Ibid., 12 November 1981, Col. 369
8 ' "Welcome Japan" Earns Charles a Rap', *Daily Express*, 12 July 1987
9 *Hansard*, 29 March 1984, Cols 403–6

10 *Hansard*, 16 February 1984, Col. 436

11 Report of Select Committee on Overseas Trade, Vol. II, p.1,381

12 'The Giants Growl a Bit', *Guardian*, 26 April 1985

13 'Thatcher Sharp with GEC Boss', *Guardian*, 26 April 1985

14 Report of Select Committee on Overseas Trade, Session 1984–85, p.42

15 Ibid., p.47

16 Young, p.362

17 *Hansard*, 3 December 1985, Col 1259

18 'Six-Month Nimrod Deadline for GEC', *Guardian*, 27 February 1986

19 'GEC Lobby Aims to Convert Tories to Nimrod', *Independent*, 29 October 1986

20 'Early Warning that Didn't Sound for Nimrod', *Guardian*, 16 December 1986

21 'Younger Demolishes Nimrod', *Independent*, 19 December 1986

22 'Weinstock Seeks Some Answers from MoD', *Daily Telegraph*, 16 December 1986

23 'Nimrod: The Big Questions', *The Times*, 17 December 1986

24 'Weinstock Likely to get the Blame', *Daily Telegraph*, 15 December 1986

25 'Early Warning that Didn't Sound for Nimrod', *Guardian*, 16 December 1986

26 Pandit, p.132

27 'The Fact that Faces Lord Weinstock', *Financial Times*, 18 July 1984

28 'GEC and Plessey Should Merge, Says Minister', *Financial Times*, 15 June 1985

29 Monopolies and Mergers Commission Report, p.25, Cmnd 9867, August 1986

30 *The Times*, 11 April 1989

31 *Daily Telegraph*, 20 January 1989

32 'The Wisdom of Weinstock', *Observer*, 7 June 1987

33 *Reflect on Things Past*, William Collins 1988

34 Confidential interview with the authors, 1996

CHAPTER SEVEN: *New World Order*

1 'Weinstock's New GEC', *Sunday Times*, 7 January 1990

2 'GEC Underperform', Salomon Brothers, August 1996

3 Lord Weinstock, interview with the authors, April 1997

4 Lord Prior, interview with the authors, September 1996

5 'Rock-Solid GEC Need Growth', *The Times*, 5 December 1991

6 'Something for Everyone in Vintage GEC Strike, *Independent on Sunday*, 28 January 1990

7 Alan Clark, *Diaries*, Weidenfeld & Nicolson 1993, p.274

8 Dick Evans, interview with the authors, 20 December 1995

9 Lord Weinstock, interview with the authors, April 1997

10 'Concerned Customer of BAe', *The Times*, 12 October 1991

11 'BAe Shares Rise on Rumour of GEC Bid', *Guardian*, 24 January 1992

12 'GEC Hints at Renewed Merger Talks with BAe', *Guardian*, 2 July 1992

13 'Weinstock Attacks Government Defence Policy', *The Times*, 22 April 1993

14 'Weinstock Stays his Hand', *The Times*, 2 December 1993

15 Dick Evans, interview with the authors, 20 December 1995

16 Ibid.

17 Ibid.

18 As chairman emeritus of GEC, Weinstock and his successor as managing director George Simpson were to pursue this course with some aggression. Early in 1997 GEC sought permission from the French authorities to bid alongside the

French-controlled electronics groups Alcatel and LAGARDERE for Thomson-CSF. When this move was blocked, GEC signed agreements with the two French groups, creating an Anglo–French defence electronics combination with the muscle and marketing clout to take on the US giants. But GEC was to be frustrated by the French National Assembly elections of May 1997, which brought the socialist leader Lionel Jospin to power and immediately put plans to privatise Thomson-CSF on hold. GEC/Thomson were also to be frozen out of an auction for the defence communications business of Siemens Plessey, which went to rival BAe in partnership with Daimler-Benz Aerospace in October 1997.

19 Jim Cronin, interview with the authors, July 1996

20 Ibid.

21 The success of GEC-Alsthom and its growing independence from the rest of GEC led Weinstock's successor George Simpson to conclude, in his strategic review of July 1997, that it could be a candidate for demerger or sale.

22 Salomon Brothers, GEC, 28 August 1996, p.8

23 Peter Gershon, interview with the authors, 1996

24 Lord Weinstock, interview with the authors, April 1997

25 'GEC at the Crossroads', *Financial Times*, 9 July 1992

26 'Making Televisions in the 1950s', *Financial Times*, 30 December 1996

27 Ron Artus, interview with the authors, 30 May 1996

28 'Why Laggard GEC Needs a New Boss', *Independent*, 2 September 1991

29 Ron Artus, interview with the authors, 30 May 1996

30 Lord Weinstock, interview with the authors, April 1997

31 Ibid.

32 GEC press release, 18 March 1996

33 'Cadbury, Greenbury and Tweedlebury', *Financial Times*, 31 December 1996

34 The first to go was deputy managing director Malcolm Bates, who retired in March. In June it was disclosed that chairman Lord Prior and veteran non-executive directors Sebastian de Ferranti and Lord Rees-Mogg were to step down, while Sara Morrison was removed from her executive role to become a non-executive director. In July, after a row over the future strategy of the group, the finance director David Newlands – once considered a possible Weinstock successor – was ousted. Moreover, Weinstock's behind-the-scenes effort to replace Prior with former Deputy Prime Minister Michael Heseltine was also thwarted. The way in which the former GEC chief's advice was ignored and in which his successor ran roughshod over his key aides and non-executive directors left Weinstock feeling frustrated, bitter and unwanted.

CHAPTER EIGHT: *The Man and his Passions*

1 Peter Reynolds, interview with the authors, 18 December 1996

2 Ibid.

3 Lord Weinstock, *Desert Island Discs*, BBC Radio 4, 23 May 1993

4 'Owners, Punters and Businessmen', *Investors Chronicle*, 14 July 1995, p.12

5 Sean Magee, *The Channel Four Book of Racing*, Hamlyn 1995, p.94

6 Alan Yuill Walker, 'Ballymacoll:

The History of a Great Stud', *The British Racehorse*, Autumn 1980

7 Ibid.

8 William Waldegrave, interview with the authors, January 1996

9 'Troy, Troy, Troy Again', *Daily Express*, June 1979

10 'Swinburn's Dark Days Banished by Turf Win', *Daily Telegraph*, 28 October 1996

11 Riccardo Muti, interview with the the authors, 9 May 1996

12 'Electric Lord on a Short Fuse', *The Times*, 12 October 1991

13 Lord Weinstock, *Desert Island Discs*, BBC Radio 4, 23 May 1993

14 Riccardo Muti, interview with the the authors, 9 May 1996

15 Lord Tebbit, interview with the authors, 11 December 1995

16 Lord Cuckney, interview with the authors, 8 November 1995

17 Louis Jacobs (ed.), *The Jewish Religion: A Companion*, Oxford University Press 1995, pp.5–6

18 Cyril Stein, interview with the authors, February 1996

19 'Britain's Richest 500, 1996', *Sunday Times*, 14 April 1996

20 Denis Healey, *The Time of my Life*, Michael Joseph 1989, p.503

21 'Britain Cursed by Cliques and Cartels', *Financial Times*, 31 December 1996

22 Lord Parkinson, interview with the authors, 1995

23 'Britain Cursed by Cliques and Cartels', *Financial Times*, 31 December 1996

24 Larry Brook, interview with the authors, 1995

25 Lord Weinstock, internal GEC memorandum, 29 December 1993

26 Jim Cronin, interview with the authors, July 1996


CHAPTER NINE: *The Record*

1 Professor Steve Davies, 'The Effects of 1992 on the Structure, Ownership and Performance of UK Manufacturing', Economic and Social Research Council, September 1996

2 McKinsey & Co., 'Performance and Competitive Success', National Economic Development Office 1988

3 See e.g. Will Hutton, *The State We're in*, Jonathan Cape 1995

4 Confidential interview with the authors, 1996

5 John Plender, *A Stake in the Future*, Nicholas Brealey 1997, p.89

6 Confidential interview with the authors, 1996

7 Confidential interview with the authors, 1996

8 Confidential interview with the authors, 1996

9 Confidential interview with the authors, 1995

10 Keith Hodgkinson and Inge Timperley, 'The Case for the Defence, Power and Telecommunications Divisions', Lehman Brothers July 1994

11 GE annual report 1995, p.2

12 Ibid., p.3

13 Confidential interview with the authors, 1996

14 Confidential interview with the authors, 1995

15 Confidential interview with the authors, 1995

16 Confidential interview with the authors, 1996

17 Ibid.

18 Confidential interview with the authors, 1995

19 Confidential interview with the authors, 1995

20 'Performance and Competitive Success', op. cit.

21 Confidential interview with the authors, 1996

# INDEX

# INDEX

## Company Man

### The Rise and Fall Of Corporate Life

ANTHONY SAMPSON

'The most luminous history of the business enterprise that we will have this year and, perhaps, for a long time to come.'

JOHN KENNETH GALBRAITH, *New York Times Book Review*

'Anthony Sampson's elegant and provocative study of the social history of corporate life, from the East India Company to Microsoft . . . is presented with all the authority and wit you would expect from a veteran commentator like the author of the hugely influential *Anatomy of Britain*.'

LAURENCE BARON, *Spectator*

'This is a fascinating book . . . The anecdotes and imagery from all the voyaging in fiction, factory and boardroom lard his analysis and turn it into a richly satisfying plum pudding of a book . . . Sampson's easy and elegant prose make this book a delight to read and savour.' CHARLES HANDY, *RSA Journal*

'A finely crafted obituary of one of this century's unsung heroes: company man.' *The Economist*

'A sparkling analysis of the breed.' ANN ROBINSON, *Sunday Times*

0 00 638068 9

## Microsoft Secrets

How the World's Most Powerful Software Company Creates Technology,
Shapes Markets and Manages People

MICHAEL A. CUSUMANO & RICHARD W. SELBY

Beyond the unquestioned genius and vision of CEO Bill Gates, what accounts for Microsoft's astounding success?

Microsoft commands the high ground of the information superhighway by owning the operating systems and basic applications programs that run on the world's 170 million computers.

Drawing on two years of unrestricted access to confidential documents and project data, eminent technology-scientists Cusumano and Selby reveal, for the first time, many of Microsoft's innermost secrets.

Forty in-depth interviews with employees enabled the authors to identify seven key strategies which demonstrate exactly how Microsoft competes and operates. They reveal a style of leadership, organization, competition and product development which is both consistent with the company's loosely structured 'programmer' culture and remarkably effective for mass-market production of software.

Managers in many different industries will discover hundreds of invaluable lessons in this superbly readable book.

'A fascinating book about a fascinating company'
                              PETER SENGE, author of *The Fifth Discipline*

'Anyone intending to approach their bank manager to fund their own software company should make this book the centre of their business plan'
                                                            *Computer Weekly*

'A unique glimpse into the company's inner workings'            *Daily Telegraph*

0 00 638778 0

*In Search of Excellence*

Lessons from America's Best-Run Companies

TOM PETERS AND ROBERT H. WATERMAN JR

The international bestseller

American know-how is alive and well and growing stronger daily. *In Search of Excellence* distills the art and science of management used by leading companies with records of long-term profitability and continuing innovation. No-one concerned with international business today can afford not to read what makes leading US corporations successful.

'One of those rare books on management'  *New York Wall Street Journal*

'Required reading'  *International Management Magazine*

'Receiving serious attention in business schools and corporate boardrooms'
*Washington Post*

0 00 638402 1

HarperCollins Business

# The Tao of Coaching

Boost Your Effectiveness at Work by Inspiring
and Developing Those Around You

MAX LANDSBERG

Coaching is *the* key to unlocking the potential of your people, your organization and, ultimately, yourself.

The good news is that becoming a great coach requires nurturing just a few simple skills and habits.

Max Landsberg, responsible for professional development programmes at McKinsey & Co in the UK, takes you through the stages needed to master and implement coaching to maximum effect. He shows how to:

- nurture an environment where coaching can flourish

- develop a team of people who relish working with you

- enhance the effectiveness of others through learning

- create more time for yourself through efficient delegation

By investing small amounts of time to provide constructive feedback, mentoring and encouragement, managers can substantially boost both their colleagues and their own performance.

With the current emphasis on helping individual employees to realize and deliver their full potential, the techniques of coaching are fast becoming essential tools for managers and other professionals. This is the first book which, in a highly entertaining and practical way, shows how to go about it.

'I'm making this useful guide required reading for my executive team'
GEORGE FARR, VICE-CHAIRMAN, American Express Company

'Practical, readable and relevant'
ARCHIE NORMAN, CHAIRMAN, Asda Group plc

0 00 638811 6

# The Sunday Times Personal Finance Guide to Tax-free Savings

*How to Make Your Money Work Hardest For You*

## Christopher Gilchrist

Are you making the most of your savings and investments?

Nobody enjoys paying tax but few people make full use of the many opportunities now available to everyone in the UK to save and invest tax-free. This guide explains the basics of tax and investment and shows how you can use tax-free plans to make more of your money, including:

- how moving your savings into tax-free schemes can boost your returns
- how to work out what you need to save for retirement and the best tax-exempt ways to do so
- the differences between lower-risk, moderate-risk and high-risk schemes and how much each could produce for you
- identifying the saving and investment plans that offer the best value for money
- the best plans for short-term and longer-term savings

Over a period of twenty years, £100 a month placed in a building society account might accumulate to £45,000. But a good tax-exempt savings plan linked to shares could turn that same £100 a month into £130,000.

Taking the right decisions now on where to save your surplus income could add tens of thousands of pounds to your personal wealth.

0 00 638703 9

HarperCollinsPaperbacks

HarperCollins Business

# Co-opetition

Two leading business thinkers use game theory to rewrite business strategy

### BARRY J. NALEBUFF AND
### ADAM M. BRANDENBURGER

The game of business changes constantly. So should your business strategy.

This is the first book to adapt game theory to the needs of CEOs, managers and entrepreneurs. *Co-opetition* offers a new mindset for business: a strategic way of thinking that combines competition and cooperation.

Though often compared to games like chess or poker, business is different – people are free to change the rules, the players, the boundaries, even the game itself. The essence of business success lies in making sure you are in the *right* game. Actively shaping which game you play, and how you play it, is the core of the innovative business strategy laid out in *Co-opetition*.

Barry Nalebuff and Adam Brandenburger, professors at Yale and Harvard, are pioneers in the practice of applying the science of game theory to the art of corporate strategy. They have devised a practice-oriented model to help you break out of the traditional win-lose or lose-lose situations, and dozens of companies – including Intel, Nintendo, American Express and Nutrasweet – have been using the strategies of co-opetition to change their game to enjoy the benefits of win-win opportunities.

*Co-opetition* will revolutionize the way you play the game of business.

'Seize on *Co-opetition*'                                                    *Economist*

'A terrific book'                                                    TOM PETERS

0 00 638724 1